Contents

THE READING CONNECTION

Proceedings of the sixteenth annual course and conference
of the United Kingdom Reading Association
University of Leeds, 1979

Editors: Gwen Bray and A. K. Pugh

WARD LOCK EDUCATIONAL

ISBN 0 7062 4069 3

First published 1980

Set in 10 on 12 point Plantin
and printed in Great Britain by
Biddles Ltd, Guildford, Surrey
for Ward Lock Educational
116 Baker Street, London W1M 2BB
A member of the Pentos Group
Made in Great Britain

Foreword

The theme of the United Kingdom Reading Association's annual conference is chosen by the President, whose last duty is to ensure the successful organization of the conference. The theme for the Sixteenth Annual Conference, held at the University of Leeds, 23 – 27 July 1979, was 'The Reading Connection'.

These proceedings reflect the range of positive contributions to the development of literacy made by many people and agencies: not only schools but also local educational authorities and national bodies; not only teaching and research into teaching methods, but also reading schemes and other materials in print or other media; and not only teaching methods but also those factors within and outside the child which affect literacy. All these, and many more interdependent links, contribute to the goal of the Association – the improvement of reading and related skills.

The conference itself creates and reinforces links and thus makes the connection stronger. These proceedings, which consist of selected papers from both main sessions and smaller group meetings, provide a record to which delegates can refer; but we hope they will also be of broader interest to those concerned, in whatever role, with the development of literacy.

Gwen Bray

Part 1

National and local influences on literacy

Introduction

The part played in the development of literacy by bodies outside the classroom and beyond the school is the main emphasis in this section. The first paper, on 'Reading and the Teaching of English', uses a historical framework to examine the factors which have led to the problems which have beset attempts to develop reading beyond the primary school. Indeed the next paper, by Geoffrey Elsmore, indicates that the recent national report on primary education reveals difficulties even within the primary school in ensuring the development of reading, as opposed to its initial teaching. There is, of course, an interesting apparent irony in the move towards some subject specialization which Elsmore reports in primary education, at a time when the challenge to subject specialization in secondary education remains strong, especially in the cause of reading across the curriculum. However, out of proposals and counterproposals comes, at least, clarification of issues leading to action.

The contribution of Christopher Tipple suggests that a great deal of activity is undertaken by local authorities at various levels in organizing and providing for the teaching of reading and other literacy skills. This paper is not, as its author indicates, a 'plug' for Leeds; although no educational authority is, perhaps, typical, the purpose of the paper is to give an inside view of what an LEA does, taking appropriately enough the LEA responsible for the city in which this conference was held. Just as one cannot readily typify the work of the LEAs, so the work of the Schools Council is also difficult to encompass succinctly. As regards the teaching of English and the development of reading, its influence nationally through projects it has supported has been considerable. A convenient list is given in *English in the 1980s* (Schools Council 1979) and John Mann refers to some of this work in the final contribution to this section. His emphasis, properly enough, is on writing as well as reading though he speaks as 'a consistent, a catholic, even a confirmed reader'. A more detailed report of one of the Schools Council sponsored projects appears in a later section of these proceedings, where the researchers report their work themselves.

Reference

SCHOOLS COUNCIL (1979) *English in the 1980s: A Programme of Support to Readers* (Working Paper no. 62) London: Evans/Methuen

1 Reading and the teaching of English

A. K. Pugh

Introduction: English and reading as subjects

Reading has not been generally regarded as a school subject in Britain, although there are some signs that it may become one (Elsmore, this volume: DES 1978). In the preface to her historical survey *American Reading Instruction*, however, Nila Banton Smith (1965) remarked that reading was the most important subject in early American schools and that it had continued to be so. Members of the British Committee of Enquiry into Teaching the Use of English (the Bullock Committee), who visited the United States to collect evidence, also found reading well established as a subject there, although they considered there were disadvantages in treating reading as a special subject in secondary education.

The Committee found, for example, that the teachers of English tended to concentrate on 'pure literature' and on 'abstract teaching *about* literature' since the teaching of reading was regarded as the preserve of the teacher responsible for that subject (DES 1975, p. 117). Although they found continuity in the teaching of reading (no 'horizontal split', in their terms) they found what they called a very sharp 'vertical split' between reading as a subject and other subjects, including English. 'Indeed,' they note, 'the teachers belonged to separate professional associations which scarcely communicated' (p. 117).

This last point might suggest a situation not so different from experience in Britain where we have a number of organizations which include the teaching of reading among their concerns, but few co-ordinated activities. However, the split in affiliation to professional organizations in Britain relates also to age and level taught, reflecting not only the fact that reading has not been recognized as a subject in secondary education but that subject specialism is not very strong in primary schools. The Bullock Report was nevertheless addressed 'to *all* teachers, whatever their subject' (DES 1975, p. 188) since the Committee considered this was the only way to do justice to its first term of reference which was 'to consider in relation to schools all aspects of

2

teaching the use of English, including reading, writing and speech' (*ibid*. p. xxxi).

The appeal to all teachers was less novel than some commentators have assumed. 'The teachers of all special subjects must be responsible for the quality of the English spoken or written during their lessons' wrote the authors of an earlier enquiry in the Newbolt Report. They continued in uncompromising if unfashionable terms to assert that 'in every department of school work, confused and slovenly English must be regarded as a failure on the part of the teacher' (Board of Education 1921, p. 24). Other government publications have included this theme of shared responsibility (see, for example, the informative if somewhat uninspiring *Language*, Ministry of Education 1954, pp. 73–4).

Unfortunately, in such a line of argument the distinction between English as a subject and English as the mother tongue, and hence the medium of learning and teaching, is sometimes overlooked. This important distinction is made in an early Schools Council Pamphlet on English (Schools Council 1965) but many reports and most authors on the subject stress, optimistically perhaps, the unity of English. They thus obscure the fact that as Keen (1978) remarks there is confusion or healthy variety according to one's point of view. The Ministry of Education pamphlet *Language* recognizes this lack of unity (DES 1954, pp. 48–50), as well it might when the chapters entitled 'English in Primary Schools', 'English in Secondary Schools' and 'English in Further Education' are subtitled, respectively, 'The Teaching of Reading', 'The Teaching of Composition', and 'Problems of Communication'. The Bullock Report set out to reflect 'the organic relationship between the various aspects of English' (p. xxxv) but in fact it contains some fairly strong switches with regard to assumptions about what constitutes English. Note, for example, the skills orientation, with hardly a mention of other aspects of development in Part Six which deals with reading and language difficulties, as compared with the emphasis on integration in development elsewhere. Or consider, closer to our concerns, the lack of clear relationship between Chapter 8 on the later stages of reading and Chapter 9 on literature.

Of course one must divide in order to examine and discuss. I argue in this paper, however, that the neglect of reading development in secondary education is due in part to the ambivalence and uncertainty about the degree of responsibility (in English lessons and more generally) which teachers of English have for language skills, including the development of reading ability. Elsewhere (e.g. Pugh 1972, 1978) I have suggested other causes for this neglect but I have chosen here, in a conference devoted to 'The Reading Connection', to look in more detail

3

at historical, cultural and ideological factors which have denied reading a place as a subject in secondary education and have given to English an uncomfortable and ill-defined role.

English and reading in the nineteenth century

The teaching of English as a school subject is of more recent origin than is often realized. Although grammar and composition in English was from time to time a part of the curriculum of elementary schools in the nineteenth century, the main emphasis for much of the period was on the three Rs as recommended in the Newcastle Report of 1861 and (financially) encouraged by the payment by results system of the Revised Code of 1862. Subjects were added later in the century to those which schools were permitted or encouraged to teach, including English literature in 1876 and English in 1888. However, until early in this century the emphasis was very much on formal grammar, which tended to mean rules of Latin grammar applied to English. Especially after the Newbolt Report (Board of Education 1921), English was regarded as consisting of literature and of composition, though one imagines that many of the earlier emphases would remain through the textbooks used and because of the approaches teachers had learned and developed. A useful fuller review of the fluctuations in 'English' in schools is given by Gordon and Lawton (1978) who take it as their first example of a 'changing subject' and add, quite rightly, that the story is not yet complete.

In the universities, which had only indirect influence on the kind of schools we have so far discussed, English had an uneven history. There was a chair in English at London University (University College) from 1828 but Oxford did not have an Honours School in English until 1894 and Cambridge had no chair in English Literature until 1912, although English could be studied there from 1890 and there was a chair in Anglo-Saxon from 1878. The development of English as a subject in the other universities and university colleges was similarly patchy with regard to the date of introduction of the subject. It was also uneven as regards what emphasis was placed on philology and phonology and what on literature.

In the last century, reading English literature was regarded mainly as a suitable recreation rather than a subject for serious study in the universities as in the public schools, although there were advocates of English in the public schools (see Hollingworth 1974). Philology and other linguistic studies were more acceptable in universities but tended to be concerned with dead languages, in part because these studies were respectable *vis à vis* the dominant classics. The emphasis on classics in

4

the public schools owed much to Thomas Arnold of Rugby, who particularly stressed the classics as a linguistic discipline rather than simply the study of authors (see Honey 1977). The class structure of Victorian England clearly encouraged this trend, for the very inaccessibility in terms of language of this learning served to prevent too much straying across class boundaries. Interestingly, and in some ways ironically, Matthew Arnold, the son of Thomas Arnold, was extremely instrumental in bringing English literature into schools. However, he too pleaded (unsuccessfully) for Latin for the ablest elementary-school children and for pupil-teachers (see Arnold 1908, p. 185, report for 1878), on the grounds that they could further their education only in this way.

There is little doubt that Victorian England used language in education to firm up its class divisions. Thomas Hardy's novel *Jude the Obscure* illustrates how educational exclusion worked, and also shows very clearly the gulf between the knowledge of elementary teachers and that required for entry to universities. The teachers, as well as the children, were denied access to the linguistic code of learning to an extent which makes any perceived differences now between the language of home and the language of school and university appear insignificant. The effects of Victorian class-distinctions made for problems in the introduction of universal secondary education (and these effects were still felt in the 1944 Act). They have contributed to neglect of reading, for the model for secondary education remained, until recently, very much the subject-based model of the university and the public and grammar school, with modification to the subjects themselves, of course.

The grammar schools of the past regarded the development of literacy as of no concern to them, since children had to be sufficiently literate in order to gain entry. The development of basic skills was, therefore, left to the Dame schools and their successors (see Davies 1973). Indeed, many of the grammar schools were obliged to keep to Greek and Latin until the Grammar Schools Act of 1840 freed them from the terms of their original founders' statutes (see Gordon and Lawton 1978, p. 10).

The elementary schools, as already noted, concentrated on the 3Rs but, especially during the period of payment by results, in an uninspired way. There was considerable emphasis in the training of teachers on rote learning and repetitive drills and this was reinforced by use of the monitorial system and by the system of payment of grants according to a child's ability to read a set text.[1] Criticism of this kind of learning was fairly common among the inspectorate, Matthew Arnold being an outspoken critic. Another inspector, the Rev. Moseley (cited Goldstrom 1972), remarked that neither children nor teachers could use their reading books for learning anything else, since they were made impervious to the meaning by frequent repetition. However, there were problems in finding a better system from the financial control point of view. The replacement of payment by results by payment by attendance was unsatisfactory, since the registers were frequently inaccurately completed, itself an indication of stress and cynicism among teachers (see Hurt 1971 on much of this).

Since the nineteenth century saw a considerable rapid growth in silent private reading in business communication, as well as for pleasure (see Pugh 1975, 1978), it is strange that the response to this growth was to continue largely to ignore reading in the secondary (i.e. grammar and 'public') sector and to teach it so badly in the elementary schools. Such apparent perversity may have been the result of other concerns than the relevance of education to work and leisure. Raymond Williams (1961, esp. pp. 141–4) stresses that the shadow of class thinking which lay over nineteenth-century education led to a disregard for its possible functional value. Williams was speaking particularly of the neglect of technical education. Rolt (1970) states what he considers to be a well-established view, when he sees the seeds of British decline in engineering planted earlier in the century than is commonly thought. He believes that a cult of amateurism fostered by liberal education had much to do with the decline. Paradoxically perhaps, he considers the general mechanistic breakdown into subjects and specialisms and the liberating effects of a largely illiberal education for the masses also contributed to Britain's rapid loss of world leadership in technology in the second half of the century.

Whatever the broader effects and causes of a lack of status for functional education, there is no doubt that reading, as an elementary-school subject, enjoyed little prestige, that teaching was uninspired and that the view of what reading involved was limited and took little account of the uses to which reading was increasingly to be put. Outside the elementary school reading was not taught and English, where it was taught at all, was a changing conglomeration of interests. These included historical, philological and literary concerns at the few universities which taught English, with more basic matters such as reading, writing, sometimes grammar and a little literature at the lower levels, with virtual neglect in grammar and public schools. The roots of twentieth-century confusion over English as a subject and as a skill lie here, as does the neglect of reading development beyond the early stage.

Reading and recent trends in the teaching of English
In this century the teaching of English has become firmly established in

schools and universities but this is not to say that the subject has necessarily attained homogeneity of topic and method either at any one time or over a period of time. The variety which exists at any one level and at any one time is itself striking, but this diversity is further increased when one takes into account the different emphases given in, for example, primary education and further education, or when one considers the teaching of English as a second or foreign language. Fortunately, we are able here to limit our concern to secondary education, except for some mention of universities.

The best approach to surveying trends would be to use evidence from classroom observation with perhaps some reference to teachers' stated objectives. Unfortunately, we appear to have little survey data, although the Bullock Report contains some information from a questionnaire survey on how time is spent in English lessons (DES 1975, ch. 25). Relevant data are also available from time-interval observation from the Nottingham Project *Effective Use of Reading* (Lunzer and Gardner 1979) and from Rutter *et al* (1979). This evidence overall supports the view that reading takes up much less than half of English lessons in secondary schools, and that sustained silent reading forms a small proportion of the short time devoted to reading. From the predominance of class reading it is reasonable to infer that the emphasis is on the subject matter and discussion of it rather than on reading skills. If it is on reading skills it will mainly develop the skills of those who are reading at a given time and, even then, it is reading aloud which is being developed.

Not only do we lack data on what occurs in English lessons but we also know little about teachers' objectives. Ten Brinke (1976) has attempted an analysis of all the 'legitimate objects' of mother-tongue teaching, with reference to three languages in four countries, but is obliged to construct his objectives by a mixture of intuition, his own experience, and interpretation of experts on the topic. It is worth noting that he finds different assumptions and practices in the different countries (Germany, Holland, United Kingdom, United States) which he surveys, thus supporting the view taken here that historical, cultural influences are strong. What Ten Brinke did not do was to follow the approach used in the United States by Bloom (1956) who devised his well-known taxonomy by asking teachers what their objectives were. This method is, of course, not beyond question if one wishes to consider validity of objectives, but it does indicate what teachers consider it worthwhile and acceptable to give as objectives.

In looking at trends in the teaching of English, we are obliged, therefore, to use mainly secondary sources. These appear to indicate three main emphases, varying according to type of school and changing over time. Dixon (1967) in his report of the influential Dartmouth seminar states that three 'models or images' for English have been widely accepted: the skills model; the cultural heritage model; and the personal growth model. He sees these as leading historically one from the other, but clearly considers that the personal growth model is not only the most recent but also the best since, he says, the others have limitations and require reinterpretation. Paffard (1978) gives similar categories as does the Bullock Report (DES 1975), though this stresses that it would be 'absurdly simplifying to say that English teaching has, without light or shade, separated itself into factions with these items as the manifestoes' (p. 5). This lack of alliance with a faction may well be truer of those who teach English without qualification, often perhaps as a subsidiary subject; as the Bullock Committee observed 32.8 per cent of teachers of English in secondary schools had no qualification in the subject. However, it is less likely that those who concentrate on English will lack, to use a word favoured by writers on the teaching of the subject, a 'commitment' to literature, personal growth, or whatever. Indeed some specialization within English may be necessary since, if one adds to the areas already mentioned a major role for English teachers, foreseen by the Bullock Committee, as coordinators of language across the curriculum, their load is clearly heavy and diffuse.

Including this last concern, we may identify at least four main current aims for teachers of English. These, with justifications and a note on any sanctions but not necessarily in order of priority, are to:

1 ensure reasonable standards of literacy (and perhaps oracy) so that children can function in school, pass examinations, get jobs etc;
2 encourage children to read literature because it is worthwhile in itself, helps develop literacy, aids personal and social development, (now less fashionably) gives access to a shared culture, leads to passing examinations and prepares for higher education in the Arts;
3 help improve sensitivity and self-respect through creative work (e.g. Clegg 1964, Holbrook 1967), personal growth (Dixon 1967), social integration (one strand of the HMI's argument in DES 1977), or socialist transformation (e.g. Searle 1977). Here the justifications are varied but stem from involvement of the child; thus at the lowest level they are to do with motivation and owe much to developments in primary education and a rejection of the hard subject-model of secondary education. Sanctions for failure in personal growth are less clear but it can be argued that such approaches are better for teaching both language and literature. However, it must be noted

that the strong opposition to examining English and stating objectives for teaching come from those who favour this kind of approach.

4   develop language for learning, in both teachers and pupils, thus giving departments of English a service role (DES 1977, p. 21) and a major contribution to coordinating language across the curriculum (e.g. DES 1975, pp. 192–3; NATE 1976) leading perhaps to some major changes in secondary education or at least in how subjects are taught (e.g. Barnes *et al* 1969, Martin *et al* 1976), which forms one justification for this approach. The sanctions are not clear and there can be no examinations as yet which directly test the success of this approach.

One obvious point to note about this list is the way in which English, from starting off as an uneasy marriage of language and literature, has accumulated other responsibilities over the years. However, in this century it is literature which has enjoyed the highest prestige, partly because it replaced the classics, partly because literature was (and remains) the aspect of English most studied in universities. Hence teachers, whether university or college graduates, could hardly escape a literary bias while divisions within English were reinforced by the continuance of distinct examinations in language and literature, a formalized division which the National Association for the Teaching of English has regularly campaigned against (see NATE n.d.). Language studies, at least until the 1960s, have not formed a significant part of the university curriculum. Thus, despite attempts (e.g. Quirk 1962) to relate work in linguistics to the teaching of the native language in schools, English language lacks the firm discipline base enjoyed to a greater extent (though not entirely) by many other school subjects.

English literature as studied in schools bears more relation to university work, although the recent emphasis on personal writing and on personal growth through literature would not find strong echoes in many university departments. The relationship was closer in the middle of this century when the effects of the acceptance of English literature as a university subject were felt in schools. The battle with the classics, regarded by many following Thomas Arnold as *the* discipline, continued long after it is often regarded as being won, i.e. in the Newbolt Report of 1921 which in the aftermath of war carried over not only what may now seem excessive patriotism but also a desire for social unity. Quoting with approval Matthew Arnold (ironically in view of his father's influence) the Report declared 'Culture unites classes' and that 'English, we are convinced, must form the essential basis of a liberal education for all English people' (Board of Education 1921, p. 6). This was somewhat qualified by '*and in the earlier stages of education* it should be the principal function of all schools of whatever type to provide this basis' (p. 19, my italics). Nevertheless, a committee which was in constitution very different from the Bullock Committee, in that it included some notable academic specialists on the subject and relatively few educationists, gave the go ahead to English.

In universities at the time, syllabus-making was avidly pursued. Two well-known books of the period which might appear to be on how to read, Quiller-Couch's *On the Art of Reading* (1920) and Ezra Pound's *The ABC of Reading* (1934) can be best understood in the context of attempts to make vernacular literature a respectable subject of study. In the expansion of English as a unifying force there was, however, an antisocietal streak. This, according to one's point of view, was a reaction following the breakdown of nineteenth-century class distinctions in education or was a result of copying the élitism and non-functionalism associated with the classics. George Sampson, one of the most influential members of the Newbolt Committee wrote, 'it is the purpose of education not to prepare children for their occupations, but to prepare children against their occupations' (Sampson 1925, p. 11).

Thus in the establishment of this liberal and unifying education in English it is possible to see traces of nineteenth-century thinking, perhaps because of the need to ape the classics. However, one finds a stronger though highly critical interest in commercialism and advertising, for example, in English in the thirties, stemming from the influence of F. R. Leavis, better known in education through the work of Denys Thompson, co-author with Leavis of *Culture and Environment* (1933), and author of many subsequent educational works including school textbooks (see Mathieson 1975 for fuller discussion).

The question of élitism in literary study cannot be pursued in detail here but the point may be made that the concern with making English literature respectable led, even when the subject matter of English broadened, to a rejection of much of the mass popular culture to which children were subjected. Furthermore, the anti-industrialism of many writers influenced by the thinking of this period (e.g. Hoggart 1957) did not encourage schools to adopt an English curriculum with a strong functional bias when all the other pressures were, in any case, towards establishing English as the liberal and respectable subject.

Thus the growth of literary studies, in which there was more diversity of approach than has been indicated here, and of the social concerns which stemmed from them, helped to keep language in its place and probably deprived it of the best thinking of the time. As indicated, it is only recently that we have turned again to language study and, unlike the United States and other countries (including some European countries) more greatly influenced by American academic and educational emphases, we have paid relatively little attention to reading either in its own right or as an aspect of the study of language. Also, it could be argued further that the priority accorded to reading literary texts in schools has not provided a good preparation for the types of reading which need to be undertaken in adult life. Even worse, it has been argued that the treatment of English literature in schools has not helped in developing positive attitudes to reading particularly because of the distaste with which children's own preferences have been treated (see, for a review, D'Arcy 1974).

Conclusions and suggestions

Enough has been said by way of explanation of the historical and cultural reasons for the neglect of reading development in secondary education to indicate that there are formidable problems in the way of a curriculum in which reading is developed in an organized way at all levels. As regards the status of reading as a 'subject', it has been seen that language has been the poor relation of literature and that, within a study of language, skills such as reading have had the lowest status. Recent thinking about the role of language in secondary education, with its implications for a breaking down of subject boundaries, may possibly lead to more attention being paid to reading. On the other hand, the responsibilities of teachers of English appear to be expanding without any greater coherence or central concern emerging. Policies for language across the curriculum seem rather unspecific and, in their early implementation, as much to do with school administration as language development. Many of those who teach English have no qualification in the subject and those who have a qualification are unlikely to know much from their own training about developing reading.

Developments such as growth of research in reading and the increase in language study in departments of linguistics in universities can lead to a better discipline base for reading and hence to its achieving status and attention. Also, the more enlightened and relevant tests of reading which the NFER is preparing for monitoring standards of reading are more likely to have a valuable 'backwash' effect on teaching than the earlier sentence-completion tests (see Gorman 1979).

This paper has stressed, however, how our current confusions are rooted in unsolved – often ignored – ideological conflicts in the past. It does not advocate that reading should necessarily be a subject in secondary education, recognizing the problems of transfer encountered in the United States, but it does suggest that it deserves more attention than it has hitherto received. Reasons for the neglect are broader than those examined here, and include the problems inherent in observing and monitoring reading as argued elsewhere (Pugh 1978). However, as noted there, we are unlikely to advance far until we have more experience of teaching reading at this level.

The Effective Use of Reading Project (Lunzer and Gardner 1979) has given some pointers to methods which could be employed, though there is criticism of them (see Spencer 1979). There is also a danger in approaches based on the reading needs of schools, which may become more current. It is to be hoped that such an approach will not result in myopic concern with immediate objectives in reading for school learning at the expense of the skills in reading, and attitudes to it, which are needed for reading for work and pleasure after school.

As for English as a subject, or a conglomeration of concerns as has been argued here, more agreement is needed on its essential aims, since the proliferation of concerns must result in dissipation of effort. The antifunctional and hypercritical (even antisocietal) stance adopted when the subject had to gain prestige is not now so necessary, but there is a danger that in losing this kind of prickliness it has also lost coherence. Judgments on the validity and coherence of aims and objectives in the teaching of English can best be made with the help of data on what actually occurs in classrooms. Some hints in literature referred to here, as well as this writer's experience of observing many English lessons, suggest that there are strong damping forces (including, for example, textbooks which few commentators mention) which even out the effect of the trends discussed here. This may mean that as regards aims even greater confusion exists than has been suggested. In any case a thorough objective study on a national scale of aims and practices in English lessons seems long overdue, as one of the prerequisites for discussion of how reading and other important language abilities can be developed in secondary education.

Acknowledgment
This paper deals with some topics which I have also treated in a draft of a contribution *The Teaching of English in Modern England* to Block 3 of the Open University course *Language in Use* (Code E263, forthcoming 1981). Dr J. L. Dobson is preparing the section entitled *Literacy and Language Teaching in the Nineteenth Century* for that course. I am grateful to Dr Dobson for discussions on the teaching of English in the last century and for allowing me to use some information, particularly on English in universities, from his draft.

References

ARNOLD, M. (1908) 'Report for the Year 1880' in Board of Education *Reports on Elementary Schools, 1852–1882* London: HMSO

BARNES, D. *et al.* (1969) *Language, the Learner and the School* Harmondsworth: Penguin

BLOOM, B. S. (1956, ed.) *Taxonomy of Educational Objectives: Handbook 1 Cognitive Domain* New York: McKay

BOARD OF EDUCATION (1921) *The Teaching of English in England* (Report of a Committee to Enquire into the Position of English in the Educational System of England, under the chairmanship of Sir Henry Newbolt) London: HMSO

CLEGG, A. B. (1964, ed.) *The Excitement of Writing* London: Chatto and Windus

D'ARCY, P. (1974) *Reading for Meaning Volume 2: The Reader's Response* London: Hutchinson

DAVIES, W. J. F. (1973) *Teaching Reading in Early England* London: Pitman

DES (1975) *A Language for Life* (Report of the Committee of Enquiry into Teaching the Use of English, under the chairmanship of Sir Alan Bullock) London: HMSO

DES (1977) *Curriculum 11–16* London: DES

DES (1978) *Primary Education in England: A Survey by HM Inspectors of Schools* London: HMSO

DIXON, J. (1967) *Growth through English* Oxford: Oxford University Press for NATE

DOUGHTY, P., PEARCE, J. and THORNTON, G. (1971) *Language in Use* London: Edward Arnold

GOLDSTROM, J. M. (1972) *The Social Content of Education 1808–1870: A Study of the Working-Class School Reader in England and Ireland* Shannon: Irish University Press

GORDON, P. and LAWTON, D. (1978) *Curriculum Change in the Nineteenth and Twentieth Centuries* London: Hodder and Stoughton

GORMAN, T. P. (1979) 'Monitoring of language performance in the schools of England and Wales' in D. Thackray (ed.) *Growth in Reading* London: Ward Lock Educational, pp. 234–9

HOGGART, R. (1957) *The Uses of Literacy* London: Chatto and Windus

HOLBROOK, D. (1967) *The Exploring Word: Creative Disciplines in the Education of Teachers of English* Cambridge: Cambridge University Press

HOLLINGWORTH, B. (1974) The mother tongue and the public schools in the 1860s *British Journal of Educational Studies* 22, 3, pp. 312–24

13

HONEY, J. R. de S. (1977) *Tom Brown's Universe: The Development of the Victorian Public School* London: Millington

HURT, J. (1971) *Education in Evolution: Church, State Society and Popular Education 1800–1870* London: Rupert Hart-Davis

KEEN, J. (1978) *Teaching English: A Linguistic Approach* London: Methuen

LEAVIS, F. R. and THOMPSON, D. (1933) *Culture and Environment* London: Chatto and Windus

LUNZER, E. and GARDNER, K. (1979, eds) *The Effective Use of Reading* London: Heinemann Educational for the Schools Council

MARTIN, N. *et al.* (1976) *Writing and Learning Across the Curriculum 11–16* London: Ward Lock Educational for the Schools Council

MATHIESON, M. (1975) *The Preachers of Culture: A Study of English and its Teachers* London: Allen and Unwin

MINISTRY OF EDUCATION (1954) *Language: Some Suggestions for Teachers of English and Others* (Education Pamphlet no. 26) London: HMSO

NATE (1976) *Language Across the Curriculum* London: Ward Lock Educational

NATE (n.d. = 1978?) *A Common System of Examining at 16+* (NATE Examinations Booklet no. 2) Huddersfield: NATE

PAFFARD, M. (1978) *Thinking about English* London: Ward Lock Educational

POUND, E. (1934) *The ABC of Reading* London: Faber

PUGH, A. K. (1972) 'Reading in the secondary schools: an unassumed responsibility' in V. Southgate (ed.) *Literacy at All Levels* London: Ward Lock Educational, pp. 81–8

PUGH, A. K. (1975) 'The development of silent reading' in W. Latham (ed.) *The Road to Effective Reading* London: Ward Lock Educational, pp. 110–19

PUGH, A. K. (1978) *Silent Reading: An Introduction to its Study and Teaching* London: Heinemann Educational

QUILLER-COUCH, A. (1920) *On the Art of Reading* Cambridge: Cambridge University Press

QUIRK, R. (1962) *The Use of English* London: Longman

ROLT, L. T. C. (1970) *Victorian Engineering* Harmondsworth: Penguin

RUTTER, M. *et al* (1979) *Fifteen Thousand Hours: Secondary Schools and Their Effects on Children* London: Open Books

SAMPSON, G. (1925) *English for the English* Cambridge: Cambridge University Press

SCHOOLS COUNCIL (1965) *English: A Programme for Research and Development in English Teaching* (Working Paper no. 3) London: HMSO

SEARLE, C. (1977) *The World in a Classroom* London: Writers and Readers Publishing Cooperative

SILVER, H. (1977) Aspects of neglect: the strange case of Victorian popular education *Oxford Review of Education 3*, 1, pp. 57–69

SMITH, N. B. (1965, revised edition) *American Reading Instruction* Newark, Delaware: International Reading Association

SPENCER, M. (1979) Effective reading *The English Magazine 1*, pp. 22–4

TEN BRINKE, S. (1976) *The Complete Mother-tongue Curriculum* London: Longman

WILLIAMS, R. (1961) *The Long Revolution* London: Chatto and Windus

Note

[1] This is the widely-accepted view. See Silver (1977) for serious criticism of this long-held characterization of Victorian classrooms.

2 From bookshelf to desk: the findings of the survey *Primary Education in England* on children's reading

G. W. Elsmore

The HMI survey *Primary Education in England* (DES 1978) covers a good deal more than children's reading. It gives an account of the work of seven-, nine- and eleven-year-olds in five broad curricular areas: language and literacy, mathematics, science, aesthetic and physical education, and social studies. It also gives information about the way primary schools are organized. A total of 1,127 classes in 542 schools were involved, chosen to be representative of all primary schools in England.

Three kinds of measurement were used to assess the children's work. The first was a measure of the range of the curriculum on offer and of the emphasis given to aspects of it; the second was a measure of the extent to which the work being done by the children was matched to their abilities. Both these measures were made through direct observation in the classroom by HM Inspectors experienced in primary education. The third measure was of performance in reading by nine- and eleven-year-olds and of performance in mathematics by eleven-year-olds. This measure was obtained through the use of objective tests administered by the National Foundation for Educational Research. I shall refer to all three sorts of measure in the context of children's reading.

What emerged from HMI's direct observation and reporting about reading was that the teaching of early reading skills was given a high degree of priority. It is clear that the teaching of early reading skills is regarded by teachers as extremely important and that these skills are taught systematically. Graded reading schemes were used in all seven-year-old classes and in nearly all of these classes reading practice was continued through the use of supplementary readers associated with the schemes. This systematic approach was continued with similar emphasis in the nine-year-old classes. By the age of eleven some children in about three-quarters of the eleven-year-old classes were still making use of graded schemes and supplementary readers.

When the second measurement was applied – the extent to which the level of task was matched to the children's abilities to perform them – the teaching of these early reading skills was overall more frequently judged to be reasonably matched than in any other area of the work looked at.

Encouraging results were produced in the reading test of eleven-year-olds. These can be compared with past results because the test used in the survey had been used to measure national reading standards in 1955, 1960 and 1970. The test is a sentence-completion type in which the child has to choose the appropriate missing word from a selection which is offered. The items become progressively more difficult. An average score of 31.13 out of a possible 60 was obtained, which was the highest score by eleven-year-olds in the series and consistent with a rising trend in reading standards, as measured by this test, between 1955 and 1977.

So far so good. This is one side of the coin. These findings indicate a good measure of success in teaching children to master the elementary reading skills. But the survey probed more deeply than this. For example it revealed that those children who found learning to read difficult were more likely to be given reading tasks suitably matched to their abilities than the children who were more able readers.

Children are taught to read but further questions have to be asked: Do they read? Do they naturally and confidently use the skills they have acquired and make use of books and printed material for a variety of purposes – both in and out of school? If the amount and range of reading material now found in primary schools is compared with that available twenty or so years ago, and if the expressed aims of many primary heads are taken as indicators, the answer to both those questions would appear to be 'yes'. The survey report states that libraries and book collections were available almost universally and in three-quarters of the classes books had been selected with care, representing a good range of fiction and nonfiction suited to the age and reading abilities of the children. Typical of statements by heads of what they intended to achieve in the teaching of language in their schools were:

To foster an enjoyment of poetry and literature and to get children to think critically about what they read.

To teach children their own language and literature and to enable them to express their own thoughts clearly, coherently and fluently.

To enable children to achieve a level of competence which will enable them to make their way when they leave the primary school.

However, observations reported by HMI do not lead to an unqualified conclusion that children do use and develop the early skills so thoroughly taught and painstakingly acquired; that they do turn to books naturally and confidently for pleasure or as a source of information as much as they might. The findings of the survey suggest that there is room for further development. There was a tendency at all ages for children to receive insufficient encouragement to extend the range of their reading. For the abler readers at all ages there was little evidence that the mor' advanced reading skills were being taught. The reading tasks which the ablest readers were given to do were too easy in about two-fifths of the classes. Only in a very small minority of classes were children dis- cussing the books they had read at other than a superficial level oı comprehension. Writing copied from reference books was felt to be excessive. Children had too little opportunity to use libraries and class collections for private reading of their own choice or for reference purposes. This is the other side of the coin. It is not entirely tarnished. For example, when the relationship between the use of books and the measures of performance in reading was examined, higher average reading scores were found to be associated with those classes who did make good use of book collections and libraries and where stories and poems were regularly read to children. (Good use of libraries and book collections was recorded for a quarter of the seven-year-old classes, just under a quarter of nine-year-old classes and just over a third of eleven-year-old classes. Appropriate use of stories and poems told or read by the teacher occurred in nearly three-quarters of the seven-year-old classes and in just over a half of the nine- and eleven-year-old classes.) These findings support the view of the Bullock Committee (DES 1975) on the place of literature:

> There is no doubt in our mind that one of the most important tasks facing the teacher of all juniors – and younger secondary pupils – is to increase the amount and range of their voluntary reading. We believe that there is a strong association between this and reading attainment and that private reading can make an important con-tribution to the children's linguistic and experiential development.

I now want to turn to the expectations that we might reasonably have of teachers' and children's attitude to reading – using books, taking them from the bookshelves to the desk for the variety of purposes already mentioned; extending the range of reading; acquiring more advanced reading skills; advancing the level of comprehension, of reference skills; and increasing the opportunity for private reading. These are all interrelated.

The first requirement to extend the range of reading is that a suitable range and variety of books should be available and easily accessible.

This requirement appears to be largely met in most primary schools. Nonfiction will need to cover all the aspects of the curriculum ranging from standard reference books for identification purposes to books that will extend the range of children's knowledge about people, places, animals, plants and manmade objects, a minimum requirement of which is that they should be factually accurate, contain clear diagrams, high quality illustration and an index, and should be suited to the age and reading abilities of the pupils. The expectation is that such books will be selected with at least these criteria in mind and that implies that teachers must know the books themselves and will be able to bring sufficient expertise and knowledge to bear upon their selection for the children they have in mind.

There should be no difficulty about finding a suitable range of fiction. Indeed the very abundance of children's fiction brings its own problem – that of selection. Again it requires teachers who have a considerable background of knowledge of children's books, who know the field, and can judge the language level and what is likely to be of interest and value to their children. Interesting plot, good characterization, human relationships and setting are all important.

The list of book titles mentioned more than ten times as having been read during the previous month in Frank Whitehead's research on children's reading interests (Whitehead *et al*. 1975) shows that the Victorian classics still retain a strong position. Among them appear the two Alice books, *The Wind in the Willows*, *Treasure Island*, *Black Beauty* and many more. Rightly so. Childhood should include encounters with Alice, Toad, Jim Hawkins and company. It should also include encounters with the great ones of ancient times found in the myths and legends of North and East, although these appear much less frequently. Is it not reasonable to expect most lively eleven-year-olds to know why the caterpillar said, 'That is not said right' to Alice when she recited, 'You are Old Father William', and to know the meaning of pun and parody; to have responded feelingly to Odysseus's triumphant victory in the great hall in Ithaca, and to understand why the last chapter of *The Wind in the Willows* is called, 'The return of Ulysses'? But nor should childhood pass by without encounter with the best of contemporary children's fiction and here many teachers appear to be on less firm ground, less discriminating in the choice of reading they make available and introduce to their children. In the best fiction children will meet not only new words and more complex language structures, but through these more complex forms, the thoughts, experiences, feelings of people who exist outside and beyond their own immediate world. Shelley said, 'A man to be greatly good must imagine intensively and comprehensively; he must put himself in the place of another and many others; the pains and pleasures of his species must become his own.' Good children's fiction is capable of starting the development of this level of feeling and imagining. Children gain from and enjoy fiction which reflects experiences similar to their own and which helps them to resolve their inner questions and conflicts safely, at one remove; the kind of gain and enjoyment that is contained in C. S. Lewis's remark, 'Nothing, I suspect, is more astonishing in any man's life than the discovery that there do exist people, very like himself.'

Availability of books is not enough. If reading skills, levels of comprehension and opportunities for private reading are to be extended then more planning of the reading programme will be necessary. Children need to be taught how to use dictionaries and reference books efficiently; how to skim passages for quick retrieval of information; how to scan passages to establish the main points; how to interpret context cues; how to anticipate and predict, to infer and to make intelligent guesses of meaning, and make sense of difficult passages. If opportunities for children to choose their own books and extend their private reading are increased, more not less oversight and guidance will be necessary, especially where fiction is concerned. Children need help with selection; they neither have the experience nor the knowledge to plan their own reading programmes. Geoffrey Trease (1964) reminds us that:

> It is a fashionable proposition that only children know what other children like. What children like is just part of the modern myth that all children are angels of instinctive wisdom and all adults are blundering, pompous fools – that the best book is the one most children like. We do not apply this criteria to adult literature or any other art form. . . . Every other art has its standards independent of box office returns.

Teachers should know what children are getting out of their reading. A list of books read can look very impressive but is no guide to what the reader has gained. But there is a need for care. Sensitive intervention is called for through discussion – and at a deeper level with older juniors than is commonly found now – with individuals and with groups rather than a routine requirement to answer questions in the form of superficial comprehension exercises (of which there are already far too many). Connie Rosen (1973) reminded us that 'Treasure Island is not a handbook of piracy and Hickory, Dickory, Dock is not a footnote on the nocturnal habits of mice. They are oblique ways of symbolizing the world of feeling.'

We had these kinds of development in mind when we suggested in the primary survey report that more might be done to build on the vital and careful work now given high priority to ensure children become literate. Doing more of anything in the current primary school curriculum is usually seen as leaving out something else. This is not necessarily the case. The primary school curriculum is probably wide enough now. What I have implied, especially for the average and more able pupils, is that what is done should be taken to greater depth rather than that content that is new to primary education should be introduced. This suggests a change of emphasis in the kind of reading programme commonly found rather than adding something extra. For example, there was evidence from the survey that some children, even at eleven, were spending considerable time on the repetitive practice of reading skills already acquired. Textbooks containing comprehension, grammar and language exercises featured in the work of almost every nine- and eleven-year-old class and in about two-thirds of seven-year-old classes. Language course kits were used for similar purposes in about half of the nine- and eleven-year-old classes. The exercises chosen were not usually connected with pupils' own reading and writing. If such exercises are done they are more likely to be effective if they are directly linked with the child's language work as a whole, including his reading, and are based on perceived need. This should make it unlikely that they feature as a routine lesson for all or call regularly on large amounts of time. Less emphasis on these isolated exercises would give more time for extending the reading activities I have outlined.

But a change of emphasis implies more than simply introducing a deeper range of reading activities. To bring about such a change requires a different kind, and in many cases, a higher level of knowledge, understanding and expertise of most class teachers. For example, not all teachers are knowledgeble about children's books, though they might be about other things. Not all teachers are lovers of books or poetry; not all teachers are certain of what they ought to do about literature and poetry or about the extensive copying from reference books. Is it reasonable to expect that this should be so? Consider the expectation we have of the class teacher in the primary school. Not only do we expect the level of expertise and knowledge needed to achieve a good reading programme and a sound language programme, but also the knowledge and expertise to organize and teach the whole curriculum to the class. Just consider what is required to plan and teach an acceptable language programme: a knowledge about language and a high level of understanding of how it is used and developed; not only an understanding of the processes at work when the spoken word is used in everyday classroom transactions, but also the ability to appraise the children's use of it and plan its extension; a thorough understanding of the reading process and a high level of expertise to teach early reading skills and to extend the children's reading. This implies the acquisition of a wide and detailed knowledge of children's fiction, of poetry and some of the range at least of nonfiction; if the children's writing is to be developed then teachers must be capable of introducing and encouraging new and more complex language forms so that children have growing access to a wide range of language from which they can choose the appropriate form for the writing task in hand. Teachers will need to have had some experience of drama and an understanding of how it can be effectively used; last, but by no means least, they will need to have understanding of how language generally, and reading in particular, contributes to and draws on other areas of learning so that, for example, the best historical fiction contributes to historical studies and good stories set in other countries enrich geographical studies.

Although all class teachers in primary schools are usually responsible for developing children's use of language and must therefore be able to operate a reading and language programme, it is surely not realistic to suppose that every teacher should acquire a wide and deep level of knowledge, understanding and expertise in this, as well as in every other area of the curriculum. The older the children, the more unrealistic this expectation becomes. This is why the notion of the specialist teacher was developed in the survey: 'A fuller use of teachers' particular strengths could make a useful contribution to the solution of this problem.' But the use of the 'specialist' was seen very much in the sense of the Bullock Committee's recommendation, 'Every school should have a suitably qualified teacher with responsibility for advising and supporting his colleagues in language and the teaching of reading.' This implies a change in the way primary education is traditionally organized in the schools; a change in the attitudes of heads and teachers that will lead to some modification in the use of teachers' talent and time, without losing the advantages of the class-teacher system. This will take time and careful planning. It will also take time for those teachers, whether already in service or newly qualified, to acquire the level of knowledge and skill needed to discharge the responsibility for language and reading in the schools. But given the firm foundation that exists there is every reason to believe that, with such developments in their reading programmes, children will not only continue to achieve an acceptable level of literacy but that they will 'maintain and extend the idea of reading as an activity which brings great pleasure and is a personal resource of limitless value' (DES 1975); that in school they will increasingly be moved to take the book from the bookshelf to the desk.

References

DES (1975) *A Language for Life* The Bullock Report London: HMSO

DES (1978) *Primary Education in England: A Survey by HM Inspectors of Schools* London: HMSO

ROSEN, C. and ROSEN, H. (1973) *The Language of Primary School Children* (Schools Council Project on Language Development in the Primary School) Harmondsworth: Penguin Education

TREASE, G. (1964) *Tales Out of School – A Survey of Children's Fiction* London: Heinemann Educational

WHITEHEAD, F., CAPEY, A. C. and MADDREN, W. (1975) *Children's Reading Interests* (Interim Report from Schools Council Research Project on Children's Reading Habits) London: Evans/Methuen Education

3 Local authority support for literacy

Christopher Tipple

Over the door of an old school in North Yorkshire is engraved the motto 'Learn or Leave'. We have moved a very long way from that, and my purpose here is to show just how far, from the viewpoint of a large local education authority. Leeds has nearly 750,000 people, 130,000 children of school age and upwards of 10,000 full-time teachers in schools and further education. Literacy, in varying degrees, is the concern of all of them.

In the first part of this paper I describe developments in schools; in the second part I shall look at the Leeds Literacy Scheme which is aimed at adults. In doing so my intention is to show how many of the precepts described by others find practical expression across the whole field of education. It is not to give a 'plug' for Leeds.

Reading skills are, of course, developing even before a child enters primary or even nursery school and Leeds has prepared a booklet to help parents of preschool children to begin to develop skills which will help their children to learn more easily. I propose to look at provision for the teaching of reading in schools along several themes. The Bullock report has been a seminal influence on our work, as will be clear.

First, in-service training. Teachers are encouraged to promote reading in all its aspects and to develop in their pupils a love of reading for its own sake and this requires a well-developed programme of in-service training. Courses are mounted on a county basis at Woolley Hall, on a city basis at the Authority's teachers' centre and, increasingly, on an individual school basis. The Authority has established at its teachers' centre a special reading centre which is now four years old. The functions of the reading centre are to:

1 carry out work which teachers would do themselves if they had the time and opportunity;
2 make available, for examination, books, reading schemes, equipment and other materials used in the teaching of reading;
3 provide an advisory/consultation service by appointment for heads/ teachers to discuss problems of organization, teaching, learning and materials;

4 make available information which is obtainable nationally but not always known to teachers locally;
5 visit schools requesting information on specific issues and to discuss these with members of staff;
6 organize pilot study/evaluation of selected published items;
7 talk with small groups of teachers, students and overseas visitors who may be specializing in the study of the teaching of reading;
8 give assistance in the organization of school reading programmes, mainly through consultation and through the availability of publications.

In-service courses on the teaching of reading at the teachers' centre have been designed to provide a programme which is both general and specialized to meet the needs of the whole staff, groups of teachers and individual teachers within a school. To achieve this aim activities have been limited to primary education in the main, though courses on remedial reading have been organized for teachers in middle schools.

Without exception all courses which are publicized are heavily over-subscribed. It has therefore been necessary to make some provision for the large number of teachers who have been unable to attend courses at the centre. To meet this need all primary schools in Leeds have received from the Authority, free of charge, five cassette tapes containing ten BBC radio programmes entitled *Teaching Young Readers*. Discussion notes and questions have accompanied each set of tapes. This material enables each primary school to organize some school-based in-service work. It also provides a common base of information to which reference can be made on any centre-based courses on the teaching of reading. For teachers of older children similar material from the BBC programmes *Reading after ten* is available on request.

A group of experienced teachers have formed a Language and Reading Development Curriculum Study Group and they have stimulated courses on a structured approach to the acquisition of prereading skills. The effect of this part of the programme, so far, has been the adoption by 36 Leeds infant schools of a programme designed to develop visual perceptual skills in young children by structuring 55 different published items. Whenever possible two or more teachers come from the same school so that the effect of courses can have a bigger impact on the head and his staff.

This programme ensures all children get a good start to beginning reading. Courses are also organized for teachers of remedial reading to seven- to nine-year-olds and a link has been forged between the work of the infant and remedial teachers, emphasizing the possibility of earlier identification and remediation.

Apart from the reading centre, secondments to long-term national courses are made and the Authority seeks to use the expertise of lecturers at the Schools of Education in the Polytechnic and the University. Several courses have been mounted based on the work of Lunzer and Gardner (1979) as set out in their research report *The Effective Use of Reading*. In this way the idea that techniques of reading are as important to the sixth former and potential undergraduate as to the middle-school pupil have been developed.

Work on reading and language is included in all induction programmes and in the training of all staff tutors. In the provision of in-service training the Advisory Service plays an all-important part, particularly within the primary tier where the three primary advisers in the Authority provide a wide range of local courses on reading and language development. In middle and high schools and in special schools other advisers promote and run courses on a wide range of aspects of reading. In particular I should mention courses in good record-keeping and more accurate assessment so teachers get better feedback about the efficacy of their teaching.

The growth of the number of school-based courses has given a valuable impetus to the progress of the building of reading policies within schools, to the nomination of particular teachers as reading coordinators and to the acceptance of the idea of reading across the curriculum. In this latter respect high and middle schools have been involved in NATE projects, in ASE projects such as LAMP and an investigation of the science register of language. Progress has not been as rapid as one would wish but the work of some local groups has shown how valuable such involvements can be.

This is a very difficult area which this Conference might be able to give some attention to. Only last week the Chief Adviser and I were interviewing a head of English department for an adviser's post in Leeds. He had tried to convince his colleagues of the importance of examining their texts from the viewpoint of readability but admitted that little progress was possible because of the internal politics of the school.

The other themes I shall deal with more briefly, beginning with screening and assessment. Leeds has a policy of screening pupils in its schools at seven plus and nine plus and this has resulted in a clear identification of children at risk. Teachers in primary and in middle schools are thus able to provide remediation at the earliest opportunities to those in need. A reading age of two years below chronological age is regarded as an indication of failure needing remediation and an average of 10 per cent of children in each age cohort has been found to fall into this category. Individual schools have also developed their own routines of diagnostic testing to focus more finely on the causes of reading failure and information on the suitability and validity of tests is available through the Schools Psychological Service, the Advisory Division and through the reading centre. The screening is carried out by schools under the guidance of the Psychological Service which is an integral part of the Advisory Division. Thought is being given to an extension of such screening to the 13 + cohort.

Much of Leeds is organized on a three-tier system of education, 5 – 9, 9 – 13, and 13+, and this gives additional importance to good liaison between the tiers. In area and local groups discussion takes place between teachers in different stages and there is a continual search for ways of bringing greater continuity to the reading curriculum. To this end, discussion documents have been produced setting out possible targets for middle schools in the range of the teaching of reading offered by a school.

Logically, the next theme must be remediation. Apart from in-service training which I have described, there is additional funding for those EPA schools where reading failure is more significant. Staffing levels in primary and middle schools have also been improved, thus allowing a greater possibility of small-group work, withdrawal groups and intensive work for those in need. Special efforts are being made to provide teaching machines such as the Language Master to a wide number of schools in the primary tier. These efforts are redoubled in the special sector of education with its more intractable cases and in special programmes to develop better language skills in deprived and ethnic minority groups.

For those children using English as a second language or using non-standard English help is given by specialist teams. A Language Development Team works in schools where groups of five- to seven-year-olds are in need of extra help to develop a fluency in English. The members of the team do not concentrate on reading to the exclusion of other aspects of literacy. The first priority is speech and although this work is done mainly in withdrawal groups, a range of activities is available to the children.

There are also Language Units for seven plus to sixteen-year-olds for English as a second language. No set reading scheme is used but Breakthrough to Literacy materials are used plus materials developed at the units, in order to help the pupils to have a sound knowledge of the language before starting on the reading scheme of their home school. A new team has recently been established comprising three teachers to help children with above average IQs who are having reading problems in the middle schools.

Another theme which deserves mention is reading development and the resources to achieve it. Leeds recognized the validity of the Bullock Report's observation that ability to cope with print often marked the end of a planned reading programme. Much work goes in at all levels to supplement the diet of reading offered to children of average and above-average ability.

Teachers are made aware of the richness of the possibilities open to them in the range of books produced for children. Apart from in-service courses this is done by publications such as *Books in Schools* which is a periodical review of children's literature carried out by teachers for teachers. Copies go free of charge to all schools. There are also travelling exhibitions of books. Typical is a collection of sixty titles suitable for pupils leaving their reading scheme. Teachers have access to exhibitions/collections of national significance such as the School Library Exhibition Collection at Wakefield.

A working party of teachers and librarians have cooperated in the production of *Choose Well* – a guide to book selection. The Advisory Division, the Tutor Librarian at the teachers' centre, lecturers in the School of Librarianship at Leeds Polytechnic, librarians in Leeds and Wakefield and lecturers in the Polytechnic and University Schools of Education all assist in this valuable work. To assist in the broader provision of books, the Authority has decided to set up a School Library Service which will offer book loans to all Leeds schools. The emphasis will, initially, be on the underpinning of topic work in schools but the service is capable of expansion to cover a broad spectrum of functions. The number of school bookshops grows steadily and children have the pleasure and excitement of owning their own books. Supplementary sums have assisted those schools in greatest need.

It is in further education that the job of tackling functional illiteracy has, in my opinion, been one of the great success stories (and there haven't been many!) of education in the 70s. The fact that this job exists demonstrates the importance of all I have been saying about work in schools.

Expert opinion suggests that there are at least two million functionally illiterate adults in England and Wales. In other words, almost 6 per cent of the adult population is either unable to read or write at all, or has a literacy level lower than that of a nine-year-old child. In our society, two million adults are severely disadvantaged at work and leisure. Two million adults cannot participate effectively in our increasingly literate society. There are probably at least 15,000 such people in Leeds.

During the summer of 1972, various people in Leeds were saying that there should be a literacy scheme to meet the special needs of people who were not attending existing classes, and a circular from the Council of Social Service appealing for volunteers was widely distributed. Thirty people committed themselves to the scheme, mainly school teachers. Since that modest beginning more than 2,200 voluntary tutors have come forward to offer help and nearly 2,400 students have been helped. The scheme has a full-time coordinator and numerous part-time organizers. Currently there are about 70 part-time teachers and 500 voluntary tutors.

Voluntary tutors are recruited from a variety of backgrounds. Each tutor is expected to undergo a selection procedure, attend a short training course and have regular in-service training. The tutor works with one student, and this work may take place in the student's or tutor's home, or in a variety of other premises – schools, libraries, youth centres, welfare clinics – in fact, in any suitable building which has a room available. The volunteer must be prepared to give a regular commitment for at least a year. In addition to the one-to-one tuition, students are taught in small groups by a qualified reading specialist. Students are encouraged to move into small groups to promote socialization and prevent overdependence on their tutor. The role of volunteer tutors in the Leeds Literacy Scheme is, however, absolutely vital to its success; without their help, it would be impossible to offer each student the individual tuition which is the Scheme's strength.

Students are referred to the Scheme from many different sources. The needs of the students coming forward differ greatly; some are totally illiterate, others need help with writing and spelling. It is a common misconception that adult illiterates are educationally subnormal; they tend to be an average cross-section of society. In the Leeds area the proportion of male to female students began at 2:1, with the majority coming forward from the 25–45 age group. This is the age group when work, careers and children are particularly significant as a means of motivating a student to seek help. The pattern is now changing to become more evenly balanced between the sexes. More unemployed young people are now referring themselves for help.

There have been three significant recent developments. First, with the cooperation of the media, particularly Radio Leeds and the *Evening Post*, a Leeds Literacy Week was held late in 1978 during which maximum publicity was given to these opportunities. Second, an adult literacy resource centre has been established. This prints the publicity and recruitment material relating to the Leeds Adult Literacy Scheme, manufactures and reproduces teaching materials suitable to the needs of adult and literacy students, compiles a regular magazine for circulation to all tutors and students, and provides a base for training tutors in the use of audio-visual equipment and teaching materials. This now actually produces 850 copies of *Leeds Reads* which is a six-weekly magazine that provides an identity for the Literacy Scheme and a communication link between the Resource Centre and participants in the Scheme. Regular features include news from the areas, dates for future events, teachers' hints, students' own work, recipes, worksheets, crosswords and puzzles. There is also *Leeds Writes* which is an illustrated collection in A5 bookform of students' own work. Worksheets have been devised to accompany these books. Three have been produced so far with the run increasing from 250 to 500. Mention should also be made of the *Adult Literacy Skills Kit*. This consists of eleven sections of graded workcards covering a wide range of interests; pop music, cooking, fiction, gardening, home brewing, know your rights, map reading, motoring, safety in the home and sport. There is a reading series called *Standards and Rebels, Books 1 and 2* plus workbooks designed with the prime intention of being used as a vehicle for teaching social sight words and functional literacy skills to beginning and advancing readers. Also produced are graded spelling booklets, a phonic crossword book and worksheets and handouts.

Thirdly, a reading and writing Drop-In Centre has been established at 6 Boar Lane which is a shop on one of the busiest streets in the city, close to the market, the bus and railway stations and a job centre. The objective is twofold. First, this is an attempt to establish contact with those who have fought shy of the Scheme so far, especially the socially disadvantaged and unemployed young people. The informal nature of the Centre encourages casual use by passers-by who may need help with filling in forms, writing letters, looking for a job etc. Some 'customers' may well have a multiplicity of problems and the staff therefore offer counselling help and refer people to the appropriate agency for further help if necessary.

The other main objective of the Drop-In Centre is to encourage clients to take advantage of the long-term educational opportunities which will be available there. Behind the 'shop front', a small room and cellar basement are used as teaching areas and for individual consultation. Clients are able to use these rooms on a self-programming basis. The staff use a counselling approach in teaching language skills and students are encouraged to take an active part in charting their own progress.

I have attempted to show something of the tremendous volume and range of literacy provision in a major local authority. Finally I would like to point to areas that need further work and initiatives:

1 A greater impact must be made on the large number of functionally illiterate people in our society. The adult literacy provision I have described is linked with the basic education programme within adult education in Leeds and the first 'graduates' of the Leeds literacy scheme took their O-level English this summer. It shows what can be done.
2 Some recommendations of Bullock still need a lot of work, notably the development of reading policies in schools; the development of different reading skills for different purposes both within a school and in life; and the deployment, and acceptance by other specialists within a school, of reading consultants.
3 There is still a paucity of substantial national courses on reading and language for teachers whom we should like to second for training as coordinators and consultants in their schools and areas, though the development of a recent one-term course at Leeds Polytechnic is very much to be welcomed.
4 Greater coordination is needed between the work in schools and the work in further education. Partly because of different traditions, partly because of the way Leeds is organized (and in this respect it is like most other local education authorities) there is a large gap between workers in these two sectors when, in truth, there is a great deal they could learn from each other. We are working on it!

References

DES (1975) *A Language for Life* (The Bullock Report) London: HMSO
LUNZER, E. A. and GARDNER, K. (1979, eds) *The Effective Use of Reading* London: Heinemann Educational for the Schools Council

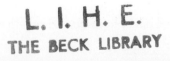

4 Hard writing – easy reading

John Mann

What a year this has been for those who are interested in reading. 1978 saw the publication of UKRA's papers on *Reading: Implementing the Bullock Report* (Grundin 1978), the Open University's anthology *Reading: From Process to Practice* (Chapman and Czerniewska 1978) and James Herring's *Teaching Library Skills in Schools* (1978). We at the Schools Council published W. K. Brennan's *Reading for Slow Learners* (Brennan 1978), and followed it with this year's splendid trilogy, Eric Lunzer and Keith Gardner (1979) on *The Effective Use of Reading*, John Dixon (1979) on *Education 16–19: The Role of English and Communications*, and a working paper on *English in the 1980s: A Programme of Support for Teachers* (Schools Council 1979a). With all this to absorb teachers will need all the support UKRA and the Schools Council can give.

Only a few weeks ago the National Book League published their report on *Books for Schools* (NBL 1979) and the British Library published *Educating Library Users in Secondary Schools* (Irving and Snape 1979). The Schools Council has just reprinted *Linguistics and English Teaching* (Schools Council 1979b), Frank Whitehead's (1977) research study *Children and Their Books*, and James Britton's (1979) *The Development of Writing Abilities*. Later this year the Schools Council will be publishing *Learning Through Talking 11–16* (Schools Council 1979c), and *Teaching Language and Communication to the Mentally Handicapped* (Leeming *et al.* 1979).

I cannot, I dare not, claim that this formidable list is comprehensive. I've deliberately omitted the Schools Council's materials in *English for Immigrant Children Project* (1969–75) and materials in Welsh as a first language at primary and secondary stages (Schools Council 1977–9a, b; Jones and Thomas 1977). There must be many others too.

The problem for teachers of language, communication and reading is not a dearth of advice, but a superabundance. I wonder whether it would be helpful if the Schools Council were to try to map the territory opened up by these explorers.

Perhaps I ought to emphasize now that I am not the man to do it. The people who attend UKRA conferences are all specialists in reading, experts in the theory of learning or the practice of teaching reading. I am not. I am at best the kind of person Virginia Woolf addressed as 'The Common Reader'. For the last forty years or so I've been a consistent, a catholic, even a confirmed reader.

Augustine Birrell (1965) thought that:

> Dr Johnson is perhaps our best example of a confirmed reader. Malone once found him sitting in his room roasting apples and reading a history of Birmingham. This staggered even Malone, who was himself a somewhat far-gone reader.
>
> 'Don't you find it rather dull?' he ventured to enquire.
>
> 'Yes,' replied the Sage, 'it is dull.'
>
> Malone's eyes then rested on the apples, and he remarked he supposed they were for medicine.
>
> 'Why, no,' said Johnson; 'I believe they are only there because I wanted something to do. I have been confined to the house for a week, and so you find me roasting apples and reading the history of Birmingham.'
>
> This anecdote pleasingly illustrates the habits of the confirmed reader. Nor let the worldling sneer. Happy is the man who, in the hours of solitude and depression, can read a history of Birmingham.

I cannot claim to have read the history of Birmingham, nor even like the late Lord Samuel to read for two hours every night before going to bed. But I would claim that an administrator needs a fair appetite for print, and a more than passing interest in the skills and arts of communication. It's as a practitioner that I'd like to explore some of my problems with you. If any of you were hoping for solutions, I would have to reply, in Jack Kerouac's words, 'I have nothing to offer anybody except my own confusion.'

My problems are simply stated. Does reading matter? Why do some people not learn to read? How can we help?

Does reading matter? We all know Pope's 'bookful blockhead, ignorantly read, with loads of learned lumber in his head'. We recognize, and flinch from, the force of Hazlitt's comments 'On the ignorance of the learned' (see Williams 1970):

> The description of persons who have the fewest ideas of all others are mere authors and readers. It is better to be able neither to read nor write than to be able to do nothing else.

A lounger who is ordinarily seen with a book in his hand is (we may be almost sure) equally without the power or inclination to attend either to what passes around him or in his own mind. Such a one may be said to carry his understanding about with him in his pocket, or to leave it at home on his library shelves.

And reading may provide an altogether different kind of escape from reality. I was interested to discover in Anthony Burgess's review (*The Observer* 8.6.79) of *Astrology and the Popular Press* by Bernard Capp, that Old Moore sold 8,200 copies in 1761 and 1,000,000 copies in 1898 after a generation of public education.

Though the 1870 Education Act had taught them to read penny newspapers, people were still happy with the rural superstitious prognostications of their fathers. In 1975 Old Moore's print order ran to 1¾ million.

We may also ask legitimately whether reading is becoming out of date. I remember about eighteen months or a couple of years ago George Steiner asking, in a review of a history of the novel in the nineteenth century, whether the novel would not soon die out, superseded by new electronic means of communication.

In that context, I was interested in a few sentences from the paper 'Reading for life' which Kenneth and Yetta Goodman and Carolyn Burke contributed to the 1977 UKRA conference (see Grundin 1978):

Oral language is sufficient for communication of hearing people in small self-contained communities. When the society and culture become complex to the point that people must preserve communication over time and communicate over space, then written language is developed.

Now of course as McLuhan and many others have observed, we can preserve communication over time, and communicate over space, without recourse to a written language. It seems unlikely that reading and writing will be as preeminently my children's means of communication as they were and are mine.

But I would not go on to argue that reading and writing are unimportant. If you are to use the bureaucratic institutions which envelop us, and to some extent become the master of your destiny, you need to be able to read and understand the gobbledygook behind which bureaucracies hide. In many jobs too you need to be able to read and communicate to good effect.

A group of Coventry teachers and advisers who recently studied the communication skills required of young entrants to engineering were astonished at what they found. These youngsters needed to be able to read and work from complex technical instructions, to use reference skills, to act on oral instructions, to contribute to group discussions, and in small firms they soon had to write letters.

For these apprentices, as for many others, reading is, in Ruth Strang's words, 'the royal road to knowledge'. Why is it that some children make little headway along this royal road?

I was interested in Frank Smith's assertion in *The Politics of Ignorance*, 'A child does not need to be very intelligent to learn to read'. This is very close to what W. K. Brennan (1978) says in the introduction to *Reading for Slow Learners:*

> Reading can be successfully taught to pupils with an intelligence quotient as low as 50–60 – and indeed some pupils with IQs below 50 have established reading skills, though usually later than their more able peers. For pupils with IQs over 50, therefore, a low level of tested intelligence cannot be advanced as the sole cause of reading failure.

Brennan suggests that environmental impoverishment, and neurological or psychological weaknesses, may also explain why some children fail to learn to read.

John Lyons (1970) has commented in his book on Chomsky that 'children acquire a command of the spoken language before they learn to read and write and they do so spontaneously without any training'. What is even more remarkable, they learn somehow to use their language creatively and are able to produce and understand sentences they have never heard before and which may never have been uttered before.

This extraordinary capacity makes it all the more puzzling that some children do not learn to read. As Jerome Bruner has said, 'Any idea or problem or body of knowledge can be presented in a form simple enough so that any particular learner can understand it in a recognizable form.'

An American anthropologist, Frederick Gearing, has recently examined the problem of how it is that only some people in any society acquire information or skills which are within the grasp of almost everyone (Gearing and Sangree 1979).

Gearing's theory is that information flows freely from one person to another unless specific barriers prevent its movement. Any such barriers are raised by the people concerned, and barriers to the flow of simple information also block the passage of all more complex information between the partners.

Blocks of this kind impede particularly the flow of information between people of different ethnic groups, different social classes, and even different localities. In consequence information which is within the intellectual grasp of all but a small minority is not widely and randomly distributed as it could be, but systematically blocked.

Gearing suggests that schooling involves two levels of know how. First come the commonplace know hows related to organizing the group. The student must first master the hidden curriculum of commonplace know hows which create and sustain the institution in which he finds himself. This hidden curriculum deals with role relations, and is therefore largely responsible for shaping the organization. If a student fails to master the commonplace know hows of the hidden curriculum he's likely to experience blocks in the flow of the more complex information which constitutes the open or formal curriculum.

If there are to be changes in the hidden curriculum there must be changes in the behaviour of the institution's old hands. In schools, the old hands are usually the teachers, and Gearing therefore suggests helping teachers to develop skills in the self-observation of their own behaviour.

This theory may explain why some children do not learn to read, as well as suggesting how they might be helped.

We need to look also for other simpler ways of helping youngsters to read effectively. But we should certainly not ignore the subtle way in which schools transmit values and attitudes.

I remember reading a good many years ago that very lively book *The Schools* by Martin Mayer (1961). He said research in New York had shown a direct correlation between children's reading ability and the amount of reading their teachers did. Perhaps our first task should be to ensure that all our teachers of reading, and that ought surely to be almost all teachers, are themselves readers. A second prerequisite is the books themselves. In their study of children's reading interests Frank Whitehead and his colleagues have shown a close and wholly unsurprising relation between the availability of books and the amount of reading children do. 'All schools,' they say, 'should recognize the powerful influence they can exercise by making books available for leisure-time reading, and many schools need to allocate more of their resources to the purchase of such books.'

Though the provision of books is a *sine qua non*, it is only the first stage in the effective use of reading in schools. Eric Lunzer and Keith Gardner have shown how much more needs to be done.

They found in secondary schools that more than half the classroom reading in all subjects lasts for only one to fifteen seconds. Pupils read a set of instructions and then start work. Reading like that cannot serve as a stimulus to reflective or critical thinking.

Extended reading does play a larger part in homework. Pupils have to memorize, make notes, prepare summaries and exercise other study skills. But at home they are working on their own, isolated from their peers and their teachers, and often without having been adequately prepared for study reading. The value of their homework is correspondingly less.

Very often, too, their textbooks and worksheets are more difficult than they need be. The way in which some books are written prevents children understanding concepts which would otherwise be within their grasp. This is particularly true of science and social studies texts.

In choosing and using books teachers may therefore find it helpful to use readability tests, of which as you will know there are now many. In his paper 'Assessing readability' George Klare (1978) said 'the evidence that simple word and sentence counts can provide satisfactory predictions for most purposes is now quite conclusive'.

This reassures me because I find some readability tests unduly complicated. I also have some doubts about the 'cloze' procedure, which involves omitting every fifth or seventh or tenth word in a text, and asking the reader to fill the gaps. This seems to me to put altogether too high a premium on choosing trite and predictable words.

What was once described as the best opening sentence ever written for a short story runs: 'Mr Jones lifted the lid of the dustbin, and looked out'. And a reviewer in *The Observer* (15.7.79) recalled that G. K. Chesterton said that ditchwater, far from being dull, was probably full of quiet fun. I'm not quite sure what Chesterton would have made of the cloze procedure.

My two authors are expert writers. They win their readers' interest with a novel idea, a paradox or an unexpected word. That is not always appropriate. In one of his essays Walter Bagehot describes the advice of an old hand to a new entrant to the East India Company. In writing despatches home he said 'the style as we likes is the 'umdrum'. The ''umdrum' is still sometimes the right and best style. I was struck a few days ago by the economy and force of a message on my television screen:

We are sorry that programmes have been interrupted.
There is an industrial dispute.
Transmissions will start again as soon as possible.

In his wartime lectures *Reading for Profit* Montgomery Belgion (1945) has a similar example taken from the Queen's Regulations of 1863. The Instructions for the Bosun read:

> He is to be frequently on deck in the day, and at all times, day and night, when the hands are employed. Assisted by his Mates, he is to see that the men severally go quickly on deck when called, and do their work well and with alacrity.
>
> Before 8 a.m. of each day, and more frequently when necessary, in reference to the service on which the ship is employed, he is to examine carefully the state of the rigging, and report the result to the Officer of the Watch, so that immediate steps may be taken to repair or replace whatever requires to be so dealt with. He is to see that the anchors are secure, and is to take care to keep a sufficient supply of mats, plats, rubbers, points and gaskets ready for immediate use; that the booms and boats are secure, and that, so far as may depend on him, the boats are ready for immediate service, and the gear in good order and constantly rove.

On board ship you cannot afford to be ambiguous or use two words where one will do. The writer has taken to heart Quiller-Couch's advice:

> Always, always prefer the concrete word to the abstract.
> Almost always prefer the direct word to the circumlocution.
> Generally use transitive verbs that strike their object and use them in the active voice.

The key to clarity, one of my mentors used to say, is PDT: people doing things.

Whether your concern is despatches or stories, it takes two to communicate, as it does to quarrel, a very special way of communicating. We need writers as well as readers, talkers as well as listeners. And I wonder whether we could help our readers more, if we grew better writers.

Those who would live by the pen must learn quickly. As C. E. Montague (1949) wrote, in *A Writer's Notes on his Trade*:

> The better bred writer begins and goes on in the faith that this is a free country where no adult need read a line that he feels to be dull; every sentence of every page is, to the writer's prescient mind a place at which one or another reader may take his spectacles off and protest that these are no sort of victuals to offer to a free white man.

A few weeks ago I happened across a little book called *Meanwhile Gardens* (McCulloch 1978). It's published by the Gulbenkian Foundation and is the wholly delightful account of how a young surveyor called Jamie McCulloch saw some derelict land in Paddington, thought it would make gardens and play areas, and made it all happen.

There are, he says, two golden rules which will get you through:

1 People first, materials and equipment next, money last.

In practice, it works like this. Get people interested; people with skills or specialist knowledge or people with friends who could be helpful. Even if they're only offering advice (anybody in the world will do that) write their names down together with the skill they're offering; type it, Xerox it, and have the copies handy. So one of the first bits of equipment you'll need access to is a Xerox machine. There are plenty about. Then go round to every conceivable builder, carpenter, garden centre, building site, warehouse and factory scrounging thrown-out materials. Tell them what you're doing, and ask if you can have the throw-outs when the time comes. If you're offered two half-bricks, accept with shining eyes and write the damn thing down. J. Sod Builders, Bricks. Don't say how many unless it's a lot.

In fact, people are fairly generous with waste material, and pretty soon your list will look quite impressive. Xerox it, show it to the next people you're getting materials from, and they begin to think, 'Hey, everyone else is chipping in, we'd better as well'. Absolutely everything goes on the list. I once spent five hours straight, trying to talk a gardener into letting us have some plants and bits and pieces. He wouldn't budge. Not a sausage. I used to work for him, so I kept trying. Nothing. I started leaving. I yelled, 'You wouldn't even let a couple of bloody toads out of your pond for the nature trail.' He grinned and said, 'To you, sixpence each. Done.' I wrote it down – Two toads for nature trail. Two days later, I was trying to get a bit of reinforcing iron from a manufacturer. There was a little pile in the corner and he said I could have it. Then he saw the list, and when he got to the toads he laughed so much he could hardly see. Then he quadrupled the iron he was giving. That's how the snowball works.

Writing like this is hard work. As William Hazlitt observed (in Williams 1970):

It is not easy to write a familiar style. Many people mistake a

39

familiar for a vulgar style, and suppose that to write without affectation is to write at random. On the contrary, there is nothing that requires more precision, and, if I may so say, purity of expression, than the style I am speaking of. It utterly rejects not only all unmeaning pomp, but all low, cant phrases, and loose, unconnected *slipshod* allusions. It is not to take the first word that offers, but the best word in common use; it is not to throw words together in any combinations we please, but to follow and avail ourselves of the true idiom of the language. To write a genuine familiar or truly English style is to write as any one would speak in common conversation who had a thorough command and choice of words, or who could discourse with ease, force and perspicuity, setting aside all pedantic and oratorical flourishes.

Or as Arthur Quiller-Couch (1946) advised:

If you here require a practical rule of me, I will present you with this: 'Whenever you feel an impulse to perpetrate a piece of exceptionally fine writing, obey it – wholeheartedly – and delete it before sending your manuscript to press. Murder your darlings.'

In rereading C. E. Montague's (1949) essays I was struck by one called 'Easy reading : hard writing'. In it he argues that hard writing makes for easy reading, citing R. L. Stevenson as his prime example. That reminded me of Stevenson's remark 'I spent the morning putting a comma in and the afternoon taking it out again.'

Such commitment may be beyond most of us. But I wonder how much we might learn about the effective use of reading if we all did a little more writing. I was weaned on the aphorism that historians learn more by writing than by reading, yet in eight years teaching I wrote hardly anything except in short bursts like our pupils' classroom reading.

That experience may not be typical. But if it is, and we have not struggled to write well, I wonder whether we fully understand the readers' problems. As Sheridan put it:

You write with ease to show your breeding
But easy writing's vile hard reading.

We know too well that many adults – some say two or three million – have rejected the vile hard reading we offered them at school. Some of the Adult Literacy Campaign's success is due to their rejection of the same hard reading. They've often substituted their own hard written materials and made for easier reading by their students.

I recently read a review which asked for what the reviewer called 'parsimony of terminology'. We might usefully pass the gist of that message to all politicians, bureaucrats and textbook authors. Let hard writing and easy reading be our slogan.

References

BELGION, M. (1945) *Reading for Profit* Harmondsworth: Penguin

BIRRELL, A. (1965, 2nd edition) 'On confirmed readers' in F. H. Pritchard and W. H. Mason (eds) *Essays of Today* London: Harrap

BRENNAN, W. (1978) *Reading for Slow Learners* (Schools Council Curriculum Bulletin 7) London: Evans/Methuen Educational

BRITTON, J., BURGESS, T., MARTIN, N., McLEOD, A. and ROSEN, H. (1979) *The Development of Writing Abilities (11–18)* (Schools Council Research Studies Series) Basingstoke: Macmillan Education

CHAPMAN, L. J. and CZERNIEWSKA, R. (1978, eds) *Reading: From Process to Practice* London: Routledge & Kegan Paul for the Open University

DIXON, J. (1979) *Education 16–19: The Role of English and Communication* Basingstoke: Macmillan Education for the Schools Council

GEARING, F. and SANGREE, L. (1979, eds) *Towards a Continuous Theory of Education and Schooling* New York: Walter de Gruyter

GOODMAN, K., GOODMAN, Y. and BURKE, C. (1978) 'Reading for life' in E. Hunter-Grundin and H. U. Grundin (eds) *Reading: Implementing the Bullock Report* London: Ward Lock Educational

HAZLITT, W. (1970) 'On familiar style' and 'On the ignorance of the learned' in Sir William Emrys Williams (ed) *A Book of English Essays* Harmondsworth: Penguin

HERRING, J. (1978) *Teaching Library Skills in School* Windsor: NFER

HUNTER-GRUNDIN, E. and GRUNDIN, H. U. (1978, eds) *Reading: Implementing the Bullock Report* London: Ward Lock Educational

IRVING, A. and SNAPE, W. H. (1979) *Educating Library Users in Secondary Schools* London: British Library Research and Development Department

JONES, M. and THOMAS, A. R. (1977) *The Welsh Language: Studies in its Syntax and Semantics* Report from the Welsh as a First Language at the Secondary Stage Project (11–16) Cardiff: University of Wales Press

KLARE, G. R. (1978) 'Assessing readability' in L. J. Chapman and R. Czerniewska (eds) *Reading: From Process to Practice* London: Routledge & Kegan Paul for the Open University

LEEMING, K., SWANN, W., COUPE, J. and MITTLER, P. (1979) *Teaching Language and Communication to the Mentally Handicapped* (Schools Council Curriculum Bulletin 8) London: Evans/Methuen Educational

LUNZER, E. and GARDNER, K. (1979, eds) *The Effective Use of Reading* London: Heinemann Educational for the Schools Council

LYONS, J. (1970) *Chomsky* London: Collins

McCULLOCH, J. (1978) *Meanwhile Gardens* London: Gulbenkian

MAYER, M. (1961) *The Schools* London: Bodley Head

MONTAGUE, C. E. (1949) *A Writer's Notes on his Trade* Harmondsworth: Penguin

NATIONAL BOOK LEAGUE (1979) *Books for Schools* (Working Party Report) London: NBL

QUILLER-COUCH A. (1946) *On the Art of Writing* Guild Books

SCHOOLS COUNCIL (1969–78) *Schools Council English for Immigrant Children Project (5–16) Scope* Stage 1 (1978): pupil material and teacher's book (2nd edition), *Scope* plays and dialogues; Stage 2 (1969–75) pupil material, teacher's book, and senior course (14+) comprising pupil material, teacher's books; (1976–8) three teacher's handbooks. London: Books for Schools for the Schools Council

SCHOOLS COUNCIL (1977–9a) *Welsh as a First Language at the Primary Level Project (5–11)* A novel *Gēl*, and the following packs of pupil booklets and teacher's notes: (1977) *Mannua Arbennig, Adar ac anifeiliaid*; (1978) *Dyddian Puiysig, Yr Ysgo*; (1979) *Lliwa Llun, Ffantasi* Llandysul, Dyfed: Gwasg Gomer for the Schools Council

SCHOOLS COUNCIL (1977–9b) *Welsh as a First Language at the Secondary Stage Project (11–16)* (1977) General teacher's guide, plus teacher's notes and pupil books on three themes; (1979) teacher's notes and pupil books on further three themes. Welsh Books Centre, Glanraven Industrial Estate, Llanbadarn Road, Aberystwyth

SCHOOLS COUNCIL (1979a) *English in the 1980s: A Programme of Support for Teachers* (Schools Council Working Paper no. 62) London: Evans/Methuen Educational

SCHOOLS COUNCIL (1979b, 2nd edition) *Schools Council Linguistics and Teaching Programme (5–7): A Teacher's Guide* Harlow: Longman

SCHOOLS COUNCIL (1979c) *Learning Through Talking 1–16* (Schools Council Working Paper no. 64) London: Evans/Methuen Educational

WHITEHEAD, F., CAPEY, A. C., MADDREN, W. and WELLINGS, A. (1979) *Children and Their Books* (Schools Council Research Studies Series) Basingstoke: Macmillan Education

Part 2

Beginning reading
at home and school

Introduction

This section is concerned with the early years, at home and in school, during which reading and other related skills are first developed. Ethel King, in arguing that reading begins at home, is not so much making a case for formal teaching of preschool reading as stressing that parents inevitably teach, as children learn, that parents can learn how to teach more effectively and that schools should involve parents more in children's education. The involvement of parents in the coordinated 'Early Childhood Services' approach in Alberta, is cited as ground for optimism about cooperation between teachers and parents.

Asher Cashdan reporting on an SSRC project on nursery education, stresses the distinction between learning at home but being taught at school. Teachers' concern for control in order to teach results in low motivation for learning, while their language and other means of control can make school seem like a foreign country for the young child. Nursery schools are the least structured schools, yet here there is insufficient structure for language development. What is principally needed, it is suggested, is to make teachers more aware of their language interactions with children. A description of such an approach is given.

The next paper, by Hans Grundin and Elizabeth Hunter-Grundin, is also concerned with the role of reading in the early years of school: indeed, they stress the importance of this stage in view of the relatively slight attention they state is given to reading later, but they also point to organizational problems in school. These originate from the apparent dualism of aims in primary education and are reflected in the usual, but not entirely satisfactory, method of hearing children read. The solution, they suggest, lies in much more use of group work, e.g. in language games, with close teacher supervision, complemented by systematic record-keeping. In addition, more formal evaluation is also advocated, and details are given on how this can be carried out.

Reading schemes are, of course, a means of organizing the teaching of reading, as Derek Thackray notes. They have been much criticized but remain in use nonetheless. This paper examines criteria developed in previous studies and applies them to several schemes. The phonic approach to reading has also been much criticized, though as Joyce Morris points out, there are important differences within phonic approaches and few would now advocate phonics as a sole method. The paper traces the historical and research background to the new phonics, which it advocates and reviews.

5   Literacy begins at home

Ethel M. King

The theme of the conference, 'The Reading Connection', suggests the importance of identifying relationships that will strengthen the effectiveness of the teaching of reading. At a previous conference the theme was 'Literacy at All Levels'. Vera Southgate Booth, commenting on the choice of that theme, stressed the connection between reading and the related skills of speaking, listening, and writing and, secondly, the cumulative effects of developing literacy at all levels. Acknowledging the importance of these connections, let us extend the emphasis in yet another direction – that of the reading connection between the home and the school.

In recent years the focus of attention seems to have shifted from the teaching of reading and writing to the learning of reading and writing. Observational data available from child-development studies have provided the basis for stimulating debate on how to facilitate learning.

During the past decade John Downing (1973) has convincingly demonstrated through his own and related research the importance of the child's understanding of language and reading in the cognitive clarity theory of learning to read. More specifically he points to the value of children understanding the *purposes* of reading and writing, something competent readers are likely to take for granted. In addition, the learner needs an understanding of the vocabulary and concepts that are used in thinking about language and print and in the instructional process.

Cognitive confusion occurs when a child has less specific knowledge or understanding than is assumed or needed, as Piaget and others have shown. Unfortunately another kind of confusion may occur which results from the kind of instructions received. The children may have the knowledge but they could be confused about how to use it or respond. We probably have all experienced the frustration of realizing later that we knew the answer, although at the time we did not understand the question. Downing (1977, p. 37) describes a successful reader as 'one who works his way out of cognitive confusion into cognitive clarity'.

In the process of acquiring literacy the learner builds on his experiences with spoken language and printed symbols. Obviously the oral basis for literacy begins at a very early age when the infant hears the language of conversation. Often remarks directed to him are related to sensory experiences. Initial, exploratory attempts at producing language often feature sound patterns marked by rhythm and much repetition. Increasingly his ear becomes tuned to the language patterns and the rate at which most children acquire the ability to produce meaningful language is truly amazing. Later, as a check on what is being read, a reader compares the encoding of the written symbols into language with his own prior acquisition of language for phonological, syntactic, and semantic consistency. This repertoire of language abilities develops from informal interaction in everyday experiences involving listening and speaking, rather than from receiving formal instruction in language.

All too often the use of the word 'education' refers to the activities that go on in the school under the direction of a teacher or the learning that is expected to occur during periods of instruction. This restricted classroom perspective is being questioned as the accumulating evidence suggests that parents as well as teachers have a major role to play as educators.

Differences in parental teaching styles have been identified due, in part, to different language patterns and sources of stimulation in the home. Parents also differ in their expectations for achievement which, in turn, relate to the child's motivation.

Children who learn to read easily tend to come from a home with a rich literary environment. The literary environment means more than the availability of books; it requires involvement with a reader. In a home where reading is a high-priority activity a child develops certain expectations about print. He comes to know the pleasures that await him between the covers of a book. He hears the language of books which will differ in varying degrees from the language he hears spoken. He learns to listen to continuous language related by a logical sequence or the unfolding of the plot of a story. He learns that you can find the answers to questions in books. He becomes acquainted with some of the features of books; how to handle them and follow a line of print. He is exposed to visual symbols, both nonverbal in picture reading and verbal in learning to recognize some words and letters. He encounters new words and new uses of words. He learns to appreciate the different effects that are created by sound patterns and rhythms. The exposure to many acceptable models of expressing ideas develops an awareness of different forms of expression and language patterns. Listening to stories provides him with models which consciously or unconsciously he may adopt into his own speech and his imagination may be stirred. One children's author described a good book as one that 'has grass and earth and familiar things on a level with a child's eye, but it also has treetops and stars to draw his gaze upward'. In time he develops a mental set towards literacy. But most important of all is the interaction with a reader.

From the descriptions of the successes in learning to read there is a remarkable degree of consistency in the findings of studies conducted in different countries. Early readers are children who have achieved some measure of success in learning to read without the benefit of instruction in a school-based programme. Among other things, the home factors which facilitated the acquisition of reading skills are important.

Durkin (1966), in her well-known study in the USA, found that parents of the few children who read early provided more help than most parents. This help was most frequently in the form of answering questions and requests immediately. Valuable also was the help from older siblings, particularly in 'playing school'. She concluded that there was no simple connection between socioeconomic class and the ability to read early. Of more importance was the presence of parents who spent time interacting with their children by reading to them and answering questions and demonstrating the values of reading in their own personal lives.

Later King and Friesen (1972) studied related questions with a Canadian sample. Similarly we found that children who had a rich literary environment at home learned to read earlier. One of the critical factors was the significantly higher level of eduction of the mother, the adult who usually had the most interaction with the young reader. Moreover, the early start in reading in the informal setting was reflected again in superior achievement in reading after a year of instruction in school.

The young fluent readers in Margaret Clark's Scottish study (1976) also came from homes where the mother spent much time with the children reading, talking, or answering questions and they used the public library frequently. All parents placed a high value on education:

. . . the parents' perceptions of education and the support and experiences they provide by measures far more sensitive and penetrating than social class, father's occupation – or even education of parents. These homes were providing rich and exciting experiences within which books were indeed an integral part. (p. 45)

Clearly there are many personal factors within the child that are interacting with the home factors to facilitate the development of literacy. For a small proportion of the children, learning to read occurs easily at home but for the larger number who acquire reading skills readily in the school setting, the same kinds of experiences are also factors contributing to their success.

Burton White (1975) claims that the requirements for adequate human development are modest during the first nine months of life but it is different when a child begins to crawl and to talk. The older a child is the less effective will be the environmental influences on his development and hence the importance of the early years.

Parents are influential teachers. For the most part they want to do what is best for their children but they need help. Whether they realize it or not, parents in a stimulating environment teach in much the same way as good teachers do; by arranging the learning environment, by serving as models, and by being readily available and willing to respond to queries. They facilitate learning rather than teach children formally.

Increasingly, the role of the teacher is being viewed differently to support the role of the parent as educator. Different approaches to family-based education of the child are receiving further study. Generally, there are three main approaches: the use of a home visitor; the involvement of the parents in a centre-based programme; or in-home programmes where three or four children meet in one home under the direction of a mother and the supervision of a home visitor.

Home-visitation programmes have perhaps received more attention from the related professions of nursing and social welfare than from education and, in some cases, these visitors are providing an increasingly broad range of services. The educational visitor, however, may provide more support in stimulating the child and the parental role through self-help techniques.

Ditchburn (1978) conducted a study to determine the best method of providing educational materials to the home and what effects different materials would have on language development and parent-child interaction. In one approach paraprofessionals with a small amount of training visited each home distributing educational toys and providing some guidance in orienting, motivating, talking, and encouraging reflection and independence. A comparable group of parents visited a preschool centre and picked up a box of similar materials with written suggestions. The third or control group was one that had access to the same materials in a centre-based programme.

While there were no differences between the methods of delivering materials to the home, as measured on a variety of evaluation instruments, parents preferred the home visitor. Having educational materials available in the home by either procedure contributed significantly to parent-child interaction. Six general kinds of materials were provided: picture books, puzzles, dolls and puppets, construction toys, toys with moveable parts, and letters, shapes and numerals. The toys which encouraged storytelling, provided aesthetic pleasure, or allowed open-minded imaginative solutions retained the child's attention and interest best. Picture books and puppets and dolls stimulated more language than puzzles and toys with moveable parts. Picture books also encouraged more parent-child interaction. In support of other studies this one also found that children preferred toys that required adult assistance or involvement. The provision of home visitors or parent education along with material resources such as a toy-lending library appears to be a useful avenue to pursue.

Initially it is wise to limit the number of adults who assume responsibility for nurturing the child. Studies of attachment relationships indicate that an important factor is sensitivity to the child's signals. In inroducing a child to new situations the presence of the mother in the room facilitates explorations. Thus, it is important to introduce children to preschool centres gradually and allow them time to explore the new environment in the presence of the mother or a familiar adult. According to Bronfenbrenner (1974, p. 55):

> The evidence indicates that the family is the most effective and economical system for fostering and sustaining the development of the child. The evidence suggests further that the involvement of the child's family as an active participant is critical to the success of any intervention program [became they] . . . reinforce the effects of the program while it is in operation, and help to sustain them after the program ends.

Clearly, the parent(s) are the first and foremost teacher. Their role as educator not only begins at home but should continue as a shared responsibility with the teacher as the child enrols in a centre-based programme at the nursery, day-care centre, playschool, kindergarten, early childhood class, or school. Parent involvement may generally be classified in three main areas: parent education, parent participation, and parents as decision-makers.

Parent-education classes have made valuable information available to parents but to date have been disappointing in changing behaviour. A strong trend has emerged in the research findings that involvement of parents directly in an early childhood programme has proven to be the best way to help them learn how to work more effectively with their children (Highberger and Teets 1974). This is not to say that teachers and parents will always have the same views. Considerable discussion and time may be needed for each to know the views of the other and to arrive at an understanding. Often differences in cultural backgrounds and values lead to different expectations between teachers and parents.

The involvement of parents enhances the programme through the assistance they provide by increasing adult-pupil interaction, by providing unique contributions to the programme in special interest areas, and by supplementing the activities later in the home. By direct involvement they observe the teacher as a catalyst for learning. They see the teacher as an active observer, one who knows when to let the child explore and when to provide guidance, one who stimulates the child's thinking and corrects misconceptions, one who arranges the environment to challenge the learner, and one who provides reinforcement when appropriate. Involving parents makes them feel more confident and responsible in the educational partnership.

Earlier reference was made to the importance of children understanding the literacy concepts and being able to respond to them. Parents who are involved in early childhood classes learn by example how to listen to children, how to discuss the important concepts, and how to identify important cues to react to in the home environment. They learn not only to read to children but to read along with them. The natural reaction of many young children listening to a story is to let his eye go to the sight of the sound; that is, he watches the face of the reader as he would a storyteller. But when parents read with their children their eyes may be directed to the source of the print and the pictures. Reading with children means that the adult can be questioned and he can facilitate interpretation between the author and illustrator and between the child and his own experiences. Parents involved in a preschool programme will often observe the teacher engaged in a reading activity with one or two children. The teacher is, in fact, modelling an activity including the verbal interaction with the child which a parent can emulate and reinforce.

Reading along with children also establishes reading as a valued activity. The parents' attitudes towards reading show in the way they talk about books, the way they discuss what has been read, and the priority placed on reading in their own lives. The family who values reading is likely to have children who *will* read once they have acquired the skills.

However, just because a child begins to read is no cause for complacency. There is little research on parent involvement specifically in reading instruction for older pupils. Dubord (1973), failing to gain the cooperation of parents in randomly-selected schools, used volunteers instead. They listened to each ten-year-old subject read three times a week for a total of about 30–40 minutes a week. In six weeks the children had made significant improvement in word recognition and comprehension scores were improving, though not to a significant level in this short period. The reaction from the pupils was positive throughout and the reaction from the parents changed from disapproval to enthusiastic acceptance when they witnessed not only an improvement in reading but also increased interest in reading. Obviously a busy teacher does not have time to listen to pupils read orally either frequently or for sustained periods in large classes. In this study the opportunity to read aloud and interact with interested adults, who by the constraints of the study were not allowed to 'teach' in the usual sense of the word, was made possible by two volunteers in the room. One could speculate that the results might have been even more gratifying if the volunteers had been parent volunteers. Conditions that foster success in learning to read are needed to sustain progress, and parent involvement and home support are among these conditions.

Many are sceptical of how we can really get parents involved and particularly those who need it most. To illustrate that some of the ideas I have suggested can be implemented, let me use the example with which I am most familiar. With a new approach to early childhood that we have adopted in the province of Alberta, called Early Childhood Services, we are now observing a great awakening of interest among the public and the parents in particular. Very simply we are attempting to coordinate all the services for the young child from birth to the age of eight and his family. Up to the legal school entrance-age the programme is voluntary but carries with it an obligation for the parents to be involved. Initially there were certain problems which might be expected arising from language and cultural differences in multi-ethnic communities, rural isolation, working single-parents, and apathy. Parent involvement includes participation on a rotation basis; parent education through television programmes, workshops, or using the facilities of parent resource-centres; and decision-making for those elected to a local advisory council which establishes the priorities in each of the programmes, whether they be school or community-based. While not fully operative for all age groups, the desire on the part of the teachers to make this coordinated approach work has led to very resourceful, innovative ideas. After three years an independent evaluation received very positive reactions from the parents and they are keen to continue as participants and decision-makers in the higher levels of education.

Reference has been made to one model but obviously the details will vary from one community to another. The significant point is that if teachers are provided with enough support to overcome their misgivings of working so closely with parents and parents are made to feel important in the partnership then the most important person, the child, will benefit.

We have looked briefly at literacy from different perspectives; and some of the theories and research findings in child development including language and reading. Further we have examined some of the ways that changes could be made through parent education, home-based programmes, and parent involvement in preschool and school programmes.

Based on the premise that literacy begins at home, parents have a significant contribution to make in initiating, supporting, and sustaining a high priority on literacy with their children.

References

BRONFENBRENNER, U. (1974) *Is Early Intervention Effective? A Report on Longitudinal Evaluation of Preschool Programs* (Volume II) Washington, DC: Office of Child Development, United States Department of Health, Education and Welfare

CLARK, M. M. (1976) *Young Fluent Readers* London: Heinemann Educational

DITCHBURN, S. J. (1978) *An Experimental Study of the Effects of Different Kinds of Home-Based Programmes for Young Children* M.A. thesis: University of Calgary

DOWNING, J. (1973) The cognitive clarity theory of learning to read *Reading, 7*, 63–70

DOWNING, J. (1977) Linguistics for infants *Reading, 11*, 36–45

DUBORD, D. A. (1973) *A Study of the Effects of Volunteers in Different Kinds of Classroom Activities* M.A. thesis: University of Calgary

DURKIN, D. (1966) *Children Who Read Early* New York: Teachers College Press

GOVERNMENT OF ALBERTA (1973) *Operational Plans for Early Childhood Services* Alberta Education

HIGHBERGER, R. and TEETS, S. (1974) Early schooling: why not? *Young Children 29*, 66–77

KING, E. M. and FRIESEN, D. (1972) Children who read in kindergarten *Alberta Journal of Educational Research 18*, 3, 147–61

WHITE, B. (1975) Critical influences in the origins of competence *Merrill-Palmer Quarterly 21*, 4, 243–66

6 Teaching language and reading in the early years

Asher Cashdan

Educational researchers often suffer from conflicting impulses. On the one hand, the rules of scientific detachment demand a strict impartiality: the investigator's duty is to define and describe and to leave value-judgments to others. At the same time, researchers often want, as educationists themselves, to draw conclusions, or even to lay down *a priori* prescriptions. In fact, both of these instincts are justifiable. What matters is not to present prescriptions as if they followed inexorably from the research, unless (which is very rare) they really do. In the nursery-school research with which I have been occupied during the last few years, there are certainly elements of both of these approaches, as I shall hope to make clear later. Our attempt at resolving the conflict has been to separate, as far as we have been able to, the two aspects. In our descriptive study, we have made a determined attempt to study what teachers actually do; in the prescriptive teaching 'experiment' we have tried to work with teachers along lines of whose value we were already convinced, albeit on what we consider sound theoretical premises. This should mean that there is relatively little room for argument over the facts, but plenty of controversy over our prescriptions. And in our discussions with teachers so far this certainly seems to be the case.

Home learning and school teaching
Even where there is close concordance between the aims of home and school and between the cultural backgrounds of parents and teachers, school is nevertheless a strange experience for any child. In the two succeeding sections, I intend to draw attention to the main respects in which this is so. Here, I would like to discuss one major feature only. At home, by and large, children learn; at school, they are taught. Not many parents lay down a curriculum for their children and proceed to put them through it. Those who do, are probably not among the most successful of parents! The best homes certainly provide a wealth of potentially educational experiences and the children make excellent use of these. The menu is, however, *à la carte*. The child decides what to

make use of and what to leave alone, regulates the richness of the diet and the frequency with which it is ingested. Parents, and other adults, are used as resources; on demand, they provide materials, advice, occasional help. The child regulates his/her own learning, usually with considerable success. (One of the best known educational platitudes is about the amount of progress, particularly in language skills, achieved by the child by the time he/she enters school.)

School is quite different in this respect. Here the menu is largely *table d'hôte*. The teacher has decided in advance what the child should learn, in what order and by what methods. Most educationists will agree that the best teachers allow maximum flexibility, tailor their curriculum to the individual child's needs and, wherever possible, encourage the child to develop in his/her own way. But such teaching is relatively rare, is concentrated in the early years and is seen as essentially transitional. In other words, nursery (and to some extent infant) teachers do see themselves as midwives, helping children to do their own learning. But in practice, this ideal is not always realized and it nearly always yields to much more 'controlled' teaching as the school years go by.

Of course this is not necessarily or entirely a bad thing. The teacher has the knowledge and the perspective to foresee what is the next move, what has longer-term value and what is mere occupation. Nevertheless it seems unlikely to be entirely coincidental that as teacher control increases, pupil motivation falls off. Some further consideration of the mismatch between teacher and pupil may make the relevant factors clearer.

School as a foreign country

While this loss of control over one's own learning may be a strange or even uncongenial experience for many pupils, it is unlikely to come as a complete surprise. Children expect school to be a place where the teacher is in charge, dictating their behaviour and learning experiences. But although not entirely surprising, the experience may still be strange and its strangeness is often increased by a number of other factors in the situation. The teacher often speaks with a different accent from the one with which the child has so far been familiar. She has a different vocabulary and different social expectations. A sentence such as 'I can see an awful lot of litter on our floor', spoken in a bright and breezy tone, may only mean 'pick up those pieces of paper'. But it encapsulates all the major differences we are thinking of: vocabulary, idiom, indirect use of language and possibly, also, differences in accent.

Many of the other ways in which school is foreign have been noted many times before and need only brief mention. They include being part of a large peer community with a very high child-adult ratio, with the attendant need to share, take turns and to postpone gratification of one's immediate needs. Focusing on communication, we note that the child has to learn to attend to adult language not apparently addressed to him/her; teachers often address themselves in a general way to small, or even reasonably large groups – for many children quite a novel experience.

Children are quick to adjust and take many new experiences in their stride. It is only when we take an extreme situation, or a number of 'estranging' factors operating at the same time, that troubles may occur. But this does of course happen. John Downing's illustration (from Clay 1977), involving a vocabulary problem only, is not that rare! It comes from a phonics lesson:

> I'm going to sove some mivvers. See these mivvers. Their names are snow and arsh. They say 'haugh'. Who knows a zasp with the tauf 'haugh' in it?

The translation follows:

> I'm going to write some letters. See these letters. Their names are sea and aitch. They say 'haugh' (as in Scottish Loch Ness). Who knows a word with the sound 'haugh' in it?

And as Downing points out, the problem may not be confined to one of vocabulary, after all the child may not know what the *translation* means!

At the heart of the educational process, at least as we practise it, is a training in thinking beyond the immediate situation. Margaret Donaldson (1978) talks of this as 'disembedded' thinking. The child is used to thinking in concrete situations, solving problems which arise in the here-and-now. In school, there is an increasing need to think beyond the immediate and the meaningful. The demand has many forms, ranging from the sorting of objects by colour and shape to advanced work in calculus. Alongside this runs the demand for the disembedded use of language – language used to classify, to generalize, to abstract. Children can cope with all of these demands, but they may easily get lost if discontinuities occur, if the steps are too big. Thus, as Donaldson points out, few of us are entirely at home with a disembedded sequence such as:

> If p, then q
> Not q
> Therefore not p

Yet a small child could argue that 'They couldn't be getting married. You have to have a man too!', which embodies the same reasoning.

In other words, school demands very strange, almost foreign behaviours. These behaviours are in fact meaningful and desirable (or many of them are, at any rate!). But the demands have to be tailored to the child's background and needs. If they are not, and if too many (and too extreme) examples are put forward at once, the child may be overwhelmed.

Teachers' demands and teachers' behaviour

If school is a foreign country, it would be very useful to be given a map. If this is not done, then those who have some bearings already will be advantaged right from the start. Yet it has been pointed out, from a variety of perspectives (see, for example, Holt 1969, Barnes *et al.* 1971) that as teachers we often fail to be explicit with our pupils. The result is that many never really understand what is being asked of them. What is worse, if they could understand, they would often be unable to comply. In other words, teachers often make demands of their pupils which are neither explicit enough, nor well tailored to their needs. Furthermore, judged by the standards applied to interactions in the world outside the classroom, the behaviour of teachers is often quite bizarre. For one thing, the teacher tends to 'hog' the conversation. The evidence for this claim is well summarized by Moseley (1972): teacher talk, in a number of studies, occupies about 60 per cent of the time and pupils speak for 25 per cent (the rest of the time being taken up by silence or confusion!). The full significance of these figures sinks in when one remembers that, in the normal classroom, the teacher is likely to be outnumbered by pupils in a ratio of something like 30 to 1. Bullock's figures (DES 1975) make the point even more dramatically: in a 45-minute period (assuming 30 pupils and 75 per cent of the time taken up in teacher talk) they expect the average pupil to have 20 seconds of talk.

My intention here is not so much to stress the value of pupil talk – this has been explored elsewhere. My point is merely to show how unnatural is the classroom situation. In the outside world, anyone who dominated the conversation to the extent we have described would soon lose their audience. But the teacher's audience is a captive one. At least, it used to be; in secondary schools throughout the country pupils are increasingly absenting themselves from the audience. They cannot easily depart, so they fail to turn up in the first instance.

Nor is this more than a surface description of classroom language. When one examines its content, it offers even more surprises. And here, there is considerable divergence between secondary classrooms and those for young children. In both, teachers are constantly asking pupils to tell them things they know already and could express better themselves. But whereas in the secondary school specific answers are insisted upon and quite reasonable pupil responses rejected because of a failure to produce the exact word or phrase in the teacher's mind, in the nursery and infant class the opposite happens. Here, any answer will do; the teacher is interested not in the pupils' response, but simply in getting children to talk, about anything, in any way they choose.

My suggestion is that teachers of young children exercise too little control over their pupils' talk while, in the secondary school, their colleagues control pupil language far too much. Both groups consider, rightly, that language plays a major role in learning. But paradoxically, both go too far. The nursery teacher is so determined not to over-structure the pupils' learning and to allow them to learn for themselves, that she fails to respond to the child's need for guidance, shaping, for what Bruner calls 'scaffolding'. In the secondary school, on the other hand, the teacher often supplies too much structure, being so determined that the pupils think and speak precisely that the need to search for one's own meanings is pushed aside.

What all teachers need to do is to devote considerable attention to the interactions between themselves and their pupils, so as to become more aware of where they are matching their pupils' needs and where they fail to do this. Even with young children, where I have suggested that teachers stand too far back, it is possible to fail to find the 'match', not just through standing too far back, but even by supplying apparently appropriate, but subtly wrong structuring.

One may illustrate this – rather cruelly I fear – in an extract from Taylor (1973), actually quoted with admiration by, among others, Clay (1977). Taylor describes a conversation between David and his teacher, in which the teacher is using the language-experience approach in the early stages of reading and writing. David is to produce some writing about the boat he has made. Taylor offers us the following conversation:

David   I want to write about my boat.
Teacher What do you want me to write about your boat?
David   Well, about my boat.
Teacher Yes, about your boat. But what do you want me to write about your boat?
David   I want you to write down about my boat. There's my boat that I made. It's red. I want you to write about that.

Taylor comments as follows:

> This conversation may go on for some time. David wants to write about his boat; but he can only express himself as he speaks, and his oral expression is not suitable for direct translation into written form. He cannot adapt his speech to a short, coherent sentence for the teacher to transcribe at his dictation. So she must suggest a form of words which will effect the transition from speech to writing.

> *Teacher* Shall I write 'I made a red boat'?
> *David* Yes, that's the boat, there on the window-sill.

> So the teacher writes 'I made a red boat', saying each word as she writes it and getting David to say each word with her.

She goes on to make a number of points about the usefulness of the exchange in terms of the child's reading development.

In fact, the whole extract worries me. Of course, this is an invented conversation, yet I agree with Taylor that it is typical – perhaps all too typical! Why am I worried? First, because I do not think that the teacher is listening carefully enough to David. If she were, she would write what he actually suggested: *About my boat*. This is a perfectly good title and does not benefit from translation into 'written form'. Secondly, there is far too much in the teacher's mind which is not made explicit and shared with the pupil. David wants to say something about his boat, or at any rate the teacher has persuaded him that this would be a good idea. If learning about reading – assembling words in suitable form, seeing words and letters being formed, having experience of what the written word signifies etc etc are important to the teacher, then these aims should be shared with the child also. The child may gradually become aware of the teacher's hidden agenda. What seems possible, however, is that he will learn from exchanges like this to be suspicious of the school process: that what he sees as significant may be taken by the teacher, refashioned without any clear rationale and handed back as something which is no longer his.

The whole point may seem a tiny, almost accidental one. Yet I think it is symptomatic. (As, again, is the intrusive 'me' in the second line of the conversation.) Some children will not easily be thrown off their stride, because they know what school is about and what it is for already; for those who do not, we need to watch out very carefully.

What nursery teachers do

In the SSRC Project in which I have been engaged with Janet Philps and my other colleagues, we spent a total of eight days in each of 25 teachers' classrooms, spread over a period of three terms, observing both teacher and child behaviour. Analysis of our observations is still proceeding, but I would like to mention some of our early findings and relate them to the theme of this paper.

The teachers were observed for three-minute periods, during which all their actions and utterances were recorded. In all, we made over 40,000 observations of which nearly 27,000 were recorded during free-play periods. After examining the data, we combined some of the categories, finishing up with 18 verbal ones and 14 nonverbal. The categories are listed in the Appendix together with the percentage incidence of each one during free play.

Of the verbal categories, 2–6 are essentially management codes, while 7–14 cover 'tutorial' questions and remarks addressed to children, as do categories 15–17. The major categories seem to be those of general remarks and acknowledgments (4 and 5), simple questions and statements, apparently requiring little thought on the child's part, and the making of suggestions (category 15). Similarly, of the nonverbal categories, the largest is housework (category 3), when the teacher is not directly involved with children at all, and the only fairly large 'tutorial' category is showing and offering (category 13).

Grouping some of these categories together, our main finding, which is in agreement with other studies, seems to be that nursery teachers do not spend a great proportion of their time in direct tutorial contact with their charges. And I use the term tutorial in a very broad sense indeed. Thus, grouping together verbal categories 7–17 yields a total of 53 per cent of our observations; even if we take away category 1 which is really an artefact, the figure rises only to just over 60 per cent. But even here, most of the observations are of short, single, simple questions and statements, rarely very demanding or followed up in interactions of any length between teacher and child. Similarly, if we add together nonverbal categories 6, 9 and 10, 12 and 13, we reach a total of just over 14 per cent, which adjusted for category 1 reaches less than 33 per cent of the total.

I must stress that it would be quite unreasonable to conclude from these figures that nursery teachers are not earning their pay or that they are failing to teach their children. But it does seem reasonable to suggest that at the time we carried out the observations (1975–6), in a range of outer London borough schools, teachers did spend relatively little of their time in 'focused' work with children. The alternative hypothesis is that teachers develop such acute powers of observation and judgment that they are able to intervene effectively, at lightning speed, to provide just the right help, question, information for each individual child, as these are needed, before passing on, equally quickly, to do the same thing for another. While we suspect that the very occasional, highly experienced and unusually brilliant practitioner can do this, it seems unrealistic to assume that it is the norm.

A particularly interesting feature of our work was the attempt we made to characterize children, not by assigning them to preformed categories of our own, but by getting the teachers to describe their own children and classify them, using the Repertory Grid technique. One of the things it enabled us to do was to place children, on the basis of their own teacher's judgment, in two categories: well-functioning (or highly-evaluated) and poorly-functioning (or poorly-evaluated). By carrying out series of observations on children in these two categories, we could now explore some very interesting questions. For instance, both in our pilot study and in the present investigation, teachers told us that they gave particular attention to those children who had greater needs – that is, those from deprived or disadvantaged backgrounds. Is this in fact the case? Our data show that in general it is not. Teachers talk as much to children they evaluate as well-functioning as to those they consider poorly-functioning. On reflection this is not too surprising: it is much easier to interact with children who reinforce the teacher than with those with whom one has to struggle. Again, one might expect that poorly-functioning children would attract simpler, more carefully tailored language from the teacher. In practice, it seems unlikely that this happens. If anything, this supports our contention that, without special training, teachers do not develop highly sophisticated interaction skills. There is no doubt, however, that well-functioning children find the teacher a more rewarding figure: on our physical distance measures they are more likely to be found within close range of the teacher in the classroom. This accords well with the research of Garner (1972, 1973) in the infant classroom.

Persuading teachers to 'experiment'
So much for our descriptive study. But our research has also included a prescriptive 'experiment'. I tend to think of this as a kind of advanced motorists' test. This is because our main purpose is to make the teacher more self-conscious about her language interaction with the child. By discussions in advance, by playing back tape- and video-recordings and by discussions after short teacher-pupil conversations, we aimed to make teachers more aware of the dynamics of a tutorial dialogue, such

as takes place whenever a teacher is interacting with a single child. We worked with half of the teachers in our group (the others serving for comparison), visiting them for half a day each week over a fourteen-week period. The rationale of our approach derives almost entirely from the work of Marion Blank (see Blank 1973, 1978) but we adapted and developed her approach in harness with the teachers, to suit the English nursery school situation. Thus, although like Blank we quite often worked outside the classroom with the teacher carrying out a planned 'conversation' with an individual child, we used these as practice sessions so as to develop skills which would be used *in* the classroom as part of the teacher's regular 'style', in the free-play situation in particular.

We worked with the following main principles:

1 Teaching to a range of cognitive demands.
2 Developing a sequential theme.
3 Selecting appropriate materials.
4 Checking the response.
5 Using the child's activity.
6 Pacing and shaping the session.
7 Managing the response.

The first and last are the crucial principles; the others are closely connected with them. In the first principle, our main concern was to make the teacher aware of the range of possible cognitive demands implicit in questions normally used with a child, and to help the teacher to select demands at an appropriate level for the particular child and for the stage of the conversation. Thus, labelling and simple function ('What is that?' 'What does it do?') are very frequently used low-level demands, whereas cause and effect ('What made the room cold?'), or rationale ('How could you tell the little girl was sad?') make much more searching demands. In our seventh principle, we focused upon the perennial problem of the conversation that 'breaks down': what does one do when an appropriate answer is not forthcoming? Essentially, the teacher must be ready with an appropriate simplification (or follow-up) to the original demand. The question has to be put again, or reorganized so that the child is now able to answer. Techniques needed here range from simply making sure that the child is attending, to a sophisticated breaking-down of the original request, resequencing it and presenting an appropriate question which the child now can answer.

An effective dialogue or conversation of this kind, whether it last for three or for fifteen minutes, inevitably involves the other principles also. Thus, a meaningful conversation will tend to stay on one theme, with a beginning and an end, will mostly centre around materials significant to the child, will involve actively doing something and will deal with verifiable situations, rather than being an opportunity for mere language practice. The conversation will be paced and shaped. That is, it will have a beginning and an end, making high demands towards the beginning – early failure is actually desirable, or there would be no purpose in the exploration! On the other hand, a joint determination to sort out the problem is developed and at the end child and teacher review together what has been accomplished.

After an initial period, in which many of the teachers found the sessions artificial and frustrating, most of them settled into the technique and found it highly rewarding. They were not being asked to change their teaching mode dramatically, rather to become aware of both the problems of a sustained conversation with a child and of how to overcome them. Most of them contributed to the development of the programme and we are producing a book – written jointly by researchers and teachers – outlining the approach in detail. Here, I should like to stress only the benefits which we hope accrue to pupils who experience this teaching approach in the classroom. We have no hard evidence of its success, so as I pointed out at the beginning of this paper, our work is based largely on *a priori* conviction. A more sustained curriculum development effort in this area may be possible later.

What we think can be achieved for the pupil, is the realization that his/her teacher is a meaningful person, who raises important questions and helps one to talk them through, by drawing on past experience, by carrying out experiments as one goes along, and by not giving up or changing the subject before a satisfactory outcome has been achieved. Essentially, we are helping children 'talk to learn' and to see that that is a large part of what school is about. And although we make heavy use of language, this is not a 'language programme'. It might in fact be better to call it a science curriculum, though the questions under investigation range from how to ice a biscuit, through washing dolls to cutting up apples. Nor do we expect our teachers to spend all their time in this type of activity; we are at constant pains to stress that what is being offered is an approach to the child which may be used as often or as rarely as seems appropriate. No doubt, too, it might be adapted for use in group situations; though we have thought it wisest at this stage to concentrate on the dialogue between the teacher and a single child.

Doing it for what it's worth
If the approach I have been outlining in the previous section is

successful, I suspect this will be more than anything else because it develops (or restores) the child's intrinsic motivation to learn, rather than relying on a blind faith in the worthwhileness of teacher-imposed learning. When, instead, pupils are 'self-running' and participate in setting goals for their learning, there can be some hope that teachers will be seen as more meaningful figures and will themselves derive greater job satisfaction from working more intensely and more productively.

I do not intend to spell out the implications for the curriculum, but I think they are undoubtedly there. Clearly, I am not advocating the entire abandonment of study for distant goals. After all, one of the main purposes of our 'conversation sessions' is to strengthen the child's handling of language and logical thinking as tools for his/her later progress. But what I am concerned to stress is that there should be meaning and hence pay-off, in the immediate situation. Thus, the child reads to learn, to acquire skills for later use, for personal growth. But reading is at least as much for immediately needed information and for present pleasure. If we forget the importance of the here-and-now, there will not be a future for which the child is being prepared – the child will no longer be there!

Finally, at the risk of repeating myself, I want to end by stressing the other crucial principle, that of explicitness. In our teacher-child dialogues we stressed the need at the beginning of a conversation to discuss with a pupil not only what is to be done, but what will be achieved thereby: 'Come and help me cut up the apple, *and we will find out about it*'. In this way, as it should be, school is seen to be both about doing things and about reflecting upon them.

Acknowledgment

The research reported in this paper was carried out by Dr Janet Philps and myself, assisted by Ms Ronny Flynn, Sara Meadows and Jennie Weaver, together with twenty-five teachers in outer London boroughs. It was supported by SSRC Grant no. HR3456 and by the Open University.

Appendix

A *Verbal Categories*

Category		% incidence
1	Nonverbal only	12.3
2	Positive directions	6.6
3	Negative directions	2.1
4	General remarks	7.5
5	Repetitions and acknowledgments	8.4
6	Positive comments	5.1
7	Simple 'what' questions	8.7
8	Complex 'what' questions	1.7
9	Other simple questions	7.0
10	Other complex questions	1.2
11	Simple factual statements	10.6
12	Complex factual statements	2.8
13	Other simple statements	5.9
14	Other complex statements	1.0
15	Suggestions	8.6
16	Instructions	4.4
17	Drawing attention	1.5
18	Missed, other	4.6
	Total	100

B *Nonverbal categories*

Category		% incidence
1	Verbal only	56.8
2	Minimal supervision	2.4
3	Housework	10.2
4	Dealing with play equipment	3.6
5	Physical child care	4.4
6	Playing	2.5
7	Affection and comfort	2.3
8	Listening/watching	1.6
9	Demonstrating	1.4
10	Helping	2.7
11	Investigating (alone)	1.2
12	Investigating (joint)	1.8
13	Showing	5.6
14	Administration (with other adults)	3.4
	Total	100

References

BARNES, D. *et al.* (1971, revised edition) *Language, the Learner and the School* Harmondsworth: Penguin Books

BLANK, M. (1973) *Teaching Learning in the Preschool: A Dialogue Approach* Columbus, Ohio: Charles Merrill

BLANK, M. *et al.* (1978) *The Language of Learning: The Preschool Years* New York: Grune and Stratton

CLAY, M. (1977) '"Write now, read later"': an evaluation' in P. Gunn (ed.) *Reading, Writing and Language* Eleanor Schonell Centre, University of Queensland

DES (1975) *A Language for Life* (The Bullock Report) London: HMSO

DONALDSON, M. (1978) *Children's Minds* London: Fontana

GARNER, J. (1972) Some aspects of behaviour in infant school classrooms *Research in Education 7*, 28–47

GARNER, J. and BING, M. (1973) Inequalities of teacher-pupil contacts *British Journal of Educational Psychology 43*, 234–43

HOLT, J. (1969) *How Children Fail* Harmondsworth: Penguin Books

MOSELEY, D. (1972) *Intervening in the Learning Process I* (E281 16) Milton Keynes: Open University Press

TAYLOR, J. (1973) *Reading and Writing in the First School* Hemel Hempstead: Allen and Unwin

7   Stimulating and monitoring early literacy

Elizabeth Hunter-Grundin and Hans U. Grundin

There exists an interesting duality of aims within our infant schools. On the one hand, the young pupils are usually free to play in a classroom which is organized to offer individual or group activities, such as play with water, clay, paint, dolls etc. Groups of from two to six children play together, and the groups are only intermittently supervised by the teacher, who must divide her attention among the various group activities.

On the other hand, it is widely accepted that during the two (or in some cases three) years in the infant school, the children must be taught to read, and it is a commonly-held view that children should enter the junior school – normally around the age of seven – able to read. Thereafter little, if any, basic reading instruction is expected to be required, except by a minority of pupils whose progress has been unsatisfactory in the infant school.

The general philosophy and ethos of our infant school have merits which are widely acknowledged. The emphasis on informal, discovery-oriented group activities is something which educators from other countries often note with admiration and envy. And the absence of an externally-imposed curriculum or syllabus makes the British infant school unusually child-centred. However, many teachers find it difficult to plan and implement effective teaching of basic language and reading skills in this context.

Although group activities are widely used in other areas of the infant-school curriculum, the teaching of reading does not usually involve group or class instruction. Typically, the infant-school teacher spends a considerable amount of time hearing *individual* children reading to her from books in the reading schemes which the school uses. (Most schools use books from several schemes; see Grundin 1980.) Even if the teacher spends about two hours a day on this kind of individual reading, each child will end up having a very small amount of reading instruction. Informal observations carried out over several years indicate that most infant-school pupils can expect to have *between fifteen and twenty-five minutes* of individual reading instruction *per week*.

It is true that most children have learned to read, to some level of competence, by the age of transfer to the junior school. But it is also true that a significant minority of pupils are not able to read on entry to junior school, and for a number of these pupils the provision for reading instruction is likely to have been insufficient or inadequate. It is commonly noted that the spoken language development of these slow or failing readers is also below average.

The problem which faces the infant-school teacher is, then, to improve the provision for systematic teaching of language and reading skills without sacrificing the play-oriented child-centred approach to early education. Direct, formal instruction of a whole class (or a large group) is not compatible with this approach, because of the great differences between individual children. To increase the amount of individual instruction given to each child might be desirable, but it is not feasible with classes of about 30 pupils and only one teacher. Various kinds of group activities with intermittent teacher supervision seem to provide the best solution.

Reading experts such as Frank Smith and Kenneth and Yetta Goodman argue that children learn to read through reading. We share this view, but we also believe that it is extremely important that the development of 'reading through reading' is seen in the wider context of language development. Many children can 'crack the code' of written language with a minimum of help from the teacher, usually because they have received and continue to receive a great deal of help and support at home. This help and support rarely takes the form of extra 'tuition' in reading. It is likely that it has been, from a very early age, an informal but extensive education in *spoken* language. Not only does this provide the child with a relatively large vocabulary of the kind needed in school, it also gives him or her a 'natural' fluency in the rhythms and patterns of our language, in the way words and phrases are strung together. This early education in spoken language makes the task of *making meaning* from printed language very much easier for the child, who can much more easily predict what certain words and word patterns are likely to represent.

For children who have this kind of help and support at home the present provision of reading instruction in the infant school is likely to be quite adequate. But other children have great difficulties in understanding what reading is all about, let alone 'cracking the code'. These children will need much more help from the teacher. They will, among other things, need help in order to develop the kind of language we use in writing, a language which in many ways is more elaborated and more abstract than the spoken language they meet outside the school. Before

68

these children can learn 'reading through reading' they will have to further develop their language through listening and speaking.

To provide sufficient practice in language skills, communication between the teacher and individual children needs to be complemented by meaningful and stimulating language communication within groups of children. This can be achieved through a variety of language games, which are fun and exciting like the other play activities offered in the infant school, but which also provide opportunities for the children to engage in purposeful and educationally-valuable speaking and listening.

In order to observe and evaluate the effectiveness of language games played by small groups of children, one of the authors (Hunter-Grundin 1979a) carried out a three-year research and development project in which an experimental curriculum involving the systematic use of such games was designed, implemented and evaluated.[1] This project was well under way before the Bullock Committee published its report *A Language for Life* (DES 1975), so it was gratifying to find that the Bullock Report endorsed several of the principles on which the experimental curriculum was based, for example: '. . . reading must be seen as part of a child's general language development and not as a discrete skill which can be considered in isolation from it' (p. xxxi); and 'There should be positive steps to develop the language ability of children in the preschool and nursery and infant years' (p. 514).

The Bullock Committee also identified objectives for language development which were almost identical with those which underpinned the language games used in the experimental curriculum. The Report (p. 67) emphasizes children's need of experience in the following uses of language:

1 Reporting on present and recalled experiences.
2 Collaborating towards agreed ends.
3 Projecting into the future; anticipating and predicting.
4 Projecting and comparing possible alternatives.
5 Perceiving causal and dependent relationships.
6 Giving explanations of how and why things happen.
7 Expressing and recognizing tentativeness.
8 Dealing with problems in the imagination and seeing possible solutions.
9 Creating experiences through the use of imagination.
10 Justifying behaviour.
11 Reflecting on feelings, their own and other people's.

A group of infant-school headteachers and teachers met frequently at the Inner London Education Authority's Centre for Urban Educational Studies (CUES) and contributed to the designing, developing and field-testing of a series of language games to be played by *groups* of two, three or four children. In the first instance, the games are taught to each group by the teacher, who also uses the occasion to 'feed in' appropriate new vocabulary to be used in the game. After this initial teaching, the games can be played by the pupils with only partial or intermittent supervision by the teacher. An audio-cassette player is required for some of the games, but this can be handled by one of the children in the group who is appointed 'playback controller' and chairperson of the discussion.

Some of the games involve series of picture cards, which can be interpreted in different ways, thus stimulating the children to tell a variety of stories. Other games use boards with many alternative routes, where the children can make progress by asking questions about specific routes. In some cases individual pupil-books are used, and a small group of children is asked to try to reach consensus by discussing various options on each page of the workbook. A full description of the games used in the experimental curriculum is given in *Literacy: A Systematic Start* (Hunter-Grundin 1979a). A series of videotape recordings showing groups of children playing the language games has been published recently (Hunter-Grundin 1979b).

The research project described by Hunter-Grundin (1979a) showed that the experimental curriculum using language games systematically was highly successful with regard to the children's reading development at the end of the second year in the infant school. All children seemed to benefit from this curriculum, but the 'working-class' pupils in the experimental school made particularly good progress during the two infant-school years.

Another important feature of this curriculum (in addition to the use of language games) was the keeping of systematic records about the children's experience of various activities and the degree to which they had mastered the tasks involved. This record keeping was based on the teachers' informal observation of individual children and groups of children. A basic reading scheme was used in parallel with the language games, and each child's progress was recorded in both language and reading activities.

Informal assessment helps the teacher to guide the child from learning experience to learning experience, but it does not tell the teacher how the progress of her pupils compares with the progress of children in other classes and other schools. In other words, the teacher's own informal assessment can establish whether or not children are steadily progressing along the road towards literacy, but it cannot tell how far along the road the children have come. In order to establish that some kind of formal assessment is needed, using standardized tests. Evaluation instruments suitable for the top infants (at the age of about seven) were developed and tried out as part of the Hunter-Grundin research project. The results showed that it is possible to test young children by means of brief and easily administered tasks which the children can perceive as games rather than as tests.

The instruments used in the research project were later further developed and standardized for Great Britain by the authors (Hunter-Grundin and Grundin 1979). The resulting battery, *The Hunter-Grundin Literacy Profiles*, consists of five tasks, none of which takes more than ten minutes to complete and which the vast majority of children enjoy doing, even if their ability level is quite low. There are four group test-tasks assessing: attitude to reading; reading for meaning; spelling; free writing; and one individual test-task assessing spoken language.

The battery has been standardized for top infants and first-year juniors aged six and a half to eight years in England, Scotland and Wales. It can be administered by the class teacher as part of normal classroom work, thus avoiding the risk of causing any disruption or anxiety. At the end of each task the children are given the opportunity to record the degree to which they enjoyed the task.

The most important test in the battery, *reading for meaning*, is a multiple-choice cloze procedure test, i.e. instead of the deletions in a conventional cloze test there are four alternative words from which the child has to choose one. This eliminates the influence of writing ability on the reading test result. In a conventional cloze test a child may know the right word that goes in a deletion, but may be unable to write it in an intelligible form; or he may be able to write the words, but the writing may be very time-consuming and tiring. The *reading for meaning* test can thus be said to be a more 'pure' test of reading ability than conventional cloze tests. Like all cloze tests, this test puts the emphasis on the ability to understand meaningful written language. It correlates highly with other published reading tests, both with word recognition tests and with comprehension tests.

One of the reasons why the *reading for meaning* test must be regarded as the most important in the battery is, of course, the fact that both educators and parents attach particular importance to the development of reading skills. Another reason is that this test assesses not only the ability to read in a more narrow sense, but also various aspects of the child's ability to understand language. It is clearly desirable that progress in the infant school should be assessed in a fairly wide spectrum of language skills, such as those which are included in the Hunter-Grundin Profiles. However, if it is felt that the available time or resources allow only one test to be administered at the end of the infant school, a test of the ability to read for meaning seems to be the best choice.

The approach to developing and monitoring early literacy in the infant school that has been briefly outlined here can be seen as an attempt to implement some of the principal recommendations put forward by the Bullock Committee, i.e. recommendations 3 and 4 which call for a systematic and organized policy for language and reading development in every school, and recommendation 1 which calls for the introduction of 'a system of monitoring . . . which will employ new instruments to assess a wider range of attainments than has been attempted in the past and allow new criteria to be established for the definition of literacy' (p. 513).

References

DES (1975) *A Language for Life* (The Bullock Report) London: HMSO

GRUNDIN, H. U. (1980) Reading schemes in the infant school *Reading 12*, 1 (in press)

HUNTER-GRUNDIN, E. (1979a) *Literacy: A Systematic Start* London: Harper and Row

HUNTER-GRUNDIN, E. (1979b) *Games for Language Growth* (a series of video tapes) Cardiff: Drake Educational Associates

HUNTER-GRUNDIN, E. and GRUNDIN, H. U. (1979) *The Hunter-Grundin Literacy Profiles* High Wycombe: The Test Agency

Note

[1] For this research Elizabeth Hunter-Grundin was awarded the 1979 Institute for Reading Research Fellowship by the International Reading Association.

8 Criteria for a reading scheme

Derek Thackray

Although reading schemes attract a good deal of criticism I think many would agree with two Bullock (DES 1975) comments. Firstly that 'the reading scheme is at the centre of reading material in young children's early experience of reading'; and secondly that 'many teachers find it an invaluable resource'. The two important common features of all reading schemes, which teachers value, are those of continuity and a rationalized structure.

The purpose of this paper is to discuss some of the more important criteria for reading schemes in the light of recent research, comment and criticism.

In chapter seven of the Bullock Report we have a full evaluation of early reading materials and reading schemes, and the weaknesses of many of our current schemes are discussed. According to Bullock reading schemes should be attractive in presentation and content; they should have words and pictures which complement each other; they should stand up to questions about how parental roles, sex roles and cultural roles are represented; they should overcome the limitations of both look-say and phonic approaches; the syntactic structures used in them should match the patterns of spoken language used by children; and the teacher's manual should indicate clearly what the reading material can and cannot do.

It is interesting to note that in the survey carried out by the Bullock Committee, the Primary Questionnaire placed considerable emphasis on the different methods, media and materials employed by teachers and the amount of time the children spent on reading, but no specific questions were put to teachers concerning the criteria of a good reading scheme. At the 1978 UKRA Annual Conference Hunter-Grundin (1978) presented the analysis of a questionnaire on reading schemes completed by 650 headteachers. In this report information concerning criteria of reading schemes was given in order of importance under two headings: *criteria of good schemes* and *shortcomings of reading schemes*.

An analysis of the criteria of good schemes and the linking together

73

of similar criteria gives a smaller number of broader areas as follows:

1 *Presentation*
Good illustrations   49% (highest % recorded is 50%)
Integration of picture and text   39%
Generally attractive presentation   33%

2 *Content*
Nature of content – meaningful and
  motivating   50%
Content relevant to child's experience   30%

3 *Vocabulary control and grading of books*
Carefully-graded vocabulary   40%
Adequate vocabulary repetition   33%
Well-graded provision, book to book,
  stage to stage   30%

4 *Other ingredients*
Supplementary readers and suitable
  back-up materials   40%
Built-in provision for word attack
  and phonic skills   34%

There is a good measure of agreement between the headteachers' views and those of the Bullock Committee regarding the criteria of a good reading scheme. Both stress attractive presentation with good illustrations, meaningful and motivating content, adequate treatment of word attack skills and more natural language structures. However it is important to note the importance headteachers place on carefully controlled vocabulary with adequate repetition and the careful grading of materials throughout the scheme.

The Bullock Committee states that it '. . . would welcome the further development of the kind of scheme to which it is as difficult to apply such simplistic labels as 'phonic', 'look-and-say', 'linguistic', etc as it is to attach such labels to the methods of competent teachers. A good reading scheme is one which provides a sound basis for the development of all the reading skills in an integrated way'. Although we have a definition of the ideal reading scheme, there is very little practical guidance given in the Bullock Report as to how to produce such a scheme. Roberts (1975) after summarizing some of the weaknesses of reading schemes discussed in the Report goes on to say that 'the discussion is so convoluted that the reader is left with the general idea that all is not well but with no clearly enunciated picture of what should be done about it'.

I would now like to discuss in turn some of the more important criteria in an attempt to help in a more practical way all those concerned with the selection, evaluation and production of reading schemes.

The prereading stage is crucial because if dealt with effectively it can smooth the way into successful early reading. The findings in a recent experiment devised by Wilson (1978) underline the importance of this stage. He was concerned to present teachers of reading with reading tasks similar to those faced by beginning readers at the early stages of a reading scheme so he presented them with some early books of *One, Two, Three and Away* (McCullough 1964) encoded in an alternative orthography using twenty-two Greek letters. One of the findings, relevant to our present discussion, was that the teachers found it very difficult to read the books in the alternative orthography and pointed out that they had not had the prereading activities to help them in their task.

It is during the prereading period that, firstly, the important reading readiness skills are developed by means of carefully-selected activities; secondly the vocabulary, sentence structures and concepts needed for the first books in the reading scheme are developed through talking and discussing; and thirdly, if key characters are used, they can be firmly established in their environmental settings by using prereaders which are carefully designed to link with the first main reader. I would like to look briefly at these three aspects of the prereading programme.

Commercially-produced and teacher-produced reading readiness materials should include the following:

1 *Visual discrimination* exercises using mainly words and letters rather than shapes, symbols, pictures, as the matching of words and letters is more closely related to the beginning reading task.

2 *Auditory discrimination* exercises involving rhyming and the matching of the most common initial consonantal sounds. As a result of Downing's (1973) work in *Comparative Reading,* there is a growing interest in the work of the Russian researcher Elkonin (1973) who stresses the importance of the child knowing the 'sound structure of spoken words' before he learns to read and before the teacher introduces written letters. In his training programme children are taught to use plain plastic tokens to represent phonemes in finding out how many phonemes there are in a word. Another stage in the programme is to teach the child to use different coloured tokens to represent vowels and consonants. Elkonin has shown that Russian kindergarten children can be trained to discriminate between vowels, hard consonants and soft consonants in Russian speech. Some of Elkonin's techniques have been adapted for

the English language in Canada (Ollila, Johnson and Downing 1974) and in this country (Pidgeon 1979).

This development ties up with recent work of Durrell and Murphy (1978) who argue that two new measures are valuable in assessing reading readiness:

(i) Awareness of letter-name sounds in spoken words. An example of a test item would be: 'Say "open" (pause) "open". (When the child has said the word continue.) What letter do you hear at the beginning of "open"?'

(ii) Syntax matching. An example of a test item would be: 'This says "Come here" (presenting a card with the words on it). Say it. Say it again. (When the child has said the words continue.) Now draw a circle round "come".'

3 *Vocabulary development* exercises to develop general vocabulary by using pictures and picture sequences, and to develop more specific vocabulary using colours, numbers, prepositions (such as 'up', 'down', 'in', 'out') verbs (such as 'jump', 'run'), and some of the technical terms used in the teaching of reading such as 'book', 'picture', 'word', 'letter' and 'sound'.

4 *Orientation* exercises to encourage movements from left to right and top to bottom.

Where the reading-readiness materials are an integral part of the reading scheme then, where appropriate, visual and auditory discrimination exercises can use the names of the children, and some of the words appearing in the first reader and again, where appropriate, the pictures and picture sequences can feature the children in their home and school environments.

Teachers are very skilled at developing the vocabulary, sentence structures, concepts and knowledge of the key characters. Their children will need to attack the first reader with confidence and enthusiasm and so experience success. In good reading schemes they are aided in this important task by some of the following: large wall pictures to which words and sentences can be attached; smaller pictures for group and individual use; figurines or models of key characters; flash cards of key sentences and words; jigsaws; and a book, or tapes, of simple stories about the characters to be read by the teachers.

If a child is faced in his first reading book with many unfamiliar words then he will derive neither meaning nor enjoyment from such an experience. On the other hand to concentrate on individual words in preparation for the first book of a reading scheme can be a rather barren and limiting exercise. Most would agree that the best way of developing the child's interest in words and knowledge of what reading is all about, is through the writing and reading of his own work. If this approach is used then the time spent on introducing the characters and the words in the first reading book need not be prolonged.

The series of prereaders form a link between the work done by the teacher to prepare for the reading scheme and the first book in the scheme. Prereaders are usually small books and feature pictures without text, or pictures with single word captions, or pictures with simple text given adequate repetition over the series of books, and there is the closest of links between the text and the illustrations. Prereaders introduce children to books and how to handle them, to picture sequences and how to follow them, to the main characters in their settings and to some important concepts about reading and key words to help their start to reading.

When evaluating the basic books of a reading scheme there are a number of criteria to be examined. Bearing in mind the criteria head-teachers feel are important, I will consider content and illustrations, vocabulary and sentence structure, the place of phonics, and comment briefly on type, punctuation and the line break.

All agree that early reading books should be attractive in both presentation and content. Current early reading materials are being presented more attractively with colourful illustrations, but as well as attracting the reader's interest, illustrations should be as unambiguous as possible in the early stages to help the child unlock the corresponding words. Illustrations must also correspond with each other in a particular episode in matters of detail as children are the first to pick up discrepancies. After the very early books the words and pictures should complement each other so the child is encouraged to examine both with care. In the later books the function of the illustrations changes again and becomes more diverse. As well as complementing the text by adding some further information, they can stimulate thinking or set the scene. Obviously as the textual load per page increases, the possibility of a close correspondence between text and illustration decreases.

Improving the content of basic readers is a much more difficult and demanding task than improving the illustrations. If children are to become involved in the episodes and stories in the basic readers they must be able to identify with the key characters who should feature quite prominently in the earlier basic books. Criticisms are constantly voiced that the content of early reading books diverges radically from the realities of the life experienced by the children reading them. One should not overstress this view as teachers report that not all working-class children take to *Nippers* (Berg 1968) and at least one experiment carried out by Ellison and Williams (1971) shows that *Ladybird* books are as attractive to working-class children as they are to middle-class children.

Children often indicate by their comments that reading is something they do outside of the reading scheme, and so the lesson to be learned is that the basic reading books should be as varied as possible in content. Stories, information, poems, plays and songs could all feature in them if there was appropriate blending of the elements to avoid bittiness.

With regard to the criteria for vocabulary and sentence structure in early basic readers in a scheme, there appears to be a conflict. In the early stages a sight vocabulary has to be gently developed and, as pointed out earlier, teachers stress the importance of a controlled vocabulary with adequate repetition. But recent research and comment stress the fact that children entering school use a wide range of sentence structures in their spoken language and because of this many advocate that children's patterns of spoken language should be matched by the syntactic structures of the early readers so that the reader will be able to anticipate and predict the syntactic structures he meets and this will help his word recognition. The problem which arises is to what extent can authors working within the confines of a limited vocabulary, which must have adequate repetition, provide the wide range of sentence structure some writers call for? Authors can avoid stilted and unnatural language, can use limited vocabularies more imaginatively, and can make the fullest use of the context to avoid unnecessary repetition; but there must be a compromise between the two conflicting demands of limited vocabulary and wide-ranging sentence structures.

Having looked at the relationship between vocabulary and sentence structure, I would like to look at vocabulary and sentence structure separately.

With regard to the choice of word lists that authors can use for controlling the vocabulary of early readers, the recent publication of the *Mount Gravatt* study (Hart, Walker and Gray 1977a) gives us word-frequency lists based on different and more realistic principles than the earlier word-frequency lists. Earlier attempts to control language in early reading material were based on word-frequency lists compiled by analysing material written for children and used by children. For example a well-known word list is that of Thorndike and Lorge (1944). This 3,000 word list was extracted from books likely to be used by children, and other American lists such as Gates (1935) and Dolch (1950) were built from Thorndike's vocabulary.

These studies simply counted the number of times a word occurred.

Words Your Children Use (Edwards and Gibbon 1964) was also compiled from material written by children, but contains lists of single words ordered according to an index that was calculated by multiplying frequency of occurrence by the percentage of children using the word; this was an improvement on the frequency count alone.

Hart, Walker and Gray (1977a) point out that although the lists mentioned above are useful, a reliance on written language as a source of material to use with beginning readers is suspect. The production of written language is a skill which is learned *after* the child comes to school, very often in conjunction with the type of language used in reading books. Comparisons between the *Mount Gravatt* lists based on children's spoken language and lists from *Words Your Children Use* are interesting. For example the 250 words most frequently used in writing, include no question markers, e.g. 'why', 'which', 'where', 'who', yet these are very frequent in the spoken language of children aged five and a half. Another example is that out of the 250 words most frequently used by this age group in the *Mount Gravatt* study, only 115 appear in the corresponding list of *Words Your Children Use*.

The other very important difference between the *Mount Gravatt* lists and earlier lists is that two- and three-word listings are given as well as single word frequencies.

Hart, Walker and Gray (1977b) write:

Studies of young children's conception of word boundaries seem to indicate that it is often the sequence of words rather than single words that are the important carriers of meaning in a sentence. It is clear also when children enter school they do not perceive a word as a separate unit according to printed conventions.

According to their findings the two- and three-word units are very consistent in the way they appear in the language development of children, and they point out that the language units used in first reading books are not the ones used by children in their spoken language.

The language units collected in the *Mount Gravatt* study were compared with those collected from the spoken language of children in Bristol. Despite superficial differences the core of frequently-used words and sentences is remarkably similar. So the *Mount Gravatt* lists are a step forward in helping authors to match the language of early readers with the spoken language of children, provided teachers feel the advantages of using two-word units such as 'I'll', 'I'm', 'it's', 'I don't', 'I got' and three-word units such as 'I'm going', 'I've got', 'I'm not', outweigh the practical disadvantages they find with contractions such as confusion caused by the apostrophe, or the conflict with the flash cards they use. One danger in using newer lists of this kind is that of neglecting the development of the early reading material to prepare children eventually to cope with the more accepted language structures found in children's books.

The language units used in the *Mount Gravatt Reading Series* (Hart, Walker and Gray 1977a) are the two- and three-word units from the word lists from the *Mount Gravatt* study, but these units are mainly at the beginnings of sentences and are not complete sentence structures. The other scheme of note, which was designed to take account of children's natural language patterns is *Link-Up* (1973) where the types of sentence structure used were based on research into the spoken language of five- and six-year-old children by investigators such as Strickland (1962) and Loban (1963). In the early stages *Link-Up* (Reid 1973) makes use of the more common sentence patterns such as subject-verb-object; it also uses linked sentences joined by 'and' and 'but', and avoids structures which belong more to the language of books, e.g. 'slowly down the road came the old man'. However there is no clear indication of the stages in the development of the language structures used as the scheme progresses.

To the best of the writer's knowledge the only comprehensive attempt to provide a scheme which grades the development of language structures is that of Bevington and Crystal (1975) resulting in a series called *Skylarks*. In this series of readers common grammatical structures and usages that children meet in everyday language are methodically introduced and organized into a sequence of six stages of increasing difficulty in syntax and meaning.

This is an interesting approach but the real problem is to match the theoretical steps in syntactic development with the developing reading abilities of young readers. For example, what structure should the average seven-year-old be able to cope with? This goal is not very practical at the present time but investigators such as Waller (1978) and Chapman (1979) are working in this area. Waller in his search for 'linguistic landmarks' designed an experiment with 300 seven- to eleven-year-old children to see the average age at which an understanding of the word 'although' is achieved in the kind of sentence structure such as 'He is wearing a coat although it is sunny'. As might be expected he found the understanding of 'although' increases from seven to eleven but he asks the question: What level of competence is deemed necessary before such a sentence is included in texts? Chapman has looked at the extent to which good and poor eight-year-old readers are able to integrate anaphoric relationships in reading continuous texts. This was studied by using the semantic field of pronouns as an experimental variable. For example, 'A bus came round the corner. It narrowly missed the pedestrians.' To understand the pronoun 'it' one has to refer back to the previous sentence and the noun 'bus'. It was found that the fluent readers could supply most of the missing pronouns whereas the nonfluent readers were less able to do so. This experiment and similar experiments help authors and teachers to realize that often pronouns are used in reading materials at too early a stage before the child can fully carry out the mental processes necessary to understand them.

When considering the teaching of phonics in a reading scheme the Survey of the Bullock Committee indicates that most teachers have an eclectic approach to the teaching of reading using look-and-say and phonic materials and methods. The Survey shows that 97 per cent of teachers use look-and-say and 97 per cent of teachers taught the simpler phonic conventions. These figures must be treated with caution as Roberts (1975) points out that they tell us little about what teachers regard as those practices which contribute to success or failure in learning to read and Southgate (1977) has serious misgivings about the phraseology used in the questionnaires.

With regard to the teaching of phonics in reading schemes, the Bullock Report makes two important points. Firstly, that look-and-say schemes provide phonic activities but usually in the form of supplementary material. The Committee states:

> They do not help a child who has difficulty when attempting to cope with the complexities of any unfamiliar words he encounters in the actual text. We regard this as a disabling limitation to many otherwise very satisfactory look-and-say schemes.

Secondly, the Committee expresses the view that if a reading scheme is well designed 'the phoneme-grapheme relationship should be self-evident and readily acquired by inductive learning with the absolute minimum of formal instruction' and 'it is better for children to learn phoneme-grapheme relations in the context of whole-word recognition at least in the early stages of reading'.

To build these important recommendations into a reading scheme suggests that an integral part of it should be a phonic strand containing material designed to encourage the reader to understand phoneme-grapheme relationships.

Because books in a reading scheme are printed, a number of decisions regarding the print have to be made, such as the typefaces (the styles of type used by the printer), the type sizes (usually given in point sizes where a point is 1/72″), the size of spaces between letters, words, lines or paragraphs, the use of punctuation marks, and the criteria to be used when a sentence runs over into a second line – the line-break.

Although over the years a great deal of research has been carried out into the legibility of print the results according to Watts and Nisbet (1974) are inconclusive because there are so many variables which affect legibility and these variables have been insufficiently controlled in the investigations reported. It is therefore usually left to the publisher, in consultation with the author, to decide in a fairly arbitrary way, the tyepeface for a series of readers. Considerations include whether the face has a script 'a' or 'g' which teachers now expect; whether it is serif or non-serif, as teachers tend to like non-serif typefaces; and whether the letters in the main, and particularly letters such as t, l, q, y, f and j are similar to the letters teachers use when first teaching children to write. Smith (1978), on the topic of handwriting, draws attention to the need for teachers to consider the kind of letter printed in the reading scheme they are using when deciding the forms of letters to teach in the early stages. But the converse is also important, i.e. publishers of early reading materials should consider the form of letters taught by teachers when deciding which typeface to use. Examples of typefaces that are usually considered for early reading materials are Univers, Gill, Futura and Optima.

Point-size usually varies from 48 or 36pt on the prereading material to 18 or 16pt in the later books of a scheme. Each time the point size is reduced it is important to reconsider the spacing between letters and words to get the balance and proportions correct.

There are conflicting views about punctuation marks. Some publishers and authors feel that capital letters (apart from proper nouns), full stops, and inverted commas should not be introduced in the first books of a reading scheme, and the introduction of punctuation marks should be gradual. The most controversial issue concerns capital letters. The argument for not introducing them at first is that children should see only one form of a letter and word shape to avoid confusion and to give the fullest opportunity of reinforcing sight vocabulary. Others would argue that it is sensible to introduce most punctuation marks from the start, suggesting it is wrong to be ungrammatical and pointing out that children see both upper and lower-case letters in public print and that many more teachers are now developing early handwriting using both forms of letters. We have examples of the gradual introduction of punctuation marks in the *Link-Up* (1973) and *Through the Rainbow* (Bradburne 1964) schemes, but most reading schemes use a good range of punctuation marks from the beginning.

When considering the line-break we find the generally-accepted view is to break the line at a break in the syntax, i.e. at the end of a phrase. For example, in the sentence 'John went to school in the car', the break would be after school. One can understand the logic of this view but recent work by Moon (1979), in which he looked at miscues made by readers caused by textual weaknesses, suggest that when a line breaks children often read the first line as a complete sentence, i.e. 'John went to school.', and start the next line as a new sentence 'In the car . . .'. Moon points out that to give an advance terminal clue in our sentence would mean a break after 'to' or 'in' and then there is a cue for continuation. Here we have two conflicting views again, but fortunately more research is now being made in this area. The commonsense view is to use the syntactic break in the early stages where reading is more word by word reading and use advance terminal cueing when there is some degree of fluency.

Having looked at some of the important criteria of the basic books in a reading scheme we can now consider briefly supplementary readers, workbooks and the teacher's manual.

The supplementary readers are a vital part of any scheme and are needed both to consolidate the vocabulary developed up to a particular level, and to provide a bridge to the next level. We have argued that the key characters should feature strongly in the early basic books, and so it is in the supplementary readers that fairy tales, folk tales, myths and legends and historical incidents can feature. Fitzgerald (1978) points out how fairy tales and folk stories transcend cultural boundaries and are found world wide in children's fiction. He writes:

> Although these literary genres are clearly of importance in the educational development of monocultural children, the fact that the literary conventions used in them transcend natural and cultural boundaries is of even greater significance for reading and reading provision in multiracial areas in Britain, because effectively these stories through these conventions emphasize that which cultures have in common and in addition provide an anchor and a crutch for newly-arrived ethnic minority group children in their new environment.

Workbooks or spirit duplicating masters are also a vital part of any scheme as they not only consolidate the skills developed in the main and supplementary readers but also develop in a systematic way all the important reading and language skills needed for developing reading. Most of our current workbooks linked with reading schemes develop phonic abilities only, but if we are to have an integrated scheme and develop all aspects of reading ability then workbooks should cover the three main areas of phonic development, comprehension and related skills, and writing.

The teacher's guide to a reading scheme should be an operating manual, the various sections being clearly distinguishable. It should present a rationale and description of the scheme and offer many practical ideas for reinforcing the work covered in the pupil's materials. It should provide models for record keeping and guidance on monitoring informal reading inventories, miscue analysis and on other methods of checking the child's progress.

Finally, and more generally, I wish to talk about bias in reading material. In Hunter-Grundin's (1978) survey 15 per cent of the headteachers mentioned bias in class, sex and/or culture as a shortcoming of reading schemes, which suggests this problem does not loom large at the moment. However there is a great deal of research and interest in this area in the States, and so it is possible that greater interest may be shown in this country in the future.

During the last decade many American educators have called for a more adequate depiction of ethnic minorities and female characters. In their view stereotyping or under-representation may transmit negative messages about minorities and females. Some recent findings there have shown publishers to be responsive to these calls and many publishers have made public statements expressing their views on this matter. However it would appear that although the number of minority characters and females has risen in reading materials, there have been no real changes. The main characters continue to behave in the same way and to say the same things.

The International Reading Association has shown interest in sex bias and its Committee on Sexism and Reading has developed a checklist to assist teachers in analysing educational materials, and also 'Inclusionary Language Guidelines' with examples such as 'fire fighter', 'police officer' and 'cave dweller'.

Our reading materials should reflect our developing multiracial society but I hope educators and teachers will never feel it necessary or useful to compare numbers of girls as against boys, numbers of coloured children as against white children, or numbers of certain kinds of actions of girls as against boys – in other words join in the witch hunt for bias which seems to be developing in the States.

All concerned with reading materials must go on trying to improve them for the benefit of the children who use them and I hope I have contributed in some small way to this end.

References

BERG, L. (1968) *Nippers* London: Macmillan

BEVINGTON, J. and CRYSTAL, D. (1975) *Skylarks* London: Nelson

BRADBURNE, E. S. (1964) *Through the Rainbow* Huddersfield: Schofield and Sims

CHAPMAN, L. J. (1979) 'The perception of language cohesion during fluent reading' P. A. Kolers, M. Wrolstad and H. Bowma (eds.) *Processing of Visible Language 1* New York: Plenum Press

DES (1975) *A Language for Life* (Bullock Report) London: HMSO

DOLCH, E. W. (1950) *Teaching Primary Grades* Illinois: Garrard Press

DOWNING, J. (1973, ed.) *Comparative Reading* New York: Macmillan

DURRELL, D. D. and MURPHY, H. A. (1978) A prereading phonics inventory *The Reading Teacher 31*, 4, 385–90

EDWARDS, R. P. A. and GIBBON, V. (1964) *Words Your Children Use* London: Burke

ELKONIN, D. B. (1973) 'USSR' in J. Downing (ed.) *Comparative Reading* New York: Macmillan

ELLISON, T. and WILLIAMS, G. (1971) Social class and children's preferences *Reading 5*, 2, 3–9

FITZGERALD, M. J. (1978) Fairy tales and folk stories: the significance of multi-cultural elements in children's literature *Reading 12*, 3, 10–21

GATES, A. I. (1935) *A Reading Vocabulary for the Primary Grades* New York: Bureau of Publications, Columbia University

HART, N. W. M., WALKER, R. F. and GRAY, B. (1977a) *The Mount Gravatt Reading Program* Sydney: Addison-Wesley

HART, N. W. M., WALKER, R. F. and GRAY, B. (1977b) *The Language of Children* Sydney: Addison-Wesley

HUNTER-GRUNDIN, E. (1978) *Reading Schemes in Schools* Paper presented at the UKRA Annual Conference, Northampton, 1978

LOBAN, W. (1963) *The Language of Elementary School Children* Champaign, Illinois: MCTE Research Report no. 3

McCULLOUGH, S. (1964) *One, Two, Three and Away* London: Hart-Davis Educational

MOON, C. (1979) 'Categorization of miscues arising from textual weakness' in D. Thackray (ed.) *Growth of Reading* London: Ward Lock Educational

OLLILA, L., JOHNSON, T. and DOWNING, J. (1974) Adapting Russian methods of auditory discrimination training for English *Elementary English 51*, pp. 1138–41 and 1145.

PIDGEON, D. (1979) 'Why put the cart before the horse?' in D. Thackray (ed.) *Growth of Reading* London: Ward Lock Educational

REID, J. and LOW, J. (1973) *Link-Up* Edinburgh: Holmes McDougall

ROBERTS, G. (1975) Early reading *Reading 9*, 2, 14–23

SMITH, P. (1978) *The Role of Handwriting in the Growth of Literacy* Paper presented at the UKRA Annual Conference, Northampton, 1978

SOUTHGATE, V. (1977) *Beginning Reading in England* Paper presented at the Twenty-Second Annual Convention of the International Reading Association, Florida, 1977

STRICKLAND, R. (1962) The language of elementary school children: its relationship to the language of reading textbooks and the quality of reading of selected children *Bulletin of the School of Education* University of Indiana, 38, 4

THORNDIKE, E. L. and LORGE, I. (1944) *The Teacher's Word Book of 30,000 Words* New York: Bureau of Publications, Columbia University

WALLER, C. M. (1978) Establishing linguistic landmarks: a feasible aim? *Reading 12*, 3, 22–30

WATTS, L. and NISBET, J. (1974) *Legibility in Children's Books* Windsor: NFER

WILSON, P. (1978) No wonder I didn't learn to read till I was about ten *Reading 12*, 3, 2–9

9 New phonics: a development from the teaching-research connection

Joyce M. Morris

This paper is in response to an invitation to give a more detailed exposition of 'new' phonics following my introduction to the subject at last year's conference under the title 'New phonics for old' (Morris 1979). It also illustrates the theme of this conference in that 'new' phonics developed as a result of the vital connection between teaching and research when tackling reading and related language problems.

At the outset, it would seem best to define the term 'phonics' which was first used by reading teachers in the early nineteenth century, and is still a source of confusion especially with the term 'phonetics'. Then, as a necessary background to answering such questions as, 'What's new about new phonics?' to proceed with a brief historical review of the main issues and events which make this development from 'traditional' and 'modern' phonics of theoretical and practical significance.

Phonics defined

First of all, it is professionally important that 'phonics' should no longer be confused with 'phonetics', which is an internationally respected science dealing with the descriptive analysis of speech sounds. It is likewise important that, in the near future, there is universal agreement in the reading field about acceptable meanings for the term 'phonics'. Meanwhile, for the purposes of this paper, phonics is defined as the substance, methods and materials of reading instruction which lead the learner to understand the relationships between speech sounds and their written symbols, thereby developing independence in the identification of printed words.

Phonics can be broadly defined as either 'synthetic' or 'analytic'. Synthetic phonic methods are part of a long tradition and are generally classed as varieties of 'traditional' phonics. They are based upon the belief that beginning readers should first be taught the sound-symbol correspondences of word elements and how to synthesize, blend or build them into whole words. Conversely, analytic phonic methods are based upon the now more widely accepted 'modern' belief that reading instruction should start with meaningful whole words. Then, through the various analytic techniques of 'modern' phonics, children are taught to apply their knowledge of sound-symbol correspondences in familiar words to the task of identifying unfamiliar words.

Nowadays, phonics rarely refers to an individual's entire method of instruction whether as teacher or learner. In other words, the necessity is recognized, as in the present context, for teaching and learning other strategies of word identification such as dictionary usage for pronunciation as well as meaning, and the use of different types of pictorial and verbal context cues including those of environmental situation.

Phonic rules or generalizations

Discussion of phonics research and practice in the professional literature naturally reflects not only the academic disciplines of the respective authors but also their nationality or, at least, the country in which they have gained relevant experience. This has important implications which are not always fully realized. For example, British writers rarely mention phonic *rules* or the more flexible phonic *generalizations*, inasmuch as they allow for exceptions. This is because in British primary schools, although teaching reading is generally part of an integrated curriculum, it tends not to be rule-orientated. Nevertheless, especially for older pupils, spelling rules such as '*i* before *e* except after *c*' are usually considered part of acceptable practice.

In contrast, on the North American continent, phonic rules and generalizations figure more prominently in publications and, presumably, in practice. So much so that, for instance, Frank Smith includes a chapter on phonics in the revised edition of his book *Understanding Reading* (Smith 1978) which would puzzle British teachers insofar as it is based on what to most of them would seem to be an incorrect statement, i.e. 'The aim of phonics instruction is to provide readers with rules that will enable them to predict how a written word will sound from the way it is spelled.' Smith then examines various aspects of phonic rules and, in doing so, reveals that his original concept of phonics is not 'modern analytic' but 'traditional synthetic' of the most old-fashioned kind. For example, he illustrates the sort of difficulty encountered when 'trying to construct – or teach – reliable rules of phonic correspondence' (p. 138) by the eleven possible pronunciations of *ho* at the beginning of the words *hope, hot, hoot, hook, hour, honest, house, honey, hoist, horse, horizon*. Not surprisingly, Smith concludes that 'phonics in itself is almost useless for sounding out words letter by letter, since every letter can represent too many sounds' (p. 145). But, how many of today's teachers would consider this to be what constitutes phonics?

Clearly, the reading connection must be used by members of UKRA and the parent association IRA to eradicate the confusion that exists because phonics has different meanings for different authors in different contexts. Over twenty years ago UNESCO tried to clarify matters in an international survey on *The Teaching of Reading and Writing* (Gray 1956). Now, significant developments during the ensuing period make it even more imperative to do so.

Historical background
Now too, it is appropriate to consider briefly what some of those developments were which led to the emergence of 'new' phonics, and which help to explain why and how 'new' phonics differs radically from previous types.

THE PHONIC REVOLT
In the early 1950s a great deal of publicity was given to what became known as the 'phonic revolt'. This took place when the search for efficient methods of teaching reading gathered fresh impetus from alarming disclosures about reading standards following the Second World War.

One of the most vociferous leaders of the phonic revolt in the USA was Rudolph Flesch whose best-selling book, *Why Johnny Can't Read* (Flesch 1955) alleged that the basic cause of postwar literacy problems was the disgraceful neglect of phonic instruction for reading and spelling. He bitterly attacked the predominant look-say methods as authoritarian, conditioning techniques which 'treated children as if they were dogs'. In his view, they were 'the most inhuman, mean, stupid way of foisting something on a child's mind' (p. 126).

Flesch included in his book instructions for teaching children to read, write and spell, starting with the sounds of alphabet letters followed by exercises using lists of graded words and the traditional technique of sounding out unfamiliar words. However, these instructions did not mention meaning or thought-getting in the context of communication although he had dealt elsewhere explicitly with this vital issue. In consequence, it was easier for Flesch's numerous critics to argue that he advocated teaching mere word-calling and had rejected the centrality of meaningfulness as, hitherto, the most important contribution to reading theory of twentieth-century research.

In Britain, the phonic revolt was led by John Daniels and Hunter Diack of Nottingham University. They also were extremely critical of prevalent look-say methods which at that time had the seal of official approval. Their criticism included the complaint of many teachers that these methods encourage children to guess at words rather than read them. But, in the main, it was directed to the fact that they ignore the alphabetical nature of English orthography in which letters are symbols for sounds.

MODERN PHONICS

Daniels and Diack did not prescribe a traditional-type phonic remedy as Flesch had done. They proposed that teachers should use a method by which children learn as soon as possible that 'the significant difference between words lies in the letters' (p. 30). This involved presenting them with whole words of the same length so that to discriminate between the words it is necessary to look at their constituent letters.

The 'phonic word method', as it was called, was incorporated by Daniels and Diack (1954) in their *Royal Road Readers* and used by them in experiments which showed it to be strikingly superior in terms of children's reading progress compared with word and sentence methods used with similar pupils. It also marked the beginning of 'modern' analytical phonics in Britain and, incidentally, the type of phonics approved in the Bullock Report (DES 1975), inasmuch as analytical phonics encourages children to learn sound-symbol relationships in the context of whole-word recognition.

REGULARIZED WRITING SYSTEMS

While the phonic revolt gathered momentum on both sides of the Atlantic and more phonic schemes were published, other innovators were advocating what became known as 'regularized writing systems'. They all felt that the traditional spelling of English is a stumbling block for children learning to read and write and, therefore, developed these regularized systems to make the task easier for pupils in the initial stages.

Briefly, some systems retain the normal spelling of words but highlight sound-symbol correspondence in various ways using different kinds of either diacritical marks or colour-coding. Other systems change the spelling of a proportion of words considered to be 'irregular' by the respective innovators and, in some cases, changes in the English alphabet are involved as in ita. Finally, there are the more radical systems for total spelling reform.

Linguistic analyses

Strange to relate, neither the regularized writing systems nor the systems of 'modern' phonics published in the 1950s and early 1960s were based on all the necessary facts about sound-symbol correspondence and word structure. This was inevitable insofar as linguistic research had not yet begun to produce some of the relevant information. For example, it had long been recognized that the representation of vowel sounds in the English writing system is a main source, and some would even say the greatest source, of difficulty for children learning to read and to spell. Yet it was not until 1962 that the first study was reported which provided a detailed inventory of the letter sequences associated with each of the twenty principal vowel phonemes of the English dialect known as Received Pronunciation or, simply, RP.

BRITISH RESEARCH

Bearing in mind the great amount of effort put into developing and publicizing regularized writing systems and 'modern' phonics, it is salutary to read what, in 1962, the British linguist Eleanor Higginbottom wrote in the introduction to the report of her pioneer study. It reads a follows:

> To my knowledge, no other study of this kind has been attempted for English; none for any language has been available to me. Correspondences and irregularities have been investigated to a limited extent by the authors of various projects for reformed spelling; but there is no detailed inventory of the sequences which occur in association with single phonemes, nor any attempts to assess the degree to which phonemes are, in general, predictable from the orthography; also no data for the frequency of occurrence of particular correlations. The correspondences treated in these projects were in any case too generalized, and involved too many exceptions, to be of much use for the accurate prediction of phonemic sequences. It is of course to be expected that the authors of these projects should lay emphasis on the irregular features of the English orthographic system rather than upon the regular correspondences.

Higginbottom's study was undertaken as part of an aerospace project for the production of a machine to 'read' sequences of printed English text and derive from them the corresponding spoken forms. In my view, this makes it even more valuable for there is no room for 'woolly' theories when dealing with machines that have to produce results. Moreover, the findings were a great help to me when developing my own system of 'new' phonics initially for the pioneer BBC television series *Look and Read* (Morris 1971, Fawdrey 1974) and now incorporated in *Language in Action* (Morris 1974).

Unfortunately, ten years elapsed before a second British study of the English writing system was published. This is by the linguist Kenneth Albrow (1972) and a contribution to the Schools Council Programme in Linguistics and English Teaching, some of whose members produced *Breakthrough to Literacy* (Mackay *et al.* 1970). He suggested in the introduction to his report that one of the main reasons why many native speakers of English find it very difficult to learn to read and write is 'the lack of an adequate theory of the orthography which can be used as a basis for teaching, coupled with the consequently inevitable lack of a systematic method for teaching the writing system' (p. 7). Accordingly, Albrow regarded his description of the writing system as an interim contribution to such a theory. As for using it as a basis for teaching, he admits that this is not a linguist's area of competence and, therefore, he leaves its practical application in schools to his teacher colleagues.

Since these teacher colleagues include the three authors of *Breakthrough to Literacy*, it is interesting to note that the phonic component of their materials is what they call the 'Word Maker'. This has many purposes listed in the illustrated edition of the Teacher's Manual (1978). However, the first purpose is to refine techniques of word recognition and help children 'replace random "looking" with systematic awareness of all the units of which a word consists'. In other words, the primary aim of *Breakthrough* phonics is the same as that of the modern, analytic, phonic-word method devised by Daniels and Diack (1974). But the method is different. It is traditional synthetic inasmuch as children are encouraged to build up words from their constituent elements. It is also different in that insert *letter* cards and insert *symbol* cards are provided for the First and Second Word Maker respectively, thereby enabling children to try to make words without, or at least before, committing their attempts to paper.

How far *Breakthrough* phonics has been influenced by the work of Albrow it is difficult to say. Certainly, it is based upon the type of linguistic facts to which he draws attention and, used differently, these could have led to a variety of 'new' phonics.

Be that as it may, to my knowledge, apart from Higginbottom, Albrow and myself, no other British researcher has carried out the kind of detailed linguistic analyses which are a necessary base on which to develop didactic materials for helping children most effectively to learn all they need to know about the orthography. Moreover, only a few scholars in other countries have carried out such analyses, although several descriptions of the English writing system have been published at various times. Most of them have been to its discredit, largely because their authors have assumed that, as Albrow (1972) points out, 'everything must of necessity be forced into one framework'. Whereas what lies behind many of the apparent complexities of the English writing system is the fact that it is polysystemic. As Albrow explains, 'It is not one system of symbols corresponding rather superficially to sounds only (or rather to sound groupings called phonemes), but a system of systems, reflecting the phonological structure of the language, with different conventions for representing the grammatically (and lexically) different elements.'

AMERICAN RESEARCH

Bearing this in mind and the international reading connection, it is interesting to note that in his book *The Structure of English Orthography* the American linguist Venezky (1970) gives a similar explanation to that of Albrow. He writes, 'The present orthography is not merely a letter-to-sound system riddled with imperfections, but instead a more complex and more regular relationship wherein phoneme and morpheme share leading roles.' Indirectly, he also supports Higginbottom's claim to have conducted the pioneer study in this area when he says, 'Since prior to the past few years no extensive analysis of current orthography has been available, it is difficult to imagine what the concept of regularity was based upon other than a simple letter-to-sound view.'

Venezky's book is based mainly on research begun at Cornell University in 1961 which involved writing a computer programme to derive and tabulate spelling-to-sound correspondence in the 20,000 most common English words. It is now continuing at the Wisconsin Research and Development Center for Cognitive Learning. Meanwhile, Venezky's work (1967, 1970) has been used by the Southwest Regional Laboratory (SWRL) for Educational Research and Development in California to develop a phonics-based reading programme for kindergarten through third grade (K–3) as part of a much larger communication skills programme. In view of the detailed linguistic analyses on which this reading programme is based it could be classed as 'new' phonics. Nevertheless, discussions at the SWRL Laboratory with Bruce Cronnell, the linguist in charge of research and design behind the programme, revealed that it differs in several ways from the variety of 'new' phonics incorporated in *Language in Action*.

In the space available, one important difference should be mentioned because phonic materials and, indeed, basal reading schemes from the USA have long had a place in British schools, and there is a tendency to consider only potential difficulties caused by variant spellings. This difference lies in the fact that the pronunciation basis of the SWRL programme is not Bostonian, which has more in common with British

Received Pronunciation than other American dialects. It is Mid-Western Standard Network English which does not have five of the vowel phonemes in RP, i.e. the vowel sounds in *cart, bird, air, ear* and *gourd*. Moreover, no distinction is made between the weak-stress schwa vowel as at the end of *boiler* and the vowel sound in *cup*.

Thus, as far as vowel phonemes are concerned, the SWRL programme is based on a 14-vowel system and *Language in Action* on a 20-vowel system, which means that the type of 'new' phonics in the British scheme reflects a greater regularity of vowel sound-spelling correspondence. Accordingly, the system of spelling pattern progression incorporated therein, and summarized later, could prove to be equally if not more advantageous for American children learning to read and to spell.

Knowledge of this kind of difference alone should encourage British teachers using American schemes to examine them very carefully. It might also encourage American teachers seriously to consider 'new' phonics from Britain in the same way as, in the past, some have tried our regularized writing systems and/or 'modern' analytical phonics exemplified by the phonic-word method.

At present, apart from *Language in Action*, there is to my knowledge only one other British scheme which can be classed as 'new' phonics insofar as it is based on detailed linguistic analyses, albeit American with regard to sound-symbol correspondence and word structure. This is the *English Colour Code Programmed Reading Course* designed by David Moseley (1970) for backward readers but not, in his view, suitable for very young or very dull children.

New phonics reviewed

Undoubtedly, there will be more choice in the years ahead to meet the requests of teachers as they realize the advantages of 'new' phonics in terms of substance, sequence and structure based on linguistically defensible information. Meanwhile, an annotated list [1] of some *general* characteristics of 'new' phonics will provide a nucleus for discussion of these advantages as a prelude to considering some *specific* characteristics of one British system, i.e. the variety of 'new' phonics incorporated in *Language in Action*.

SOME GENERAL CHARACTERISTICS OF 'NEW' PHONICS

1 Is based on good descriptions of the English writing system derived from detailed linguistic analyses of sound-symbol correspondence and word structure.

2 Has a 'standard' pronunciation base, but takes account of dialect

variation and, especially, significant differences between 'standard' British English and 'standard' American English.

3 Provides structured content from linguistically defensible information which allows for classroom practice in accord with *the principle of economy in teaching and learning.*

4 Without sacrificing 'meaningfulness' in the context of communication, is so organized in didactic materials as to give children maximum help in building-up knowledge that there is pattern and order in the written language.

5 Is presented in a professional manner without linguistic errors and confusing references. In particular, a clear distinction is made between the phonological and visible systems of English with regard to vowel and consonant *phonemes* (sounds) and vowel and consonant *graphemes* (letters).

SPECIFIC CHARACTERISTICS OF ONE BRITISH SYSTEM

1 Has a research-based reason for every detail. Areas of research include:

(a) The phonemic system in children's speech as the basis for all higher-order linguistic structures.

(b) The speaking, reading and writing vocabularies of young children.

(c) The relative frequency of the alphabet letters in sample texts.

(d) The perception by children of alphabet letters in various contexts.

(e) The different and/or complementary roles of letters in words.

(f) The dynamics of word play in children's language and in children's literature.

2 (a) Provides a sound linguistic structure for economy in teaching and learning against a background language-experience approach.

(b) At its sound-symbol base, this structure is the result of first analysing relationships between the 44 phonemes (20 vowel sounds plus 24 consonant sounds) of Received Pronunciation (RP) and the graphemes representing them in Traditional Orthography (TO). The analyses naturally cover affixes and affixation processes, stress and word structure, compounds and contractions.

(c) The resulting correspondences total 396 but, according to the criteria established, less than 10 per cent are classed as 'divergencies'. In other words, the analyses support the contention of a number of linguists that, in the main, 'English spelling is a reliable system based on both sound-to-spelling correspondences and on morphological principles'.

3 (a) Uses *key words* singly with illustrations and in verbal context to act as *mnemonics* for 'regular' sound-symbol correspondences. This strategy starts, with the alphabet materials, for the sounds represented at the beginning of words printed on picture story cards and spirit duplicator masters.

(b) The vocabulary in these materials and the associated picture story books is not restricted to 'regular' words.

(c) Findings from the areas of research listed above account for the unusual grouping and sequencing of the Initial Letter Books as follows:

Group 1 Tt; Yy; Hh; Ww; Rr; Gg/Jj; Ss/Zz; Cc/Kk/Ss
Group 2 BD/bd; PQ/pq; MN/mn; VW/vw; EF/ef; IL/il; UN/un

4 (a) Vocabulary is not restricted to 'regular' words in the rest of the foundation materials which incorporate a system of spelling pattern progression as part of the 'new' phonics approach. Instead, *spelling patterns are highlighted in the titles and texts of story books by children's writers* who use a good deal of word play to focus attention on what needs to be learned.

(b) The system of spelling pattern progression reflects the fact that vowel phoneme representation in TO is a source of much greater difficulty for beginners than consonant phoneme representation.

(c) The system of spelling pattern progression begins with a division of monosyllables into major sets as follows:

Set A Words in which the vowel letter corresponds to a so-called short vowel sound, e.g. *cat, hen, pig, dog, pup.*

Set B Words in which marker, modifying, or 'magic' *e* signals that the preceding vowel letter corresponds to a so-called long vowel sound, e.g. *lane, kite, robe.*

Set BB Words in which vowel digraphs correspond to so-called long vowel sounds, e.g. *nail, eel, road.*

Set C Words in which the rest of the vowel phonemes (10) are represented in different ways, e.g. *hoop, cart.*

Within each of the above sets of spelling patterns, the system develops monosyllabic words with consonant clusters of various kinds. For example, the sequence in *Set A* is as follows:

(i) Double letters or their equivalent; pu*ff*, ba*ck*.

(ii) Consonant clusters which occur both at the beginning and at the end of words; *sk*ip, ri*sk*; *sp*ot, li*sp*; *st*op, lo*st*.

(iii) Other consonant clusters of two or three letters which occur at the beginning or at the end of words; *cl*ub, *cr*ust, *scr*ap, *str*ap; ste*ps*, sta*nds*, bli*nks*.

(iv) Consonant digraphs which occur both at the beginning and at the end of words; *ship*, fi*sh*; *ch*op, la*tch*; *th*in, mo*th*; *th*en, wi*th*.

Next, within each of the major sets of spelling patterns, disyllabic words are introduced; for instance, present tense forms of verbs, such as *slipping* (Set A), *making* (Set B), *painting* (Set BB), and *shouting* (Set C).

The system also allows for the sequential introduction of words containing so-called silent letters, in addition to 'silent' marker *e* words. Thus, words such as *knit* and *thumb* (Set A) are followed by *knave* and *comb* (Set B).

5   The system uses a *differentiation approach* rather than a single sequence approach, e.g. King *Dan*, the *Dane*.

The way ahead with 'new phonics'

Much more could be said about the variety of 'new' phonics incorporated in *Language in Action* and, doubtless, it will be said in future publications. So far, the results of this development are very encouraging, but what about the way ahead?

Certainly, research supports the view that phonics is here to stay, and teachers continue to advocate the phonic method although often without stipulating to which of the many types they refer. For instance, Ann Dubs (1977), Head of the Reading Centre at the well-known Woodberry Down Comprehensive School writes, 'Many children entering secondary school have acquired a large sight (or whole-word) vocabulary, yet are still unable to read a new word when they come across it. They have not learned how to identify the sounds of the letters or groups of letters in that particular word.' She then goes on to say, 'Staff should use the phonic method of reading words, and should teach syllabification. Difficult words should be approached this way even with older and more competent pupils' (p. 185).

Hopefully, the staff of that school and British teachers in general will ask more questions about the types of phonics available, starting with the phonic material in their own classrooms. Hopefully also, they will learn about 'new' phonics which emerged too late to be mentioned in the *Bullock Report* (DES 1975). Then this development from the teaching-research connection will have come full circle, in that it was the questions of teachers in the first place which prompted the long years of research from which 'new' phonics, British style, was born.

References
ALBROW, K. H. (1972) *The English Writing System: Notes Towards A Description* Harlow: Longman

DANIELS, J. C. and DIACK, H. (1954) *The Royal Road Readers* London: Chatto and Windus

DES (1975) *A Language for Life* (The Bullock Report) London: HMSO

DUBS, A. (1977) 'The phonics approach' in M. Marland (ed.) *Language Across the Curriculum* London: Heinemann Educational

FAWDRY, K. (1974) *A Personal View of BBC School Broadcasting* London: BBC

FLESCH, R. (1955) *Why Johnny Can't Read* New York: Harper and Row

GRAY, W. S. (1956) *The Teaching of Reading and Writing* UNESCO

HIGGINBOTTOM, E. M. (1962) A study of the representation of English vowel phonemes in the orthography *Language and Speech* 5, 2, 67–117

MACKAY, D. *et al.* (1970) *Breakthrough to Literacy* Harlow: Longman

MORRIS, J. M. (1971) 'Television and reading' in J. E. Merritt (ed.) *Reading and the Curriculum* London: Ward Lock Educational

MORRIS, J. M. (1974) *Language in Action* Basingstoke: Macmillan Education

MORRIS, J. M. (1979) 'New phonics for old' in D. Thackray (ed.) *Growth in Reading* London: Ward Lock Educational, 99–110.

MOSELEY, D. (1970) *English Colour Code Programmed Reading Course* London: Natinal Society for Mentally Handicapped Children

SMITH, F. (1978, revised edition) *Understanding Reading* New York: Holt, Rinehart and Winston

VENEZKY, R. L. (1967) English orthography: its graphical structure and its relation to sound *Reading Research Quarterly* 2, 75–106

VENEZKY, R. L. (1970) *The Structure of English Orthography* The Hague; Paris: Mouton

Note

[1] In the space available this is in condensed form exactly as distributed to delegates although it was elaborated upon during the presentation.

Part 3

Integration and extension

Introduction

The development of reading at all levels has always been a concern of the UKRA. Eileen Pearsall examines some broad definitions of reading and suggests ways in which reading interest and skill may be developed in the first school. This involves her in drawing on various sources, including a project concerned with secondary reading, *The Effective Use of Reading*, sponsored by the Schools Council. The final report of another Schools Council Project *Extending Beginning Reading*, is awaited: however, Vera Southgate Booth and Sandra Johnson report here on one aspect of the work of that project, the diagnosis of phonic strengths and weaknesses. A new test was devised for the research and findings are given here for 367 children aged seven to nine years. The authors consider that children's poor knowledge of phonic rules is a cause for concern, but their suggestions specifically exclude a return to phonic drills. Rather they stress the importance of uninterrupted fluent continuous reading.

Jennie Ingham reports on the Bradford Book Flood Experiment which was intended to measure the effects of providing middle schools with a more than adequate supply of books to permit fluent reading. The paper is mainly concerned with the recording and analysis of children's reading. However, discussion of the categories employed also involves presentation of some data, mainly in the form of children's responses to the Record Form which is also given. Roger Beard is also concerned with children's literature, arguing that it does not receive due attention from those concerned with reading teaching. He applies James Britton's classification of language functions – poetic, expressive, transactional (Britton 1970) – to discuss not only reading literature but its relation to children's own narrative and talk.

Marian Tonjes provides a review of American research into reading flexibility, i.e. the matching of rate and purpose in efficient reading. Paying particular attention to terminology, which is often confused in this area, she provides a checklist for developing materials or tests for reading flexibility. The checklist can also serve, of course, as a basis for discussion of the skills and strategies which, it is posited, are employed by the effective reader.

Finally, Frank Smith argues against rigid categorization into separate language skills. His context is North-American language arts programmes but the discussion has bearing on the debate about the specialized teaching of language in Britain (mentioned in this volume by Elsmore and Pugh). The categories of reading, writing, speaking and understanding speech are not thus separated in the learner's mind, nor should they be for the convenience of school organization. To do so, Smith contends, is to ignore the relationship between language and life and to fail to draw on the purposeful and intentional nature of language.

Reference
BRITTON, J. (1970) *Language and Learning* London: Allen Lane, Penguin Press

10 Reading extension in the first school

Eileen Pearsall

The question of extended and efficient reading is one which is occupying the minds of a good many people today. In considering the question I will first try to show why this interest has arisen, and then I shall look at the implications of the question for teachers of primary school children in the five to nine age range.

Most of our children come to school unable to read, and yet within two years they have come to terms with those strange marks which we call print – marks which behave in completely different ways on different occasions – and they have turned them into meaningful sounds. I think this is a remarkable feat. This achievement is, of course, the result of a good deal of hard work on the part of both the teacher and the child, but it is an achievement which brings a great deal of satisfaction to both. The child delights in showing off his skill to anyone who is willing to listen and the teacher finds great joy in seeing a young child curled up in the book corner lost in a book. Such a child is on the threshold of reading and the world of books is open to him.

It must be a matter of deep disappointment for teachers of young children to learn that many children do not travel very far beyond that threshold. It would seem that, despite the good foundations which are laid, on the whole adults are not readers. There are many who cannot meet the reading demands of everyday life. It is known, too, that after the age of ten children tend to read less and less for pleasure and, despite the fact that the number of books borrowed from public libraries is increasing, it has been found that very few adults – only about one in five – sometimes read a book right through. Moreover, though university students constantly need to refer to books, their lecturers complain that many of them are unable to use books efficiently and that they tend to panic when faced by a number of books on a given subject.

How can we account for the mismatch between children's early ability to master the mechanics of reading and their later inability to use reading in everyday life? One could argue that as children get older they are introduced to an ever-increasing range of interests. They therefore

103

have less time for reading and their initial reading skills are not developed. There is some truth in this argument, but it is not the whole answer for many of those children who learn to read effectively also take part in a wide range of activities.

I believe that the chief reason for the nondevelopment of early skills is the all too commonly-held interpretation of the term 'reading'. Reading tends to be thought of in terms of early reading, and the teaching of reading is generally considered to be the responsibility of teachers of young children and it ends once the child is able to read aloud with reasonable accuracy and at a reasonable speed. There is, however, all the world of difference between being able to read and being a reader. Sarah, who is seven, and who can read *The Times*, may surprise her parents by her ability to read the printed page, but can she really be said to be a reader?

A good many definitions of the term 'reading' have been given. The Bullock Report (DES 1975) refers to three possible definitions. In the first place it suggests that reading might be thought of as a response to graphic signals in terms of the words they represent. By that definition Sarah is reading because she is able to turn the symbols on the page into words. But reading is more than reading words. Reading is a form of communication. When an author writes he does so because he has something to say. The words we read contain a message for us. Reading may then, the Report suggests, be defined as a response to text in terms of the meanings the author intended to set down.

For example, if I am able to read the words in a report and to understand both the words and the statement contained in them, then the author has passed on to me a piece of factual information. Communication has taken place. There are, however, some who would say that this is not the end of the reading process. A purely literal interpretation of the words is not enough. Reading is a thinking process – a process in which we should be actively involved. We should react to what we read, bringing to the passage our own background knowledge and experience and making the passage part of our experience. We should, in fact, read beyond the words and as the result of our reading we should, to some degree, effect a change in ourselves. We may learn something new, we may modify our thinking, we may have an emotional experience or we may formulate a whole range of further questions.

It might be said, therefore, that reading is 'a response to text in terms of the meanings the author intended to set down plus a response to the author's meanings in terms of all the relevant previous experience and present judgments of the reader'. This is a very complex definition. But reading is a very complex activity, demanding a whole range of skills beyond the initial skills involved in converting written symbols into sound. We can get some idea of what this means if we analyse all that is involved in any piece of research, from the moment of entering the library to the final writing of the statement. We need, for example, to employ location skills, which enable us to find, from the thousands of books on the library shelves, the passages which are relevant to our study. We need to be able to read those passages both fluently and flexibly and to employ comprehension skills which enable us to read between and beyond the lines and by so doing to make the information and the ideas contained in the passages part of our own thinking and feeling. We need to be able to evaluate and appreciate what has been written and, finally, to store the information so that we can use it in drawing our conclusions and in making the final statement.

If we think about it, it is as unlikely that these skills will be acquired without help as it is that the early skills will be acquired without their being taught. Nevertheless, in the past, such help has rarely been given. Today we are becoming increasingly conscious of this lack and of the need to develop in children extended reading skills. Teachers are becoming both concerned and interested, and a certain amount of research is taking place. Work which has already been undertaken includes two Schools Council projects, both of which were started in 1973. One of these projects, directed by Vera Southgate Booth, investigated the teaching of reading in the early junior years. Its findings, which are awaited with great interest, are due to be published in 1980. The second project, The Effective Use of Reading, directed by Professor Lunzer and Keith Gardner, considered how average and above-average readers in the ten to fifteen age-range actually used reading in school and what might be done to improve an existing competence. The findings of this project (Lunzer and Gardner, 1979) have relevance for teachers of primary as well as teachers of secondary children.

It is interesting, for example, to find that in the secondary schools visited by the project team, neither teachers nor children gave reading a high rating as a tool for learning. Indeed, except in English lessons, reading played a small part in the day's activities. Some use was made both of textbooks and reference books but the readability level of the textbooks was generally beyond that of the children and the reference books were used in a somewhat haphazard way. Even though the children had been told how to locate information they tended to take books from the shelves at random rather than make a purposeful selection and they sampled rather than studied the contents. They read the printed text without really thinking about it and, in general, their overall gain was insignificant.

Perhaps the most interesting fact that emerged, and one which surprised the research team, was that it is not possible to break down comprehension skills into subskills and to develop them one at a time. Like reading, writing and talking, these skills are interrelated and one needs to work on a broad front. The key to comprehension really lies in the pupil's ability and willingness to reflect upon what he reads. The research suggests that, using appropriate strategies, the teacher is able to increase this ability and to improve the quality of the child's 'conversation with the text'.

Clearly then all teachers have a responsibility to develop children's reading skills so that they are able to enjoy and use reading in later life. How can we begin to do this in the primary school? There are no ready-made or proven answers. What I hope may happen is that teachers will work together to provide ideas which will lead to the formation of a body of knowledge such as we have about teaching the initial reading skills. My intention is simply to put forward one or two suggestions to stimulate thought and discussion.

First and foremost it is necessary to create in children a positive attitude towards reading; secondly it is necessary to develop reading strategies. Most young children, when they begin to read, enjoy reading and get a thrill as they move from book to book. It is very important that they maintain this joy in books and that reading becomes such a part of their lives that when at nine, ten and eleven, they are introduced to new interests, they continue to enjoy reading. In creating a desire to read, the environment of the school and that of the classroom are all-important. Teachers of young children know the value of giving children access to attractive, colourful books that are well displayed. They know, too, that when children are surrounded by interesting objects, both natural and manmade, their curiosity is aroused and, if there are books carefully and strategically placed, they readily turn to them to seek information. But it is not sufficient simply to provide a wide range of books, however attractive and however varied. It is necessary, too, to create a reading climate. Reading needs to be seen as a normal activity – an activity engaged in by adults as well as by children.

Here the teacher's own enthusiasm and example are very important. Her attitude to books – the way she handles them, talks about them, goes to them to find things out, shares them with her class – has a great influence upon the children who become infected by her respect for books and by her love of words. She can also give encouragement by showing each child that she is genuinely interested in what he is reading; that she is pleased to chat about books she has read and to suggest further titles and new authors. This means that she must not only make time to talk with children but she must also find time to familiarize herself with the books that are on the shelves. Such an approach demands a great deal from the teacher but it results in great gains on the part of the child.

Having whetted their appetites for reading the teacher must provide the children with adequate reading opportunities. They need time to read – time to browse and time to settle to long spells of concentrated reading – and they need a place to read, somewhere that is quiet and comfortable where they are able not only to read books for themselves but where they can also listen to recorded stories and poems.

Having created the climate and provided the opportunities for reading, how might we help the children to develop reading skills? Before attempting to answer this question, perhaps it might be useful to ask another. Teachers of young children are highly successful in developing early reading skills. Why are they so successful? There are, perhaps, four reasons for their success. In the first place the teachers put reading high on their list of priorities. Secondly, they have high expectations of their children and they expect that they will learn to read. Thirdly, they have carefully analysed the skills involved in early reading. Fourthly they have worked out strategies and methods through which the children might acquire these skills. Might it be that the same ingredients could produce successful results at the succeeding stage?

With this in mind it might be helpful to look again at the skills which are basic to mature reading and to consider how far we are able to lay the foundations for these in our work with young children. These include the ability to:

1 read fluently
2 read in various ways
3 locate information
4 read critically
5 reorganize what is read
6 evaluate the material read
7 store material.

Mature readers are fluent readers. Young readers, however, tend to read somewhat haltingly because, for the most part, they build and read single words. When you and I read, we see, on the whole, not single letters but groups of letters, and not single words but groups of words. Though we may not be conscious of so doing, we are reading one phrase and looking at the next and we are constantly making use of our knowledge of sentence structure, of the rules of grammar and of letter patterns. We know, for example, that there is a limited range of letter combinations which could be used to complete a word which begins 'correct. . .', and automatically our minds select these possibilities from all the other letter combinations which exist. We select, for example, 'ion', 'ive', 'ing', and from these we take the appropriate one. In the same way we often read the first part of a phrase and complete it not by reading the rest of the phrase but by completing a well-known pattern such as 'by and . . .', 'cup and . . .', 'Once . . .'. As well as being helped by letter and word pattern we are also helped by the meaning of what we are reading. We know what word or words are coming next; the sense tells us. Can we, then, as the children read to us, help them to look ahead to see whole phrases, to use context cues and to make intelligent guesses?

While we are encouraging the child to read fluently, how can we also encourage him to read critically, to comprehend what is implied as well as what is stated, to relate what he reads to what he knows, to predict what might happen next and to have views upon what he has read? In short, how can we help him to reflect upon what he reads? One answer is that we can do this through discussion – through the questions we ask.

The answers to some questions are easily found in the text and need little, if any, thought. They are the kind of question so often found at the end of passages for comprehension in English textbooks. If one knows the technique it is fairly simple to score full marks for answers to this type of question but one is not necessarily any wiser at the end. With another type of question it is not possible to find direct answers in the text, however carefully one reads. They can only be answered by using clues found in the text, by using one's own knowledge and by putting 'two and two together'. Yet other questions require answers which certainly cannot be found in the text; one can only give answers if one has absorbed the text and thought about it.

At what stage in his reading should we encourage a child to get behind the print in this way – to think about what he reads? I think we cannot start too soon. Could we, perhaps, start before he can read print at all, when he 'reads' his picture books? For example, pictures are used by Dr Joan Tough in her work on the development of children's spoken language. The material devised for the Schools Council Communication Skills in Early Childhood Project (see Tough 1976, 1977) contains sets of pictures, each of which tells a story in serial form. By discussing the pictures with the child, Dr Tough aims both to appraise his skill in using language and to provide an opportunity for him to interpret and think about the pictures. The questions she asks lead the child to extract the central meaning, to make judgments on this, to project himself into other people's feelings and to predict what is likely to happen. Since there is an overlap in the skills needed in spoken language and in comprehension we may well find that a good deal of Dr Tough's work, particularly her ideas on the teacher's use of questions, is extremely helpful in developing reading skills.

Could we also, perhaps, use some of the strategies suggested by the Schools Council Effective Use of Reading Project? One of these is based on looking for order and sequence. A story is cut into a number of sections and the child or group of children is asked to put the sections into a logical sequence. This can only be done if each section is carefully studied. This, too, is an idea which we use with very young children when we give them a set of pictures and ask them to order these so that they tell a story. Could we, perhaps, follow through this early activity into the reading stage, first asking the children to order single words to form a sentence, then single sentences to form a passage and finally simple passages to form a story?

Another strategy suggested by the Project is the use of 'cloze procedure'. Here the children are asked to supply missing words in a text. This strategy can be used to assess a child's reading ability and also, particularly when used in a group situation, to encourage both fluent and thoughtful reading. However, children can only employ context cues and read critically if the material they are given to read resembles their own speech form and contains words and ideas which they understand. It would seem important, therefore, that even when children have got through their initial reading scheme they are guided to some extent in what they read so that some of their reading, at least, is at an appropriate readability level. G. W. Elsmore spoke of the need for guidance in the choice of fiction: guidance is equally necessary in the case of nonfiction. As we have seen, critical reading demands a good deal of the child. If he is grappling with meaning he should not, in addition, have to grapple with vocabulary and syntax. It is often difficult to find suitable reference books for young children and there would seem to be a need for more books in which the content is of sufficient depth and interest to satisfy the child whilst the language is accessible to him.

Perhaps one of the ways in which we can help a child to read critically is to encourage him to read purposefully. A child does, of course, often have a genuine purpose in mind when he starts to read – perhaps he saw a hedgehog on the way to school and wants to find out about hedgehogs. With this end in view he either finds, or is given, a book on hedgehogs and he starts upon his task. The next stage we know only too well – he laboriously transfers the words from the printed page to his own book. It is understandable that he should do this because his purpose for reading is far too broad. Faced with a complete book he has nothing to help him to be selective in his use of the information it contains. In the early stages we need to pinpoint, one by one specific aspects that he might look for. We might ask him, for example, 'What does the hedgehog eat?', 'Why has it prickles?', 'Where does it live?'. If the child reads in order to answer a definite question he will be able to identify relevant information in the text. In time, as he becomes accustomed to reading with a question in mind, we can encourage him to formulate his own questions and so define his own purposes for reading. It is important, of course, that the child becomes able not only to select but also to use information found in books. This is a difficult process, but if he is reading in order to answer a predetermined question he will find that, whether he is telling someone what he has found out or writing it down, he needs to rearrange the various pieces of information he has extracted.

Initially, when he sets out to answer his simple question, 'What does the hedgehog eat?', the child may need to be directed to the page upon which he will find the information. As he progresses, however, he can be helped to find the book and the page for himself. He will need, for example, to be given some knowledge of the system employed for storing books so that he can locate the books relevant to his study. He will also need experience in using a table of contents and practice in using an index. This latter skill we start to develop when we give the young child a word book in which we write all the words he needs, beginning with 'a' on the 'a' page and so on; and we develop it when we introduce him to a simple dictionary.

As the child skips over the 'a' words and the 'b' words and then starts reading carefully the 'c' list in order to find which page in his book deals with 'cats', he is actually beginning to develop another skill – the skill of scanning. I do not think that many children in the five to nine age range will develop this skill much beyond this early stage, nor will they develop the ability to skim. They will, however, be able to develop some flexibility of reading pace, as they read silently more quickly than they read aloud and as they read and reread some passages with particular care in order to obtain greater depth of understanding.

The two final skills I mentioned – the ability to evaluate the material read and the ability to store material – are also advanced skills for which only a few nine-year-olds will be ready. I do think, however, that we can encourage children to question what they read and not to take a statement or an idea as being correct simply because it is in a book.

In considering reading extension, I think two things become evident. In the first place it is clear that teachers in primary schools have a responsibility to help children to begin to acquire the higher order skills; secondly, it becomes apparent that the skills involved are closely interrelated. They cannot be taught in isolation and, by the same token, the whole group of skills cannot be taught as an isolated aspect of the curriculum. These skills should, whenever possible, be taught as part of the child's general experience and in situations which are meaningful to him.

Though until recently the field which we have been considering was relatively unexplored, a good deal of research and thought is taking place today. We are realizing increasingly the truth of the statement 'We are all of us learning to read all the time'. We have accepted the need for teaching extended reading techniques but what we have not done, in any structured way, is to work out the implications of this in practical terms. There is a need for both experimentation and for the pooling of ideas.

References

DES (1975) *A Language for Life* (The Bullock Report) London: HMSO

LUNZER, E. and GARDNER, K. (1979) *The Effective Use of Reading* London: Heinemann Educational for the Schools Council

TOUGH, J. (1976) *Listening to Children Talking: A Guide to the Appraisal of Children's Use of Language* London: Ward Lock Educational for the Schools Council

TOUGH, J. (1977) *Talking and Learning* London: Ward Lock Educational for the Schools Council

11 The phonic competencies of children aged seven to nine years

Vera Southgate Booth and Sandra Johnson

Introduction

The Schools Council Project Extending Beginning Reading was carried out over the four years 1973–7, based at Manchester University. Analysis of all the data and writing up the findings has taken an additional two years. The report will be completed by December 1979 and published in 1980/1.

The project was focused on average readers in the first two years of junior education, i.e. children aged seven to nine plus. The main aims were to:

1 discover exact details of these children's competencies and the ways in which they utilized their reading skills;
2 locate points at which difficulties occurred and the strategies children used to overcome these difficulties;
3 note the methods their teachers employed to help them to 'extend' their proficiency during the first two years of junior education, as well as the progress the children made during this period;
4 examine in the children habits and attitudes likely to encourage them to utilize fully their reading abilities, currently and after they have left school.

The project was entirely school-based and in the course of the research many different probes were made into ongoing teaching practices and their results, as judged by children's reading competencies and the uses children made of their increasing skill in reading. Little has so far been published about the project apart from two short papers previously presented to UKRA Annual Conferences – Southgate (1976) and Southgate *et al.* (1978). The current paper on children's phonic competencies is a brief report on one further aspect of the investigations. It should be emphasized, however, that the diagnosis of phonic strengths and weaknesses represented only a very small proportion of the total project.

Preliminary investigations
During the first two years of the project the research team worked with two large teachers' reading research groups consisting of some 440 and 260 teachers respectively. Preliminary work undertaken by these 700 teachers on phonic skills concerned:

1 their pupils' mastery of the sounds of the letters of the alphabet and of various letter combinations and phonic rules;
2 the feasibility of utilizing 'nonsense words' as a diagnostic phonic testing device.

The findings highlighted those areas of phonic weaknesses in children aged seven to nine years which merited further investigation. They also confirmed the use of 'nonsense words' as a useful diagnostic assessment technique.

Although a number of available phonic tests employ the device of 'nonsense words', when closely examined none was found to be exactly what was required for children in these two age groups. Accordingly, a new diagnostic phonic test, particularly suitable for children aged seven to nine years, was devised, tried out in schools and revised.

The new diagnostic phonic test
The new test consisted of 55 nonsense words. The range of items was such that the poorest reader of seven years would be able to 'read' some of the items, whilst only the most proficient readers of nine years would be likely to score all items correctly. The nonsense words were devised so that they had the format, construction and rhythm of English words, which means that when pronounced they would seem plausible English words. In other words, English-speaking children would find it possible to 'get their tongues round them'.

The test was diagnostic in character. While it could not hope to provide the teacher with a complete picture of a child's total knowledge of phonics, it could indicate areas in which the child was confident and, even more important, highlight those areas in which his knowledge was either doubtful or nonexistent. These latter areas could then form part of the basis of the teacher's forward teaching plans for the child in question.

Children's mastery of the following phonic skills could be assessed by administering the test:

1 The common sounds of the letters of the alphabet in the different positions in words which they usually occupy;

113

2   Blending sounds together in simple three-letter words;
3   Combining together, in a word pattern, two and three syllables;
4   Phonic rules to which there are few exceptions, for example the pronunciation of 'ee', 'ing', or 'ph';
5   Rules which, although they have certain exceptions, are nevertheless in fairly common use; for example, the rule that a silent 'e' at the end of a monosyllabic word such as 'cake' often causes the preceding vowel to have its long sound.

The seven categories of phonic skills being tested in the nonsense words fell into the groups shown in Table 1.

Table 1 Categories of phonic skills tested in new diagnostic test

No. of items	Categories of skills	Example
5	consonant blends	sp
5	consonant digraphs	sh
10	vowel digraphs	ee
5	murmur vowels	er
5	rule of silent 'e'	as in m*ake*
3	silent letters	'k' as in *k*nife
7	common word endings	ing

In addition there were five examples each of words of one, two and three syllables. As certain vowel digraphs have alternative, common pronunciations in different words in English, e.g. *ea* as in t*ea* or h*ea*d, *ow* as in c*ow* or belo*w*, either pronunciation in the nonsense word was counted as correct.

Each child was tested individually, after being given introductory instructions about the items being 'silly' words, as they didn't make any sense at all. If, during the testing, a child appeared to be trying to make an item into a known word, the tester would say: 'Don't try to make it into a word you know. You won't know any of these words. They are not real words.' The words were presented singly in the order of difficulty which had been established in the pilot trial. The following are examples of nonsense words included in the test: hix, plon, roxer, kide, shaff, towk, exchinfer, umbasade.

Children tested

The third year of the project represented an intensive study in twelve schools. The phonic test was one of a battery of tests used in first- and seond-year junior classes in ten of these schools. It was administered to four randomly-selected children in each of three bands of reading ability – above average, average and below average – in each class (reading ability based on *Southgate Group Reading Test 2* (1962) administered in September 1975). All the testing was undertaken by the three members of the research team.

The original testing took place early in February 1976 and, in order that some measurement of progress might be made, the test was repeated with the same children in July 1976. The total number of children tested in February was 434, but by July, owing to absences, holidays and removals of families, this number was reduced to 367. It should, however, be noted here that the reduction in sample size was evenly distributed across all three ability bands.

Results of the testing

PERFORMANCE OF THE SEXES
It was interesting to note that there were no apparent differences between the performances of boys and girls on any aspect of the new diagnostic phonic test.

AREAS OF WEAKNESS
1   *Order of difficulty of rules*
The main value of a diagnostic test lies not in its ability to measure children's success in various areas, but rather in its uncovering of the weaknesses or failures of individual children, so that the teacher's attention may be directed to those precise areas of phonic knowledge in individual children where tuition and practice are needed. The method of scoring adopted in this test made it possible to isolate those areas least well known by the children and to establish a general order of difficulty of the sound categories and phonic rules tested. Starting with the most difficult they were found to be:

Category	*Examples*
vowel digraphs	'ee' 'ow' 'ou'
long vowels	as found in 'm*a*ke' and 'b*i*te'
murmur vowels	'er' 'or' 'ar'
common endings	'ck' 'ing' 'ight'
silent letters	as found in '*w*rite' '*k*nock'
consonant digraphs	'sh' 'ch' 'th'
consonant blends	'sp' 'pl' 'tr'

In the context of the difficulty of phonic rules, teachers might also find it useful to know that within each category, the following examples in the test showed the highest failure rate:

vowel digraphs	*ou* (as in sh*ou*t)
long vowels	*u* (as in t*u*ne)
murmur vowels	*ir* (as in s*ir*)
common endings	*tion* (as in ac*tion*)
silent letters	*b* (as in lam*b*)
consonant digraphs	*ph* (as in *Ph*ilip)
consonant blends	*qu* (as in *Qu*een)

2 *Success and failure rates*

As was to be expected the failure rate in every category was highest for children of below-average reading ability, whilst above-average readers had much lower failure rates. Similarly, in respect of age, second-year children were consistently better in every category than first years.

In the least well-known category – vowel digraphs – on average 74 per cent of first years and 50 per cent of second years recognized fewer than eight of the ten examples included in the test. But when the children were grouped according to reading ability, it could be seen that among first years this same failure rate for vowel digraphs was as follows:

Children of below-average reading ability (BA)	95 per cent
Children of average reading ability (A)	85 per cent
Children of above-average reading ability (AA)	42 per cent

This same pattern of success and failure rates was noted in every category.

The categories which showed the greatest evidence of *total* failure, that is lack of success with even one item, are set out in Table 2.

Table 2 Percentages of children who failed to get even one example correct in various sound categories

Category	Date	1st Years				2nd Years			
		BA	A	AA	All	BA	A	AA	All
Long vowels	Feb.	34	13	1	14	9	—	—	2
	July	14	2	—	4	9	—	—	3
Silent letters	Feb.	25	19	5	16	17	4	1	7
	July	25	7	3	10	9	—	—	3
Murmur vowels	Feb.	25	10	—	12	12	—	—	4
	July	13	2	—	4	5	—	—	2

It is not surprising to find that the 'rule of the silent *e*' in a monosyllabic word, which usually converts a preceding vowel to its long sound, turned out to be the most difficult (14 per cent of all first years showing total failure), nor that it was the below-average readers who most frequently exhibited no knowledge of this rule (34 per cent). What is more surprising is that 13 per cent of average readers and 1 per cent of above-average readers in the first year failed to respond correctly to even one example of the rule. These figures had at any rate improved between February and July and, by the second year, every child was able to succeed with at least one of the items in this category.

That murmur vowels might cause some difficulty was perhaps also to be expected, but it was rather disturbing to discover that 12 per cent of children, half-way through their first year, did not even know one of the five murmur vowels – not even the easiest one 'er', which is in such common use (25 per cent of below-average readers – 12 per cent of the whole age group). Fortunately, by the second year most of the children recognized at least one of the murmur vowels, even though many children had not mastered them all.

In the best-known category, i.e. consonant blends, all the second-year children of above-average reading ability were successful with four or five of the five examples included in the test. Even with first years, only 1 per cent of those of above-average reading ability failed to reach a success rate of 80 per cent of the items.

In the light of one of the findings from the first teachers' reading research group, it is not surprising that 11 per cent of first years and 4 per cent of second years were virtually unable to blend together such common combinations of sounds as the digraphs 'sp' and 'tr'. The teachers had found that only 35 per cent of their first-year pupils and 45 per cent of second years knew the sounds of all 26 letters of the alphabet, and that the number of errors made extended as far as 21 and 22 must surely have been a stumbling block in blending together the sounds of two letters in an unknown word. In addition, it was noticed in administering the new phonic test that certain children aged seven to nine years still confused 'b' with 'd'.

EVIDENCE OF LACK OF DIAGNOSIS

While, in general, the results of testing children's phonic competencies indicated an overall improvement in the performance of second years over first years, there were, nevertheless, certain indications of lack of diagnosis of children's phonic weaknesses on the part of teachers. Many of the results, particularly those relating to children of below-average reading ability, showed little improvement for second years over first

years. For example, 95 per cent of below-average readers in the first year failed to reach the 80 per cent success rate referred to earlier for vowel digraphs in the test; the equivalent proportion in the second year was 79 per cent.

Other comparisons in the research confirmed this finding. For instance, in February, 25 per cent of below-average first years failed to recognize even one of the silent letters; and five months later in July, the figure was exactly the same. The figure of 17 per cent of below-average readers in the second year failing to recognize one silent letter in February also indicates little improvement over children one year younger. Individual children's weaknesses in this respect could very quickly have been remedied, had teachers been fully aware of them. Two of the silent letters tested are in fairly common use in reading materials used by children of these ages, and are also frequently used by the children in their own writing. For example: silent k as in knock, knit, knob, know, knight, etc; silent w as in write, writing and wrong.

These findings should not, however, be taken to indicate that teachers in the intensive study schools did no phonic teaching. On the contrary, their daily logs and the researchers' own observations in classrooms showed that nearly all teachers did some phonic teaching but this was usually class teaching rather than teaching based on the diagnosis of individual weaknesses.

Summary

1   The results of the new diagnostic phonic test indicated that while many children aged seven to nine years, especially those of above-average reading ability, demonstrated a working knowledge of certain common phonic rules, the phonic skills of other children – particularly those of below-average reading ability – were so sketchy that in certain areas they succeeded on fewer than 80 per cent of the examples in the test. In general, the categories of phonic skills least well known were vowel digraphs, the rule of the 'silent e' and murmur vowels, in that order; followed by common endings of words and silent letters.

2   Some children exhibited total failure with certain common phonic rules in that they were unable to succeed with even one item in the category. While the majority of such children were of below-average reading ability there were nevertheless a proportion of average readers, and even a sprinkling of above-average readers, who showed total failure to recognize such categories as long vowels, silent letters or murmur vowels.

3   Children were most successful with the category of consonant blends, but even here 11 per cent of first years and 4 per cent of second

years were successful with fewer than 80 per cent of the examples included in the test. As certain children, even among second years, did not know the sounds of all the letters of the alphabet, their inability to blend two sounds together is not surprising.

4   There was some evidence of lack of adequate diagnosis of their pupils' phonic weaknesses on the part of teachers, in that only a proportion of the weaknesses shown by first years had been overcome by children in their second year. This suggests that either teachers were unaware of the particular weaknesses of individual children or that the phonic teaching provided had been ineffective because it was not aimed at the precise problems experienced by individual pupils.

Implications for teachers
1   As it has been shown that some first- and second-year junior pupils show a complete lack of knowledge of the simplest and/or most common phonic rules in the English language, while even.average and above-average readers in second-year classes have not achieved complete mastery of these rules, the implications for teachers of children aged seven to nine years are absolutely clear. Diagnosis of *individual* children's phonic strengths and weaknesses is the first essential step – and the new phonic test has proved an effective instrument for this purpose. The aim need not be to test every child in the class at the beginning of the school year, but a start should certainly be made, as rapidly as possible, with the least competent readers. Accurate records of individual weaknesses should follow diagnosis and be updated as skills are mastered.

2   Steps then need to be taken to teach children those skills which are found to be weak. Class teaching will only be the appropriate means for doing this if the entire class is ignorant of the rule in question. In most other cases group teaching of only those particular children who have shown lack of mastery of certain sounds or rules would be most effective. The actual members of the group would vary on different occasions, depending on which children had or had not mastered the skill in question. In certain cases individual tuition would be called for.

3   The fact that the smallest number of phonic deficiencies are usually displayed by children of above-average reading ability also means that once a teacher has diagnosed and rectified the few phonic weaknesses among the most fluent readers in her class, further attention can be devoted to providing appropriate phonic tuition for average and below-average readers.

4   Teachers might wonder whether the findings of the research project Extending Beginning Reading has led us to advocate a return to phonic

methods of teaching beginning readers, or for that matter, ineffective older readers. Nothing could be further from the truth. The total findings of the project have strengthened our belief that the major portion of the reading programme for seven- to nine-year-olds should be exactly that – uninterrupted reading of books the children understand and enjoy. It is fluent reading which aids comprehension, rather than stumbling, halting progress. If comprehension is the ultimate goal of extending beginning reading, the practice of continuous fluent reading, rather than hesitant oral reading with frequent halts for coaching, will be most likely to achieve this goal. Therefore, we have concluded that periods of phonic teaching, when required, should be brief. Probably no more than five to ten minutes once or twice a week, should be all that is necessary – and just for those particular children in whom specific phonic weaknesses had been diagnosed.

At the particular stage of reading competency which the majority of children aged seven to nine years have reached, it would seem that the semantic cues in the text relating to meaning, and the syntactic cues relating to grammatical structure, are more important than the phonic cues – although the latter certainly play a part in the global understanding of what is read. We would agree with Smith, Goodman and Meredith (1976) who stated:

Most of the simple panaceas in reading instruction are not methods but sets of tactics that emphasize the learner's use of one set of cues or a group of related cues. Phonics, for example, is a set of tactics for handling letter cues. These tactics, if they are based on a sound understanding of letter-sound relationships, can be fitted into a method of reading instruction. But phonics is not a complete method of reading instruction. . . . Any strategy of reading instruction based on a single principle or tactic is incomplete, no matter how valid the principle.

References

SMITH, E. B., GOODMAN, K. S. and MEREDITH, R. (1976, 2nd edition) *Language and Thinking in School* New York: Holt, Rinehart and Winston

SOUTHGATE, V. (1962) *Southgate Group Reading Tests: Test 2 – Sentence Completion Test* Sevenoaks: Hodder and Stoughton Educational

SOUTHGATE, V. (1976) 'Extending Beginning Reading: An outline of the research project' in A. Cashdan (ed.) *The Content of Reading* London: Ward Lock Educational

SOUTHGATE, V., ARNOLD, H. and JOHNSON, S. (1978) 'The use of teachers' and children's time in *Extending Beginning Reading*' in E. Hunter-Grundin and H. U. Grundin (eds.) *Reading: Implementing The Bullock Report* London: Ward Lock Educational

12 Recording children's responses to books in the Bradford Book Flood Experiment

Jennie Ingham

The aim of the Bradford Book Flood Experiment (1976–9) is to examine longitudinally the effects on children's literary skills, interests in, and attitudes towards books of 'flooding' or saturating their classrooms with non-textbooks. Two pairs of matched control and experimental schools have been involved in a pretest, post-test design; approximately 5,000 additional books were placed with the second-year middle-school children, initially aged ten years, in each of the experimental schools.

In addition to undergoing various tests of reading ability and reading attitude, each child (n = 357) was required to complete a questionnaire (Reading Record Form: see Appendix 1, p. 129) each time the child read a non-textbook. Whilst the main purpose of keeping such a record was to enable us to compare the reading habits of the children in control and experimental schools, it was also hoped that it would be an intrinsically valuable exercise in that it would provide a developmental picture of the reading habits and interests of a substantial number of children.

It was decided that the Reading Record Form should fall into two parts, the first to be completed at the time of choosing a book; the second to be completed after the child had finished with the book, thus avoiding a reliance on children's memories, which is a feature of several previous studies (e.g. Jenkinson 1940, Carsley 1955). Our case studies revealed that whilst memory of book titles is often vague and short-lived, awareness of authors is often lacking.

Many previous studies of children's reading interests have employed the 'one-off' survey approach (Jenkinson 1940, Carsley 1955, Yarlott and Harpin 1970/71, Whitehead *et al.* 1977). Such a study, if conducted on a large scale and with rigorous sampling procedures, can yield highly generalizable results, but will, inevitably, fail to provide a detailed developmental picture of the reading habits and interests of a particular group of children. Whitehead *et al.*, both in their interim and final reports to the Schools Council (1974, 1977), acknowledged the need for 'a longitudinal study of a much smaller number of children in order to follow through their reading over a period of several years . . .'. Possibly, this will be one of the achievements of our experiment.

One of the disadvantages of the survey approach is that it does not reveal the possible wide variety of reading undertaken by a particular child. It is no exaggeration to say that a thirteen-year-old might read a *Moomintroll* book one week, *Mike and Me* or *The Ogre Downstairs* the next, read nothing at all voluntarily for a few weeks, dip into encyclopaedias or books on sport for maybe half a term, read *Watership Down* and *Plague Dogs* in rapid succession, and return to Roald Dahl by way of a breather. The return to old favourites in times of academic strain or emotional disturbance etc is well known. In Peter Hollindale's citation of *The Journeying Boy* by Michael Innes, we find that the boy has compiled a reading list, which demonstrates a pattern of reading behaviour remarkably similar to the patterns found amongst some of our more able subjects:

Please deliver at once by special messenger one pair of binoculars for bird-watching and a good camera (not box). Please also send these books: *Biggles Flies East, Biggles Flies West, Biggles Flies North, Biggles Fails to Return*, Bertrand Russell's *History of Western Philosophy*, George Moore's *Daphnis and Chloe, Biggles and the Camel Squadron*, Bleinstein's *More and More Practical Sex*, Blunden's *Life of Shelley*, also *Atalanta in Calydon, Biggles in Borneo, Women in Love*, and any close translations of Caesar's *Civil Wars*.

The Reading Record Form has made feasible a detailed examination of the reading interests of a substantial number of children as they passed from childhood to adolescence. A greater insight into the reading habits and interests of outstandingly avid or reluctant readers has been gained via case studies of thirty-three children.

Another reason for keeping a longitudinal record of children's reading and, thus, attempting to have the children record every title, was so that we should avoid the practice of having the children tick broad subject categories of books preferred (see Jenkinson 1940, Smith and Harrap 1957, Butts 1963, Inglis 1969, Yarlott and Harpin 1970/71) such as 'school stories', 'animal stories', 'love and romance' or 'adventure'. (We note that Whitehead *et al.* reached the same conclusion: see pp. 110–11 of final report.) Although the responses resulting from this method of data collection lend themselves relatively easily to computer analysis (we have approximately 1800 authors and approximately 4000 titles), there are many disadvantages to this method, in particular the oversimplification inherent in such a reductionist approach; for, whilst some books fall readily into topic or subject categories such as 'science fiction' (e.g. the *Dr Who* series) or into 'detective stories' (e.g. *The Hardy Boys* or the *Nancy Drew* series), many others defy categorization at this level. For example, how would one categorize *The Shrinking of Treehorn* or *The Ogre Downstairs*? Are they 'fantasy' – in the former, a child gradually shrinks and later turns green; whilst in the latter children fly and toffee bars, a pipe and doll's house people become animate? Or are they 'social realism'/'family life', since they deal with often painfully real situations encountered by many of their readers? One could ask similar questions about *The Blah, Freaky Friday, A Billion for Boris, The Ghost of Thomas Kempe, Marianne Dreams* and myriads of other books, which cross subject boundaries, but all of which use fantasy in order to illuminate and contain realistic problems, often of human relationships. In *Freaky Friday* and *The Ogre Downstairs*, for example, empathy is portrayed at a level of concrete operations by means of magic, just as budding hypothetical thought is given a helping hand in *A Billion for Boris*. Books of this type both provide 'an imaginative insight into what another person is feeling' and confront 'the reader with problems similar to his own . . . at the safety of one remove' (Bullock Report, DES 1975, p. 125). The means of achieving this should not be judged by adult standards, however.

The other aspect of oversimplification which we wished to avoid by rejecting categorization by subject area or topic (again cf. Whitehead *et al.* 1977) was the lumping together of the diversity of books, differing on so many other dimensions, which would be likely to fall into one category. For example, within the category of 'animal stories', in the middle school we should probably find *Harvey's Hideout, Mrs Frisby and the Rats of Nimh, Dogsbody, Tarka the Otter, Charlotte's Web, The Midnight Fox, Watership Down* and *Animal Farm*, only one of which is purely and unconditionally an animal story. Perhaps even more disparity would be found within a category of 'school stories' which included *What Katy Did, The Eighteenth Emergency, Jennings* and *Pardon Me, You're Stepping on My Eyeball!* There are as many differences within a subject category as there are between categories and it is patronizing of us to assume that we can regard children's books or children's reasons for choosing books in this simplistic way. What we should try to achieve is an examination of both implicit and explicit reasons for book choice in all their complexity.

It is perhaps worth mentioning briefly that the ticking of subject categories could cause a distortion of results if children succumb to peer-group pressure (and adult socialization) and give sex-stereotypic responses; this is less likely to occur if a child is invited to record responses to each individual book. For instance, a boy who might respond favourably to *The Midnight Fox* or *Dogsbody*; or to *A Very Long Way From Anywhere Else* or any of Paul Zindel's books, would be unlikely to express a preference for 'animal stories' or 'love stories'.

The importance of allowing the children to explain what it was that attracted them to a particular book, on as many dimensions as they thought fit, prompted a deviation from the multiple-choice format of the rest of the Reading Record Form, both for response to the question 'Why did you choose this book?' and at the end of the questionnaire where they were invited to make further remarks about the book. In a pilot study, we did try a multiple-choice format for this question, but reverted to our original idea of a free response, as the large number of boxes ticked seemed to indicate that we were furnishing children with reasons which, otherwise, would not have occurred to them; also, verbal questioning regularly supplied reasons not included in our list. Although we realized that for purposes of computer analysis of what eventually amounted to approximately 15,000 returns we should be forced to condense the free responses into a manageable and meaningful number of categories, a process inevitably involving a degree of subjectivity, we can, nevertheless, claim that the categories are derived from, not imposed upon, the children. Thus, hopefully, we have equipped ourselves with some of the tools for exploring the reasons behind the popularity of certain authors. In addition, of course, we are in a position to quote actual reasons or additional remarks (see Appendices 3 and 4, pp. 132–4).

In fact, the categorization of reasons for book choice went through three trial stages before inter-coder agreement was reached on the basic categories to be found in Appendix 2. The major area of disagreement was resolved when the two categories (a) Interest in an activity/object e.g. horses, football; and (b) Interest in a sort of story, e.g. horse stories, football stories, were merged and became category 4. A record was also kept by the coder of type of book in terms of fiction; nonfiction; poetry/plays; jokes/puzzles.

All the data from the three years' returns of the Reading Record Form are now on file in the computer, so that all responses can be examined in terms of school, school class, age and sex, as well as for the most popular authors for any or all possible subgroups. Against the lists of books most frequently enjoyed will be set lists of books available in each school, for we agree with Whitehead *et al.* (1977) that availability is adult-controlled in many ways and that this adult control frequently underlies popularity ratings which can easily be accepted by the reader as 'an undiluted expression of children's reading preferences'.

From a preliminary analysis of the returns of the Reading Record

Form for the first year of the experiment, it has been interesting to note that sex differences in responses to the questionnaire have been minimal. However, there is some indication that the returns from children in the experimental schools, with a greater and wider selection of books, are less likely to reveal major differences between boys' and girls' lists of most popular authors than the returns from children in the control schools, with a smaller stock of books including a relatively larger proportion of classics. Naturally, it is easier to classify books like *What Katy Did*, *Little Women*, *Heidi* and *Ballet Shoes* as girls' books or *Coral Island*, *Treasure Island* and *Kidnapped* as boys' books, than it is to so classify books by Roald Dahl, Norman Hunter, Betsy Byars or Paul Zindel.

An examination of the responses to those books rated as one of the best ever read or as not liked at all demonstrated a high degree of internal consistency which seems to favour the reliability of the children's responses. For example, those books rated as 'one of the best' were usually taken home, completely read, not found very difficult, discussed with others, especially peers, recommended to friends, and often inspired the child to read another book by the same author. The reasons given for book choice also appear to bear a logical relationship to the degree of enjoyment experienced by the child, i.e. a child was likely to have fairly realistic expectations of a book which he enjoyed, in that he had some kind of prior knowledge of the book, whether because he had heard part of it read aloud, by the teacher or on *Jackanory*, or because he had read several pages before borrowing it. Also, peer-group recommendation was less likely to lead to disappointment than was recommendation by an adult (cf. Pugh 1971). It will be interesting to discover whether children become more expert at choosing a book which they will enjoy given a wide choice of readily-available reading material, and whether this expertise develops in control schools also as a result of completing the questionnaire for three years!

Certainly, our preliminary analyses have raised many interesting hypotheses both for ourselves and for future researchers. Hopefully, our study will enable us to examine 'ways in which books can be analysed and meaningfully described so that one can predict with some accuracy the reception which a book will receive' (Pugh 1971). If there is 'a strong connection between voluntary reading and reading attainment' (Bullock Report, Ch. 9) then positive reinforcement for voluntary reading is vital.

References

JOURNALS/BOOKS ABOUT CHILDREN'S READING

BUTTS, D. (1963) What do some boys and girls read and why? *Use of English 15*, 2, 87–90

CARSLEY, J. D. (1955) The interest of children (10–11 years) in books *British Journal of Educational Psychology 27*, 13–23

DES (1975) *A Language for Life* (The Bullock Report) London: HMSO

INGLIS, F. (1969) *The Englishness of English Teaching* Harlow: Longman

JENKINSON, A. J. (1940) *What do Boys and Girls Read?* London: Methuen

PUGH, A. K. (1971) Secondary school reading: obstacles to profit and delight *Reading 5*, 1, 6–13

SMITH, W. H. and HARRAP, G. G. (1957) *A Survey of Boys' and Girls' Reading Habits* London: Harrap

WHITEHEAD, F., CAPEY, A. C. and MADDREN, W. (1975) *Children's Reading Interests* London: Evans/Methuen Educational for the Schools Council

WHITEHEAD, F., CAPEY, A. C., MADDREN, W. and WELLINGS, A. (1977) *Children and Their Books* (Schools Council Research Studies Series) Basingstoke: Macmillan Education

YARLOTT, G. and HARPIN, W. S. (1970–71) 1000 Responses to English Literature 1 and 2 *Educational Research 13*, 1, 3–11 and *13*, 2, 87–91

CHILDREN'S BOOKS

ADAMS, R. *Plague Dogs* Penguin 1978; *Watership Down* Puffin 1973

ALCOTT, L. M. *Little Women* various editions

BALLANTYNE, R. M. *Coral Island* various editions

BUCKERIDGE, A. *Jennings Stories* numerous titles Collins

BYARS, B. *The Eighteenth Emergency* Puffin 1976; *The Midnight Fox* Faber 1970; *The Pinballs* Bodley Head 1977

COOLIDGE, S. *What Katy Did* various editions

DAHL, R. *Charlie and the Chocolate Factory* Allen and Unwin 1967, Puffin 1973; *Charlie and the Great Glass Elevator* Allen and Unwin 1973, Puffin 1975; *Danny: The Champion of the World* Cape 1975, Puffin 1977; *James and the Giant Peach* Allen and Unwin 1967, Puffin 1973; *Fantastic Mr Fox* Allen and Unwin 1970, Puffin 1970; *The Magic Finger* Allen and Unwin 1966, Puffin 1974

DICKS, T. *et al. Dr Who Series* various titles Target Books

DIXON, F. W. *Hardy Boys Series* various titles Grosset and Dunlap

HEIDE, F. P. *The Shrinking of Treehorn* Kestrel 1975

HOBAN, R. *Harvey's Hideout* Cape 1973

INNES, M. *The Journeying Boy* Gollancz 1970

JANSSON, T. *Moomintroll* books various titles Benn/Penguin

JONES, D. W. *Dogsbody* Macmillan 1975; *The Ogre Downstairs* Macmillan 1974

KEENE, D. *Nancy Drew Series* various titles Collins

KENT, J. *The Blah* Abelard Schuman 1974

LE GUIN, U. *A Very Long Way From Anywhere Else* Gollancz 1976

LIVELY, P. *The Ghost of Thomas Kempe* Heinemann 1973

O'BRIEN, R. C. *Mrs Frisby and the Rats of Nimh* Puffin 1975

ORWELL, G. *Animal Farm* Penguin 1963

RODGERS, M. *A Billion for Boris* Hamish Hamilton 1975; *Freaky Friday* Hamish Hamilton 1973

SPYRI, J. *Heidi* various editions

STEVENSON, R. L. *Kidnapped; Treasure Island* various editions

STORR, C. *Marianne Dreams* Faber 1958, Puffin 1964

STREATFEILD, N. *Ballet Shoes* Dent 1968

WHITE, E. B. *Charlotte's Web* Puffin 1967

ZINDEL, P. *I Never Loved Your Mind* Bodley Head 1970; *My Darling, My Hamburger* Bodley Head 1970; *Pardon Me, You're Stepping on My Eyeball* Bodley Head 1976; *The Pigman* Macmillan 1971

Appendix 1: Reading Record Form

WHAT I THINK ABOUT MY BOOK

Your name .... Your class ....

Title of book ....

Author ....

Date you began this book ....

ANSWER THE FIRST TWO QUESTIONS WHEN YOU CHOOSE A BOOK TO READ

1 *Where did you get this book from?* Tick one box below.

The public library	...	...	...	...	...	☐ 1
The school library	...	...	...	...	...	☐ 2
The books in the class	...	...	...	...	...	☐ 3
It belongs to me ...	...	...	...	...	...	☐ 4
It belongs to a brother or sister	...	...	...	...	☐ 5
I borrowed it from a friend	...	...	...	...	☐ 6

2 *Why did you choose this book?*

ANSWER THE REST OF THE QUESTIONS WHEN YOU HAVE FINISHED WITH YOUR BOOK

Date you finished with this book ....

3 *Did you take this book home to read?* ... ... Yes/No

4 *How much of the book did you read?* Tick one box which applies to you.

I read all of it	...	...	...	...	...	☐ 1
I read over half of it	...	...	...	...	...	☐ 2
I read less than half of it ...	...	...	...	...	☐ 3
I read a few pages	...	...	...	...	...	☐ 4

5 *What did you think of this book?* Tick one box which applies to you.

It was one of the best books I have ever read … … ☐ 1

I liked it very much … … … … … ☐ 2

I quite liked it … … … … … … ☐ 3

I did not like it much … … … … … ☐ 4

I did not like it at all … … … … … ☐ 5

6 *How difficult was it to read?* Tick one box which applies to you.

Very difficult … … … … … … ☐ 1

Quite difficult … … … … … … ☐ 2

Not difficult but not easy … … … … ☐ 3

Easy … … … … … … … ☐ 4

Very easy … … … … … … ☐ 5

7 *Did you talk to anyone about this book?* If you did, put a tick against the people you talked to.

Your class teacher … … … … … ☐ 1

Another teacher in school … … … … ☐ 2

Your friends … … … … … … ☐ 3

Your parents … … … … … … ☐ 4

Your brothers and sisters … … … … ☐ 5

I did not talk to anyone about it … … … … ☐ 6

8 *Have you told your friends that this is a good book?* … Yes/No

9 *Would you like to read another book by the same author?* … … … Yes/Don't Know/No

10 *If there is anything else you would like to say about your book, write it here.*

Appendix 2: Final category system for coding children's reasons for book choice

1 Child has read other books by the same author (or books edited by a particular person) or mentions the author's name as a factor affecting his/her choice.

2 Child has read other books in the same series, or mentions that there are other books of 'the same kind', e.g. *Narnia*, Secret Seven, Famous Five, *Mrs Pepperpot*.

3 Child has read part of the book before choosing and found it interesting, e.g. contents, jacket, first page etc.

4 Child interested in an activity or object or certain type of story. (If child does not specify the interest or type of story he must use the expression 'type of story' to be included in this category.)

5 The book's appearance, title, cover, typography, level of difficulty etc influenced choice.

6 Child knows something of the story before reading the book (but has not read books in the same series if one exists – or *other* books by the same author – although he may have read the book under consideration before) e.g. child has read book before, seen/heard it on TV as a story read or serialization, has heard some of it read by a teacher before etc.

7 Book recommended by someone.

(No category 8)

9 Miscellaneous reasons.

10 Information given but *no reason*.

11 Compulsory reading.

0 No information given at all.

Appendix 3: Typical reasons for book choice (Original spelling and punctuation preserved)

1 (a) I chose this book because I know the author rights good books. (Carolyn Keene *Nancy Drew*)

  (b) Because I like Enid Blyton books.

  (c) Because I had a book by the same make and I liked it. (W. H. Chalk)

2 (a) I like *Famous Five* books and I have not read this one.

  (b) Because I read another *Jackie* book. *Final comment:* I wish there were more Jackie books in class.

  (c) I chose this book because I like reading Hardy boy books.

3 (a) I chose this book because when I read the ilastration it sounded very exciting and there would be a lot of adventure to share with the children in the book. (Ruth Tomalin *A Green Wishbone*)

  (b) I chose this book because I read the editors blub and it sounded very exciting.

  (c) I chose this book because I read the first page and it was good.

4 (a) I chose this book because I like playing with string. (*Why Don't You: String Games*)

  (b) I had just drawn a map of the barrier reef of Australia and I got a book about diving in the barrier reef. (Willard Price *Diving Adventure*)

  (c) Because I like cowboys.

5 (a) I chose this book because I liked the title *Journey to Jupiter* and the cover looked good. (Hugh Walters)

  (b) I chose this book because the written looked hard so I chose it.

  (c) The picter took my eye. (Roald Dahl *Charlie and the Chocolate Factory*)

6 (a) I chose this book because once a teacher only read part of the book and that part of the book was very good so I disided to read the rest of it. (Christianna Brand *Nurse Matilda Went to Town*)

  (b) Be cassi saw it on Telleevigan.

  (c) Because I have read it befor.

7 (a) I chose this book because Amanda recommended it to me.

  (b) I chose this book because my friend Susan said it was a good book so I thought I would choose it. *Final comment:* I think my friend was right it was a good book. (Joan Aiken *The Kingdom Under the Sea*)

Appendix 4: Unusual reasons or usual reasons expressed in unusual ways, and some interesting final comments (original spelling and punctuation retained)

1   *Final comment:* I enjoid the book very much because I have read it three times before I would recommend the book to any boy but not a girl. (Kenneth Ulyatt *North Against the Sioux*)

2   *Final comment:* It was a super book and when I picked it up I couldn't put it down. It was the best book I have ever read the writer captured the scenes so well. (Honor Arundel *The Girl in the Opposite Bed*)

3   *Final comment:* It was not as good as Bettinas Secret because I would put this down when it was teatime but I read Bettinas secret over tea. (Doris B. White *The Family that Came Back*)

4   *Final comment:* It was a fantastic book by a very creative author. I read it from cover to cover in 2 nights and an afternoon. (Carolyn Keene)

5   *Reason:* I chose this book because the teacher read it to us and I enjoyed it so much that I wanted to read it again. (Roald Dahl *Charlie and the Chocolate Factory*). *Final comment:* I am going to read *Charlie and the Great Glass Elevator*.

6   *Reason:* I chose this book because I thought it would be good because it was a new version. (Anne Edwards (ed.) *A Child's Bible: Old Testament*). *Final comment:* I did not like it because it seemed to go on and on about the same thing.

7   *Reason:* Joan Lingard is a very good writer and I like the way she makes ma feel as though I was there. (*Into Exile*)

8   *Final comment:* The book is very funny and it is easy to get into the situation that the boy is in. (John D. Fitzgerald *More Adventures of the Great Brain*)

9   *Reason:* I chose this book because I think I'm rather romantic so I like love stories. (Julius Lester *Two Love Stories*)

10 *Reason:* I choose this book because I am a schoolboy so I got a book on schoolboys to see how they behaved. *Final comment:* There was some bad language in this book. But it was very interesting. There was something happening all the time. (Petronella Breinburg *Us Boys of Westcroft*)

11 One boy's reasons:

Because I like Dogs	Because I like dogs
Because I like Dogs	Because I like <u>DOGS</u>
Because I like <u>Dogs</u>	<u>BECAUSE I LIKE DOGS</u>

12 *Final comment:* The sort of thing it had in the book was accountant – insect who is good with figures abundance – A waltz for cakes.

13 *Reason:* Because I like poimes and words that rhyme. *Final comment:* I like the song of the Jellicles and the Rum Tum Tugger Best. (T. S. Eliot *Old Possum's Book of Practical Cats*)

14 *Reason:* Whell Miss Ashby wrede chumley so it simde just my tiyp of reding. (Joan Crammond *Dear Zoo*)

15 *Reason:* I pit it because we were erin abote muscles. (*The Human Body* Macdonald Educational)

16 *Reason:* I got it because my friend recommended it to me. *Final comment:* This book was rubish and I did not like it attal becase it was not ecsiting and it is not my tipe of book. (child read it all – Willard Price *Amazon Adventure*)

13 Literature, life and language skills

Roger Beard

Introduction

This paper explores the notion of 'the reading connection' in terms of the relationship between literature, life and language skills. It argues that children's literature is sometimes not studied as extensively as it could be in books, courses and conferences on reading, and it emphasizes the teaching potential of a consideration of the nature of literature and its relationship with children's own experiences.

The main part of the presentation illustrates how James Britton's classification of language functions can provide a helpful teaching framework for developing writing and talking in the classroom, with literature being used as a starting point. A number of examples of junior-school children's work will be used, from my own teaching experience.

Reading and literature

Although there has been a considerable increase in the number of reading courses available to teachers since the Bullock Report (Marder 1976), literature rarely features prominently in them. Instead, the emphasis tends to be on the development of reading skills and their application to nonfiction material or 'reading for learning'. Successive books on the teaching of reading have only given brief passing attention to literature.

There is a similar tendency in the United Kingdom Reading Association's annual conferences. Several conference proceedings of recent years have not contained a single paper on children's literature (e.g. Latham 1974; Moyle 1975; Gilliland 1977) and where such papers are included they rarely number more than one or two (e.g. Merritt 1971; Southgate 1972). In fact, there is a wide difference in the focus of attention of professional associations concerned with literacy, a phenomenon noted by Michael Marland (1978):

. . . at a meeting of the National Association for the Teaching of English there are few if any members of the United Kingdom

Reading Association or the National Association for Remedial Education. The teaching of reading is seen as related to remedial work, but not to literature (a very funny split that).

There are a number of ways in which this tendency to leave literature aside seem anomalous. Firstly, Margaret Clark's (1976) study of young fluent readers indicated the value of sharing stories with their parents and making extensive use of local library facilities from a very early age: 'Repetition of the same story read to a child has many values, not least the sensitizing of the child to the features of book language which is probably a far more valuable preparation for school than any attempts at teaching the child phonics or even a basic sight vocabulary' (p. 104).

Secondly, at a time when teachers seem to be incorporating a number of reading schemes into individualized teaching approaches, there is considerable scope for the inclusion of individual books from children's literature at appropriate points, as Moon's (1979) lists show.

Thirdly, it is widely acknowledged that the post-war years have seen a 'golden age' of children's literature (Ellis 1968). Townsend wrote in 1972 (p. 22) that 'British (children's) books are better today than ever before' and many of these highly regarded stories of Aiken, Cresswell, DeJong, Garfield, Garner, Lively, Pearce and so on are available in the cheaper paperback editions. It is therefore surprising that books, courses and conferences on reading do not consider the ways and means of exploiting the rich provision for the development of pupils' voluntary reading which, the Bullock Report (DES 1975, p. 126) asserts, is strongly associated with reading attainment.

Finally, literature can play an important role in developing children's reading comprehension. If we take the suggestion of Frank Smith (1978) that comprehension involves the 'reduction of uncertainty', the narrative form can provide a particularly coherent and engaging basis for encouraging the anticipations and predictions which are a vital part of this process. Walker's (1974) group prediction activities can perhaps make explicit the kinds of related thinking involved.

A theoretical structure

Perhaps one reason for the relative neglect of literature in books, courses and conferences on reading is that a theoretical structure has not been adopted to embrace 'reading for learning' and the reading of literature. Yet a theoretical structure which makes this possible does exist, that of Britton (1970, 1975). Britton sets out a continuum which is built around three language functions, the expressive, the poetic and the transactional, which can be applied to speech or writing.

Poetic ◄——— Expressive ———► Transactional

Expressive language is the central function, the one which is 'close to the self', verbalizing consciousness and displaying a close relation with listener or reader (Britton 1975, p. 90). *Poetic language*, for example poetry, songs and stories, creates a 'form' by using language as an art medium (Britton op. cit.); *transactional language*, for example reports, essays and notes, is the language of informing, persuading, advising: the language of 'getting things done'. The continuum has much of social and psychological as well as linguistic interest. There is much more to the structure, but these fundamental terms will serve for the present discussion. Literature thus becomes principally defined as 'poetic' language; the subject textbook predominantly 'transactional'. The framework is adopted by the Bullock Report's chapter on writing but regrettably it is not crossreferenced adequately to the chapters on literature, reading or talking. What follows may rectify this a little, taking up the beginnings made by the Grugeons (1973, 1977).

It should be pointed out that the continuum and the research associated with it have been subjected to fierce criticism (Williams 1977) to which Britton has recently replied (Britton *et al.* 1979). The points of issue are largely esoteric and are too complex to do justice to here. Similarly, Whitehead (1978) has expressed grave reservations on Britton's work, including a concern that as a result of it teachers may believe 'that when they have assigned their pupils' language to a category they have accomplished something'. Whitehead feels it is far more important to be able to 'spot what is good (whatever its kind or category) and to reward and reinforce the growing point' (Whitehead 1978, p. 20). What follows is an illustration of how Britton's work can provide a helpful 'framework' for the very process of fostering such growth. The remainder of this paper will illustrate how Britton's ideas have been of assistance in my own teaching, both in schools and in a college.

An important advantage is that the continuum provides a frame of reference for the exchange of ideas on initial and in-service courses. In an in-service course for twenty-five teachers, I have known over 20 'types' of written language to be put forward, with many overlaps and ambiguities. Britton's framework helps formulate a broad basis for discussion.

A further advantage is that the continuum has implications for differential assessment of children's own writing. The stress on 'form' in poetic writing helps keep story writing, poetry and 'creative writing' distinct from the more utilitarian criteria involved in the assessment of the 'action effected' by transactional writing. Both assume different kinds of 'audience'. In expressive writing the criteria will be more 'child-centred' and the teacher's role more likely to be that of a 'trusted adult' than 'examiner' (Britton 1975, p. 66).

As well as theoretically encompassing 'literature' and information texts, the continuum allows for links to be forged between reading and the other language skills, listening, talking and writing. This paper will concentrate on the links between reading and writing. In the classroom, this is likely to be particularly effective if the relationship between literature and life is exploited.

Literature and life

If we take literature as 'words to create a symbolic representation of human experience' (Grugeon 1975, p. 95) we can place virtually any form of narrative on the same dimension. Thus the story told in the streetcorner chat can be seen as differing from a novel only in the degree to which the experiences described are fashioned into a verbal artefact, as well as the obvious difference in the medium used. The origins of famous novels in an author's personal experiences are often acknowledged, as with Laurie Lee (1975, p. 49): 'In common with other writers I have written little that was not for the most part autobiographical'.

We need to bear this in mind when teaching children, for as Nancy Martin (1976, p. 210) says, 'The trouble with most school writing is that it is not genuine communication'. Too often perhaps, the development of writing abilities in the junior-school age range is based uneasily on arbitrarily imposed 'compositions' or artificially pumped up 'creative writing'.

Literature and language skills

The Grugeons (1977) provide a useful distinction between 'narrative processes' and 'narrative products' to help formulate a more promising perspective on teaching children. This distinction can be related to Britton's continuum. Poetic products can be used to elicit narrative processes, formulated in expressive language. The hearing of a story or poem can lead on to children sharing incidents, thoughts and feelings which belong to established narrative themes. Children from a wide range of backgrounds will have a whole range of stories 'worth the telling' and the sense of audience in the classroom is likely to increase the effectiveness of that telling. As Philippa Pearce (1975) says, 'The idea of a story springs from what has been seen and heard and done and felt and thought, going back for weeks, months, perhaps years'.

See for example Judy's (age nine) response to hearing Meindert

DeJong's *Shadrach*. She wrote a long account of a pet she treasured, ending

> But by the next week, Candy had chewed up another pair of gloves, eaten a piece of string and her collar and lead. So the next night, Daddy went and gave her to a farm. I could not sleep that night and the next day I had red rings round my eyes with crying. The next morning I felt I had lost my heart. I had lost Candy but I will never forget her.

Elizabeth (age eleven) was in a class to whom I read Alan Garner's *Elidor* and the episodes concerned with moving house prompted her to write in an uninhibited, expressive way similar to Judy:

Utter chaos

yes it was utter chaos when we had our extension.

Floor boards were heaved up. half the roof was take off. And I had to have all my brothers in my bedroom. It was rather exciting though.

But in the night it was terrible. Mostly because I'v got a double bed and I had to share it with my brother Lawrance. Talk about battles. We had a battle every night of the week for six months. We would have an argument and tug-of-war with the bed clothes. It was absolutely utter chaos.

Responses to poetic products can lead to quite sophisticated products of the children's own, where their experiences are shaped into poetic language, bypassing the expressive foundations which some children may need first.

On hearing the narrator's introduction to Dylan Thomas's *Under Milk Wood*, Carl (age nine) wrote:

Night in a country village

The silence of the nights descent is frightning.
The erie hooting of the owl as he sits upon his perch.
The moonlight passes over the stoops.
Then the gentle breathing of the night animals suddenly ceases.
The intruder is the dawn.
The badger rushes to his set and sleeps.
Now over the creatures of the night there is silence.
As silent as the nights descent in comes the busy morn.

Helen Cresswell's *The Nightwatchmen*, was behind Diana's (age ten) sensitive piece of blank verse.

The tramp

I'm a tramp
Dirty, cold, tired, hungry
Wandering through London
Dirty alleyways
Children
Yelling and shrieking
For me
No home to go to
No warm fire
No comfortable bed
No hot food
Curtains drawn
Hiding from me
The cosy glowing light
Of the flickering lamp
A hedge
Hard and uncomfortable
But
I wrap up in my sack
Asleep Dreaming.

In another way, the outcomes of the shaping and sharing of everyday experience in expressive language can be consolidated by references to literature.

Janet's (age nine) 'worst experience' was extended into reading Philippa Pearce's short story 'In the middle of the night' (in *What the Neighbours Did*).

Something I will never forget

About three weeks ago on Friday.
I fell off the bars.
First of all I wasn't crying because I was shocked.
I had hurt my nee bad.
I went to tell Miss Robinson.
She took me inside.
She put a plaster on my nee then.
I sat down in the classroom.

Blood was dripping on to my sock
I couldn't bend it a long time.
I just managed to walk home.
My nees better now.

Karen (age eight) opted for a more poetic form immediately, when
writing on fog. Her writing has features similar to Carl Sandburg's
'Fog' (in Williams 1972) to which she was later referred.

Fog

The fog hang's from tree to tree
From branch to branch
It was like an evil spirite
Changing them to a ghost
    Garding
        each other
The grass was growing up into a carpet of foam
A mack looking like a little bob
    Now
        it is
            going.

The classroom context
The individuality of these children's writing may indicate that the
teaching organization behind their work, which is taken from several
mixed-ability classes, was relatively open-ended. I always maintained
the reading of a 'class serial' but also regularly introduced books by
reading selected passages and providing two or three paperback copies
of each for children's voluntary reading. Book- or author-based talks
once a term by the county assistant librarian performed a similar
function.

The children would write for at least thirty minutes at some stage
during the morning in a partially integrated day. On most days choice
was theirs, although I did encourage exploration of literature-based
themes. An 'ideas corner' was set up for the few who 'did not know
what to write about'. The writing produced by individuals, links with
literature and general points arising would be dealt with in daily class
discussions. A number of useful anthologies exist to refer children to or
to read aloud to complement their writing, for example those of
Maybury (1970, 1972) and Williams (1972).

Transactional writing was largely kept for the afternoon local-study project sessions. There was some direct teaching in English, for example in spelling and in the occasional 'creative writing' session. However, the nature of the main bulk of the writing was chosen by the children themselves and this did lead to some longer pieces of work than the single lesson with its arbitrary title might allow for. I also found that the children's involvement in the task of writing was increased by the provision for and encouragement of 'drafting'. The 'messiness' of this tentative stage in writing is often taboo in classrooms, yet even in educated adults it remains a regular part of the process of most writing tasks. It was certainly an important part in the writing of this paper.

Conclusion
This paper has been concerned with establishing some important points between literature, life and the language skills, particularly writing. It is hoped that the inclusion of a number of pieces of children's work and details of classroom organization has given a useful practical slant to what has largely been a theoretical discussion. Here, the theoretical framework of Britton was adopted; others will prefer different models for curriculum planning. What is important, however, is that some sort of a framework is established, applied and critically evaluated. Without this kind of analytical process, the teaching of reading and other language skills will lack an important quality: a sense of direction.

References
BRITTON, J. (1970) *Language and Learning* London: Allen Lane

BRITTON, J. *et al.* (1975) *The Development of Writing Abilities 11–18* Basingstoke: Macmillan Education for the Schools Council

BRITTON, J. *et al.* (1979) 'No, no, Jeanette' *Language for Learning, 1*, 1, 23–41

CLARK, M. M. (1976) *Young Fluent Readers* London: Heinemann Educational

DES (1975) *A Language for Life* (The Bullock Report) London: HMSO

ELLIS, A. (1968) *A History of Children's Reading and Literature* Oxford: Pergamon

GILLILAND, J. (1977, ed.) *Reading: Research and Classroom Practice* London: Ward Lock Educational

GRUGEON, D. and E. (1973) *Language and Literature* (Course E262 Language and Learning Block 5) Milton Keynes: The Open University Press

GRUGEON, D. and E. (1977) *Narrative, Literature and Literacy* (Course PE231 Reading Development Unit 8) Milton Keynes: The Open University Press

LATHAM, W. (1974, ed.) *The Road to Effective Reading* London: Ward Lock Educational

LEE, L. (1975) *I Can't Stay Long* Harmondsworth: Penguin

MARDER, J. (1976) The Bullock Report: a record of in-service activities in related fields *British Journal of In-Service Education 3*, 1, 18–25

MARTIN, N. *et al.* (1976) *Writing and Learning Across the Curriculum 11–16* London: Ward Lock Educational for the Schools Council

MARLAND, M. (1978) Learning to read and reading to learn *The Guardian* 26 September

MERRITT, J. (1971, ed.) *Reading and the Curriculum* London: Ward Lock Educational

MOON, C. (1979, 10th edition) *Individualized Reading* Reading: Centre for the Teaching of Reading, University of Reading

MOYLE, D. (1975, ed.) *Reading: What of the Future?* London: Ward Lock Educational

PEARCE, P. (1975) 'Writing a book' in E. Blishen (ed.) *The Thorny Paradise* Harmondsworth: Kestrel

SOUTHGATE, V. (1972, ed.) *Literacy at all Levels* London: Ward Lock Educational

SMITH, F. (1978, 2nd edition) *Understanding Reading* New York: Holt, Rinehart and Winston

TOWNSEND, J. R. (1972) 'The present state of English children's literature' in A. Davies *Literature for Children* (Course PE261 'Reading Development' Unit 2) Milton Keynes: The Open University Press

WALKER, C. (1974) *Reading Development and Extension* London: Ward Lock Educational

WHITEHEAD, F. (1978) What's the use indeed? *The Use of English 29*, 2, 15–22

WILLIAMS, J. (1977) *Learning to Write or Writing to Learn?* Windsor: NFER

BOOKS FOR CHILDREN

CRESSWELL, H. (1969) *The Nightwatchmen* London: Faber

DEJONG, M. (1957) *Shadrach* London: Lutterworth Press

GARNER, A. (1965) *Elidor* Harmondsworth: Penguin

MAYBURY, B. (1970, ed.) *Wordscapes* Oxford: Oxford University Press

MAYBURY, B. (1972, ed.) *Thoughtshapes* Oxford: Oxford University Press

PEARCE, P. (1972) *What the Neighbours Did* Harlow: Longman

THOMAS, D. (1954) *Under Milk Wood* London: Dent

WILLIAMS, E. (1972, ed.) *Dragonsteeth* London: Arnold

14 Adaptable rates and strategies for efficient comprehension: the effective reader

Marian J. Tonjes

Introduction

Interest in reading rate is far from new. In the past hundred years we have systematically explored such varied aspects as eye movements, perceptual span, the role of purpose, the use of mechanical devices, speed-training programmes and rate flexibility. Results from this research have too often been mixed, inconclusive or contradictory.

The purpose of this paper is twofold: to suggest the need for clarifying our terminology in one area, that of reading flexibility; to recommend the use of a checklist which attempts to identify and pull together from current research those facets deemed necessary when developing accurate materials or tests for rate flexibility.

Terminology

The effective, mature reader is one who is both flexible and efficient in terms of rate and strategies. Looking at these terms, first of all, being flexible means having the ability to select not only the appropriate rate to fit a particular purpose but also to select a strategy that best suits that purpose. Being flexible means being adaptable, able to adjust in response to new circumstances. Actually, if you study closely the definitions and synonyms for 'flexible' it is not as precise a term as adaptable is. 'Flexible' means the ability to be bent, twisted or turned without breaking, or the ability of people or things to accommodate to another's wishes or conditions. Synonyms are adaptable, malleable and pliable – not necessarily what we are after here. On the other hand, 'adaptable' means changing to become suitable to a new or special use or situation, and its synonyms are flexibility, adjustment and responsive alteration. Adaptable appears to be a more precise term.

Secondly, the term 'efficient' comes from the Latin 'efficere', meaning 'to effect'. While being a synonym for 'effective', 'efficient' more clearly stresses the ability to perform well and economically in terms of time, energy and materials. Effective is a more general term.

Finally, although the terms 'rate' and 'speed' have often been used interchangeably, 'speed' is actually a misnomer that has caused general misconceptions with the general public over the years. Speed, meaning very rapid movement, has among its synonyms hurry, hasten, quicken and accelerate. On the other hand the term 'rate', which comes from the Latin 'rata', meaning 'calculated', is a measured quantity (occurring within limits of a fixed quantity of something else) and denoting a continuum from slowest to most rapid. If we continue to insist on Speed Reading Courses we should also be instituting snail-paced ones. ('How to be a slow reader' has its possibilities – just think of savouring that description, that thought . . .) One last comment concerning the term 'rate'. It should not be thought of merely in terms of words per minute that the eye has moved over, but the rate of comprehension, or how rapidly purpose is achieved; how long it takes to comprehend for a given purpose, and that purpose includes the type of comprehension needed as well as personal reasons for reading.

Research on flexibility

One point clearly emerges from thirty years of considering flexible reading rates: that is, it is a complex phenomenon with much work still to be done.

Miller (1978) has delineated some of the problems with assessment and teaching procedures based in part on faulty interpretation of existing research. First of all, *existing* rate tests have given us misleading information as to efficiency level because they generally measure only one aspect of rate, and rate is never a unitary concern. Tests rarely take into account all three factors of reader, text and familiarity with the material; nor do they consider that flexibility means change or strategies as well as rate; and they have rarely taken into account such factors as psychological set in influencing results.

It is difficult to rely with confidence on some of the research evidence when we realize the deficiencies of many of the testing instruments used. Are those readers who have been classified as inflexible actually quite flexible when you consider, as McCracken (1965) suggested, their intra-article or internal flexibility? Even though their overall rates may differ hardly at all, perhaps they have slowed down or speeded up several times within the article.

Recently rate adjustability was shown in two studies by Samuels and Dahl (1975) and McConkie, Rayner and Wilson (1973). Their findings supported the fact that students do adjust their rate according to the type of test or questions they anticipate. This provision for reader set has long been ignored. Rothkopf and Coatney (1974) found that students who were given difficult material to read first, read succeeding material more slowly. The effect was not as strong when easier material was read first.

La Berge and Samuels (1974) accounted for an increase in efficient reading in terms of the gradual automating of processes. In their model, at the lowest level, visual information is analysed by feature detectors. We look at a feature of a letter or letter combinations and process it by activating codes stored in visual memory. The reader who encounters unfamiliar letters while his attention is focused on meaning will slow down in order to focus on the letters. Efficiency then means gradually automating the skill processes to speed up comprehension.

Weiner and Cromer (1967) found that poor readers were often bogged down in reading word-by-word, not segmenting into phrases or organizing into semantically meaningful units. This list-type of reading naturally led to a slow rate, often with minimal comprehension. On the other hand Samuels, Begy and Chen (1975–6) found that better readers processed visually presented words at a faster rate than slower readers when each group was given familiar words flashed on a tachistoscope. The better readers appeared to be able to use context and letter cues more efficiently. They picked up on the redundancy of the language. It is important to remember here that when decoding becomes an automatic process, attention can then be focused on meaning.

Much research has been done in the areas of eye movements, visual and perceptual abilities (Jensen 1978). However, these areas have often viewed reading in a constricted sense looking mainly at the first part of the reading process or the visual impressions of print and neglecting or underemphasizing the experiencing of the meaning of that print.

Today eye movements and subvocalizations are seen merely as expressions of reading ability, not symptoms of good or poor readers. Yet much of the material and teaching methods still reflect the old notion of stepping-up eye movements, widening perceptual spans, speeding up fixations and the like. Here is an excellent example of where practice has not caught up to the research.

A checklist for developing instructional materials or tests for reading flexibility: problems and possible solutions

Scattered throughout the literature are many valid research findings concerning reading flexibility. However, as just mentioned, materials and tests have not as yet taken all of these into account. To address this problem I offer as a first step, a checklist (see Appendix, p. 150) developed in an attempt to pull together the fragments.

Using the checklist as an organizer the problem areas are: set, material readability, content orientation, rates, comprehension check and two general aspects of flexibility.

SET

Until recently we have not provided for reader set or background preparation, thus leading to ambiguous or erroneous conclusions concerning adaptability (e.g. the longstanding belief that there is little rate adaptability among fluent readers).

1   *Practice* Do we ensure understanding of procedures and what to anticipate?
2   *Purpose* Little provision has been made to ascertain that readers truly understand the purpose, or actually use it when reading. Also is the purpose a personal one (for escape) or a comprehension purpose?
3   *Strategies* What reading strategies are most efficient for the purpose – e.g. skimming to get an overview or a cognitive map? Which type are used – e.g. key words, introduction, subheadings, summary and questions?
4   *Time* We need to get away from measuring reading time spent in terms of words per minute and look at alternatives such as time to read a content chapter, or time per page.
5   *Length* Many of the testing and practice materials are short selections not approximating actual reading tasks required of students. There is not necessarily an automatic transfer from short selections to lengthy ones.

MATERIAL READABILITY

Material readability is broken up into six categories. The first three, sequence, concept load and typographical features, should be self-explanatory. Style, on the other hand, needs further clarification. This might better have been called 'modes of discourse', and the question asked, 'Is a range included such as personal essay, report, explanation, etc?' The other two categories, 'interest in the subject' and 'prior experience' are crucial connections. We have all experienced occasions when because of lack of interest our attention wandered and comprehension suffered. On the other hand, because of prior knowledge of a subject it is possible to answer questions correctly even when barely reading the material. This is easily checked by asking the reader prior to reading how well he knows the subject.

CONTENT ORIENTATION

It is recommended that practice headings for adaptability contain material similar to the actual textual demands of the reader and that the opportunity is given to practice on a wide variety of content subjects.

RATES

Hill (1979), in a recent text, delineated six types of what he termed modes, each implying the use of a different technique. The first three (skimming, scannning and rapid reading) are typically found in discussions of rate. The fourth, 'personal reading', might be considered by some as average or normal reading. Finally, he has differentiated between two slower rates which he calls analytical evaluative reading and study reading. The former is usually used when higher-level reasoning is required and can be combined with other modes, especially with study reading. The last mode is a combination of study and reading where learning and remembering are essential. The reader uses a planned strategy such as SQ3R or one of its derivatives.

COMPREHENSION CHECK

1 Questions generally used with flexibility materials are mostly at the literal level where the reader is asked to feed back stated information. Since our purposes often go beyond the facts we should be asking the higher-level questions, too.
2 Understanding something as we read may be a different task from being able to recall it later on. Do we take this into account?
3 One of the most successful teaching strategies I have found in terms of adaptability is to have the reader skim first for the main ideas before rereading for details in a timed situation.
4 We often appear to be over-concerned with the ten questions for comprehension. I suggest we alternate at times by asking readers to summarize main points.
5 How well we comprehend can be strongly affected by external environmental conditions such as some commotion outside, the temperature of the room, or internal psychological conditions such as anxiety. The reader should have the opportunity to note this before reading in a timed situation.

ADAPTABILITY

Everything preceding this category has dealt with an aspect of adaptability. This final area asks basically only two questions concerning types of adapting: internal, or the variety of rates within a selection (McCracken 1965) as opposed to the generally-accepted concept of the external which denotes one overall rate, generally in words per minute of a selection.

The other aspect, negative as opposed to positive, is a more rare phenomenon. Negative here means going against normal expectations, such as speeding up for study reading or slowing down when the purpose is merely to get the gist.

Finally:

1 Do not be so dependent on existing rate materials, mindlessly accepting what is written, but develop your own, using the type of material you expect your students to handle effectively.
2 Show students how to develop an awareness of the time needed with a particular strategy depending on their purpose or level of desired effectiveness.
3 Give students process directions (the 'how to') describing the strategies, purpose, rationale and sample questions.
4 Please do not ask them to read 'to find the needle in the haystack!'

Appendix: Checklist for developing instructional materials or tests for reading adaptability

There is ample evidence of the need for developing instructional materials and tests that reflect the principles consistent with the concept of reading adaptability. The following is proposed as a guideline for teachers and curriculum specialists when selecting or developing reading adaptability materials.

SET

1	*Practice*	Is practice provided initially in reading similar material and answering similar questions? (warm-ups)
2	*Purpose*	Is the purpose clearly stated? (e.g. main ideas, details)
		or
		Are a variety of purposes proposed, allowing the reader to select?
		Does the reader accept and hold on to the purpose?
3	*Strategies*	Are strategies suggested based on the purpose selected? (the degree of effectiveness needed)
4	*Time*	Is the reader asked to estimate the amount of time needed in terms of WPM (words per minute), time per page or time per selection?
5	*Length*	Are selections long enough to approximate actual reading tasks? (2,000 + words)

MATERIAL READABILITY

1	*Sequence*	Are the selections sequenced from easy to difficult in terms of reading levels as determined by readability formulas?
2	*Concept load*	Has the material been selected with an eye to the density of concepts or their abstractness?
3	*Typographical features*	Has good use been made of such structuring devices as introductory previews, summaries, subheadings and graphics?
4	*Modes of discourse*	Is a range of modes of discourse included, such as the personal essay, report, explanation?
5	*Interest*	In practice materials may a student select the material which appears to be of most interest?
6	*Background experience*	Is some connection made between the reader's prior knowledge of the subject or topic and the comprehension score attained? (Does the student check before

reading whether the subject is known well, slightly, or not at all?)

CONTENT ORIENTATION

1 *Similarity*   Is material similar to actual textual demands of the reader?
2 *Variety*   Is there a variety of content subjects from which to choose? (science, home economics, poetry, etc.)

RATES

Do materials include articles conducive to using one or a combination of the following rates:

1 *Scanning*   For particular cues to answer specific questions.
2 *Skimming*   Combining scanning and rapid reading to preview, get an overview or gist.
3 *Rapid reading*   To gain a general understanding, or main ideas using continuous contact with the text.
4 *Personal reading* For enjoyment, relaxation or general information.
5 *Analytical-evaluative reading* Detailed, intensive examination of content, critically analysing and using higher-level reasoning.
6 *Study reading*   Using a planned attack, a combination of techniques such as found in the study systems SQ3R or PQRST.

COMPREHENSION CHECK

1 Are questions at the lower, literal level? (Higher order questions are important, too.)
2 Is provision made for responding without looking back as well as allowing the reader to reread for answers?
3 Is the value of rereading stressed by such exercises as having the reader skim first for the gist and then reread for details?
4 In lieu of responding to questions is there ever an option of asking the reader to summarize the main points?
5 Is there provision for the reader to note after reading the external environmental conditions (noise, heat, etc.) and his level of anxiety or need?

ADAPTABILITY

1 Is internal adaptability (variety of rate within a selection) recognized in some manner? This can be accomplished by asking students to:
   (a) mark (after practice) where they are in their reading at intervals of every 15 seconds.

(b)   estimate how many times they slowed down for better comprehension or skimmed over a section.
2   Is negative adaptability (going against normal expectations) accounted for by asking if the reader ever speeded up for study reading or slowed down for personal reading when his purpose did not require it?

References

BERGER, A. and PEEBLES, J. (1976) *Rates of Comprehension: An Annotated Bibliography* Newark, Delaware: International Reading Association

BRAAM, L. S. and SHELDON, W. (1959) *Developing Efficient Reading* New York: Oxford Press

BROWN, J. (1974) 'Techniques for increasing reading rate' in J. E. Merritt (ed.) *New Horizons in Reading* Proceedings of the Fifth International Reading Association World Congress on Reading, Vienna, Austria, 12–14 August, 158–65

COHEN, K. M., WEST, R. F. and MARSH, G. (1978) *Models of Efficient Reading* Newark, Delaware: International Reading Association Series on the Development of the Reading Process

ELLIS, N. C. and MILES, T. R. (1978) Visual information processing as a determinant of reading speed *Journal of Research in Reading 1*, 2, 108–20

HARRIS, T. L. (1974) 'Reading flexibility: a neglected aspect of reading instruction' in J. E. Merritt (ed.) *New Horizons in Reading* Proceedings of the Fifth International Reading Association World Congress on Reading, Vienna, Austria, 12–14 August, 27–35

HILL, W. R. (1979) *Secondary School Reading: Process, Program, Procedure* Boston: Allyn and Bacon

HOFFMAN, J. V. (1978) The relationship between rate and reading flexibility *Reading World*, May, 325–8

JENSEN, P. E. (1978) Theories of reading speed and comprehension *Journal of Reading 21*, 7, 593–600

LA BERGE, D. and SAMUELS, S. J. (1974) Toward a theory of automatic information processing in reading *Cognitive Psychology* 6, 293–323

MCCONKIE, G. W., RAYNER, K. and WILSON, S. (1973) Experimental manipulation of reading strategies *Journal of Educational Psychology* 65, 1–8

MCCRACKEN, R. A. (1965) Internal versus external flexibility of reading rate *Journal of Reading* 8, 208–9

MCDONALD, A. S. (1963) Flexibility in reading *International Reading Association Conference Proceedings* 8, 81–5

MILLER, P. A. (1976) *The Effect Upon Reading Rate of Variations in Purpose, Familiarity and Difficulty: An investigation of reading flexibility at the community college level.* Unpublished doctoral dissertation: University of Minnesota

MILLER, P. A. (1978) 'Considering flexibility of reading rate for assessment and development of efficient reading behavior' in S. J. Samuels (ed.) *What Research Has to Say About Reading Instruction* Newark, Delaware: International Reading Association

NACKE, P. L. (1971) 'Assessment of flexible efficient reading' in F. P. Greene (ed.) *Reading: The Right to Participate* Twentieth Yearbook of the National Reading Conference, Milwaukee: National Reading Conference, 256–65

RANKIN, E. F. (1970–71) How flexibly do we read? *Journal of Reading Behavior 3*, 3, 34–8

RANKIN, E. F. (1974) *The Measurement of Reading Flexibility: Problems and Perspectives* Reading Information Series: Where Do We Go? Newark, Delaware: International Reading Association

RANKIN, E. F. and HESS, A. K. (1970) The measurement of internal (intra-article) reading flexibility *Reading Process and Pedagogy* Nineteenth Yearbook of the National Reading Conference, Vol. 1, 254–63

RANKIN, E. F. and KEHLE, T. J. (1972) 'A comparison of the reading performance of college students with conventional versus negative internal (intra-article) reading flexibility' Twenty-first Yearbook of the National Reading Conference, Milwaukee: National Reading Conference, 51–8

ROTHKOPF, E. Z. and COATNEY, R. P. (1974) Effects of readability of context passages on subsequent inspection rates *Journal of Applied Psychology* 59, 679–82

SAMUELS, S. J. and DAHL, P. R. (1975) Establishing appropriate purpose for reading and its effect on flexibility of reading rate *Journal of Educational Psychology*, 67, 39–43

SAMUELS, S. J., BEGY, G. and CHEN, C. C. (1975–6) Comparison of word recognition speed strategies of less and more highly skilled readers *Reading Research Quarterly*, 11, 72–86

SMITH, H. K. (1965) The development of effective, flexible readers *Proceedings of the Annual Reading Conference* Chicago: University of Chicago Press, 159–68

SMITH, H. K. (1964) The development of evaluation instruments for purposeful reading *Journal of Reading*, October, 17–23

WEINER, M. and CROMER, W. (1967) Reading and reading difficulty: conceptual analysis *Harvard Education Review* Autumn, 37, 620–43

15   The language arts and the learner's mind

Frank Smith

There is widespread concern about how the 'language arts' – reading, writing, speaking, the comprehension of speech, and possibly also the appreciation of literature – should be integrated in the school curriculum. But there is a more fundamental question of how these different aspects of language must be brought together in the learner's mind. The problem is not one of defining terms – it is hard enough for a teacher to say what precisely constitutes reading, writing, and so forth, except as particular activities in classrooms – but of relating the activities that go under these labels to everything else the learner can understand and do. Unless the various aspects of language, and our efforts to teach them, are integrated in the learner's understanding, then there will be no learning in any case.

The categories of the language arts are arbitrary and artificial; they do not refer to exclusive kinds of knowledge or activity in the human brain. Reading, writing, speaking and understanding speech are not accomplished with four different parts of the brain, nor do three of them become irrelevant if a student spends a 40-minute period on the fourth. They are not separate stages in a child's development; children do not first learn to talk, then to understand speech, then to read, and then to write (or any variation of that order). And the four aspects of language do not require different 'levels' of cognitive development. The labels are our way of looking at language from the outside, ignoring the fact that they involve the same processes within the brain. In the same way a variety of physical activities may be distinctively labelled as standing, sitting, running, jumping, crawling, swimming, skiing, and so on, although all, from the inside, involve the same muscular systems operating in basically similar ways. How does language look from the inside, from the point of view of a child trying to understand and interact with the world as a whole? How does a child perceive language?

I do not believe that language, in any of its manifestations, is regarded as something 'different' by children. Children do not learn language differently from the way they learn anything else, nor are they motivated to learn about language for different reasons. Indeed, children do not want to learn 'speaking', 'listening', 'reading' and 'writing' as isolated skills, or as abstract systems; they want to understand the world in a far more general sense and to achieve their own ends in a far more general sense, and the learning of language in any of its external aspects is entirely coincidental. Language only becomes complicated and difficult to learn when it is separated from other, more general, nonlanguage events and activities in the world.

My argument in this paper is that there is only one essential pre-condition for children to learn about language, and that is that it should make sense to them, both in its content and its motivation. Children come to understand how language works by understanding the purposes and intentions of the people who produce it, and they learn to produce language themselves to the extent that it fulfils their own purposes or intentions. Where language does not make sense, where it has no apparent purpose, not only will children fail to learn from it but they will actively ignore it. This applies from the very beginning of language learning.

Learning about spoken language
Research into the language development of infants has tended to concentrate on the language they produce. Thousands of studies have charted infant progression through babbling, one-word utterances, two- and three-word utterances and the first rudimentary grammars. Far fewer studies have focused on the language that infants understand, although comprehension is always more extensive than production. We can all understand language that we cannot produce. There is a reason for the bias in children's language research – production is easier to measure. It is not difficult to count and categorize children's utterances, but it is almost impossible to quantify the language they can under-stand. (For the same reason, and just as unfairly, children's language competence at school is often evaluated from how they speak rather than by what they understand.)

How do infants begin to learn about spoken language? The paradox is that in order to learn language they must first understand it. Children do not first learn language as an abstraction, or as a 'skill', which they then employ to understand what people are saying. They learn language by understanding the purposes to which it is put. Obviously no one can *tell* an infant how language works, or what it can do; children have to find out about language themselves, by *making sense* of it. And this is the way that children learn about the world in general, about everything in their experience – by hypothesizing what must be going on, anticipat-ing what might occur, and observing to see if they are right. Always children learn by relating what is new to what they understand already (Smith 1975).

There is only one way children can make sense of the language they hear around them in the home, at play, and on television, and that is by capitalizing on the fact that the language is often closely related to the situation in which it occurs. Children use the situation, including their perceived intention of the person speaking, for clues to what is being said. This is the reverse of how adults normally perceive language. We think language spoken around us describes situations and indicates speakers' intentions. Parents say 'Would you like some milk?' if they want to offer their child some milk; they say 'Where's the diaper pin?' when they are searching for a diaper pin. But for the infant this relationship between speech and situation can be used the other way. The fact that the parent is offering milk suggests the purpose of saying 'Would you like some milk?' The fact that a parent is searching for the diaper pin indicates the probable meaning of 'Where's the diaper pin?' There is no need for anyone to tell the child anything. The child can go from the situation to the probable meaning of the statement and from the meaning to the probable language system that produced the statement. Children can even find out if they have made a mistake. If they think mother said 'Would you like some coffee?' and father gets up and puts the cat out, they know a mistake has been made, and can learn.

If language is meaningful, if it is uttered for a purpose, then the situation in which it is uttered permits the child to deduce its probable meaning and also find out whether the deduction is correct. Thus the child can get on with the difficult business of working out the relationship between utterances and their meaning, the rules of language, without direct adult guidance or correction, simply by hearing and *seeing* meaningful language in use.

Halliday (1973) points out that children learn language and its uses simultaneously; the two cannot be separated. The fact that children have mastered language with some uses – particularly to express the interpersonal relations so important in a child's early life – does not mean that the child can comprehend language used for other purposes, especially the more detached, descriptive, impersonal language of school.

What are the uses to which language can be put? There is no simple answer because language can be used in support of every human intention; it is an all-purpose tool (Smith 1977). Language can be used to convey information, to request information, to dispute it, to deceive, to change the world, to change someone's mind, to describe an actual object or state of affairs, to invent or enjoy a possible object or state of affairs, to entertain oneself or others, to express or assist oneself, to convey a certain impression of oneself, to show how one feels about someone else, to show how one feels about oneself. There is no end to the uses to which language can be put.

But if language has no perceived use, then it will not be learned and cannot be learned; the perceived use is central to the understanding and the learning. Children must understand the intention. If they can see no purpose to an aspect of language, if they cannot see that it makes any difference, they will not attend to it. It is because children are only concerned with the purposes to which language can be put that they grow up speaking language and not imitating the noise of the vacuum cleaner. Children learn language *because it is there*, part of the world around them, and because it makes sense in that world. Language and the rest of the world are inseparable. Babies can no more ignore the language about the milk than they can ignore the milk that comes with it. They will only ignore language that does not make sense, that exists as noise only.

Learning to speak

While infants are striving, so successfully and apparently effortlessly, to understand the speech around them, they are learning to produce speech that can be understood. And paradoxically again, in order to learn to speak so that they can be understood, they have to be understood apart from the language they produce. To learn to talk, children have to make their intentions obvious.

It is revealing to reflect upon the uses to which small children put their growing competence in language during the first few years of their lives. They do not learn to talk in order to get their needs met; this they can do perfectly well without language. No baby starves or freezes for want of words. Nor do children develop language ability in order to communicate; they do not exhibit a great passion for conveying information that their listeners might not be expected to know. Instead they spend most of their time saying the obvious. They say 'There's a pretty cat', 'Lookit the big truck' and 'Daddy go walk' when they know perfectly well that you see the cat, the truck or father walking. That is the whole point. When the listener knows what the child is trying to say, that listener can directly or indirectly provide feedback for the child – we can say 'No that's a pretty *dog*', or 'Yes, daddy *has gone for* a walk', correcting the child's hypothesis about the world and about adult language. If the adult did not understand the infant's purpose in making the remark, the adult could not correct the remark. Therefore, there is no point in a child saying something which has no purpose, where the intention is not obvious, because then there can be no possibility of learning. When the intention is obvious, the child can learn about language and the world.

Children strive to find out more about the world in a very general and personal sense. They want to understand the world in which they live, the world as it impinges on them, and since they are part of that world – indeed they are at the centre of it – they want to understand themselves and how they make a difference to the world. They want to understand their relationships with other people, but they also want to understand their own powers. Language is a way of acquiring all these understandings; it is not the only way, but is always one possibility. Sometimes language may be the best way to learn, for example, to find out if an object is safe to touch. Sometimes language may be less adequate, for example, to find out if someone really cares for you. But language can always be put to work, provided the intention behind the language is apparent. There is no point in language without a purpose; with meaningless language there can be no comprehension or learning. Children will neither attend to nor willingly produce and practise language which does not seem to have a point. They are only interested in language that is an integral part of the world; language cannot be something that is 'different'.

Learning about written language

Reading and writing are often regarded primarily as school activities but their roots must lie outside the school, and to the extent that school makes something different or unique of reading and writing, the more it will interfere with children's attempts to understand them.

Two aspects of written language must be distinguished where reading is concerned. One is the written language which occurs in books (which is often thought to be the only kind of written language with which 'reading' – as a school subject – is concerned), and the other is a quite different kind of written language (which frequently does not have a formal grammar at all) which I shall call 'signs'. By signs I mean almost all of the writing that surrounds almost all children in their homes and in the world around them – the labels on products in kitchens and bathrooms, the signs in streets and shopfronts and department stores, and the print of television guides, catalogues, sports programmes and telephone directories. I want to call all this written language 'signs' because it is directly related to the nonlanguage situation around it. The label on the toothpaste tube indicates the contents of the tube; the sign 'footwear' in the store is related to the department in which it occurs, and the print in a television guide or catalogue describes a particular programme or product. All of this print, in other words, functions in exactly the same way as the spoken language of the home and street which is the basis for children's learning to understand speech. It is part of the world in general, intimately related to the situations in which it occurs, and it can therefore both motivate and guide a child in learning how it works.

There is growing evidence that children at the age of three, before they are able to read in any formal sense, can be well aware of the purpose of this kind of written language. They can use the situations in which signs occur to hypothesize their probable meaning (Smith 1976, Ylisto 1977), just as they have been able to use the situations in which speech occurs to indicate its probable meaning. Readers think the label indicates the contents of the tube, but children can use knowledge of the contents of the tube to indicate the probable meaning of the label, and again can find out if they have made a mistake. A boy who goes through the door marked 'girls' does not need a teacher to correct his reading. Why should very small children pay attention to the print around them before they are able to read? Again, because print is part of their world and they can discover that it is put where it is for a purpose. Signs are not arbitrary like the pattern of the wallpaper or the decoration on the shampoo bottle. When children can deduce intention behind print they can hypothesize its probable meaning and learn. They will not disregard print unless they are persuaded that it has no meaning (because it has no obvious purpose) or unless they find that meaning is irrelevant (because they are instructed to concentrate on words, not sense). But if children are unable to perceive purpose in print, they will find it difficult to attend and impossible to learn, no matter how much a teacher urges them to concentrate upon the words on the board or in the book.

In other words, children expect the written language of signs and labels and catalogues to work in exactly the same way as the spoken language they hear around them in the home; they will attend to it for the same reasons and try to understand it in the same way. Print is not for them something that is different, a unique category of experience, but something that serves very general and understandable purposes in predictable ways. There is no difficulty about integrating an understanding of this kind of written language with a child's knowledge of speech because it works in the same way as the spoken language with which the child is familiar, and is understood and learned in the same way.

The written language of stories and newspapers is a different matter because it is not directly related to the situation in which it occurs. This kind of written language, which might be called *text*, is related to situations remote in time and place from where it occurs (like a newspaper report of yesterday's hockey game) or even related to situations which are completely imaginary (like stories).

But once again there is a necessity about the written language of texts. Every word in a story or newspaper article is there for a purpose, but now the purpose is related to the content of the story or article in which it occurs. The *context* determines the meaningfulness of each word. You cannot arbitrarily change words in a story any more than you can randomly change signs in a supermarket or the wrappers on candy bars; each word is where it is for a reason. We do not have to understand the reason the words were put where they are when we read a story – we just have to understand the story (at least until we are expected to do more complicated things at school under a heading like 'English' or 'literary appreciation'). Usually it is only when we fail to understand that we are reduced to asking 'What is the purpose of these particular words; what are they doing here?' If children cannot detect a reason for words they are trying to read, if there seems to be no underlying intention, then they are in trouble. And very naturally they are likely to turn their attention away from the text. Why not? They are gaining nothing from it.

The written language of texts does not work in the same way as the print of signs, and written language in any case is not quite the same as speech. (The differences are relatively superficial, but we can always tell if someone is reading aloud rather than speaking spontaneously.) Therefore a child's ability to learn to read texts will depend on a prior familiarity with written language, which can only be gained by being read to. Being read to, in fact, enables children to see sense in written language, in books and magazines and newspapers, because they can see that it has a purpose. Again, it just becomes assimilated with everything else that they know. Meaningful texts, like meaningful situations, are those where a child can find clues to possible meaning and evidence that a mistake has been made. When children have to be corrected by someone else – because they do not find the situation sufficiently comprehensible to correct themselves – there is a certain indication that they are engaged in a task which is essentially devoid of purpose and meaning to them, and no learning will take place.

Learning about literature
Similar considerations apply as children are introduced to literature. Unless they are familiar with the language (and also the general content) of what they are expected to read, they will experience great difficulty

in reading. Certainly there will be no enjoyment. The only way to acquire a starting familiarity with the written language of various kinds of literature is to have heard it read aloud. Just as children cannot learn to read and learn subject matter at the same time – one of them must be a base for learning the other – so students will not learn how to read and enjoy literature if they are unfamiliar with the language and conventions of the literature they are trying to read. Learning always involves relating the new to something that is known already.

Provided understanding is possible, and there is no undue apprehension about the consequences of making mistakes, children will learn about literature in the same way that they learn about the world in general, and for the same reasons. Literature offers new ways of exploring the world and new worlds to explore – the stuff a child's brain thrives on. Children can immerse themselves in novels, plays and poetry with the same enthusiasm with which they immerse themselves in the world, and learn accordingly. It is depressing to think how much so many children must have suffered, growing up unable to find pleasure, worth or sense in literature.

Learning to write

Writing is often considered the final and most difficult aspect of language, partly because it is often not taught – at least not with any great expectation of success – until children appear to have considerable competence in reading and spoken language, partly because writing ability in any case often seems to lag far behind. But apart from relatively trivial aspects of the physical act of writing – such as the fact that small infants find it hard to hold and control a pencil – there is no reason why fluency in writing should not develop concurrently with fluency in other aspects of language. They have the same roots; the urge to make sense of the world and of oneself.

It is worthwhile to ask why so few people write well (compared with the number who can read) and why even fewer seem to enjoy writing. There are two possible explanations. One is that writing is such a difficult and unnatural activity that relatively few people have the years of training and special talent that it requires. The other possible explanation is that writing is a natural and rewarding activity that just about everybody is born capable of learning, but that for many people, something goes wrong.

I think the second explanation is more likely, because writing does basically nothing more than speaking does (so there is no reason for it to be thought unique in any way) and because almost all children find the beginning of writing satisfying. They enjoy making marks on paper, they are impressed by its permanence, and they wonder at the power of print that it can even represent their own name. Teachers know that one of the hardest things to do with a young child's writing is to throw it away; the writing is part of the child. To children, writing can be as satisfying and as natural as singing, dancing, play-acting, painting, and modelling with clay or mud. It is not something different or special; it is not a unique kind of tool.

So why should children grow up reluctant to write? Perhaps for the same reason that so many grow up reluctant to sing, to dance and to play; at least publicly. We become self-conscious about activities that once were spontaneous, and we become too concerned about our own and other people's evaluation of what we do. We are inhibited. Many adults find it difficult to begin to write because they are afraid they will not do it well, or because they will have nothing to say. It is as if they have a school teacher on their shoulder waiting to criticize every word that comes out. They will never write well if they do not write at all, and they are reluctant to write at all for fear they will not write well.

Writing tends to be laborious in any case. It is tiring physically, demands more concentration, and it is slow; perhaps ten times slower than the speed at which we comfortably manage to read, speak or listen to speech. We can only become proficient at writing by practice, and we can only write proficiently when we write spontaneously and relatively fast (leaving all the cumbersome attention to spelling, punctuation and neatness to a later draft). Too much of what happens at school, I am afraid, tends to slow writing down. Writing does not become better if we slow down, it becomes harder.

Why should anyone learn to write; what does it do? We sometimes talk about writing as if it were a poor substitute for speaking. But writing can do everything that speech can do, which means that it can be used in support of every human intention. Sometimes writing seems more reliable than speech, which is why it is preferred for laws and contracts; sometimes it is not so desirable – it seems less efficacious for maintaining personal relations. But writing clearly has one great advantage over speech – its relative permanence. We have more leisure to reflect upon ideas when they are written down. Another obvious advantage of writing over speech is that the producer and the receiver can be separated in time and space. But I see an even greater advantage that is rarely considered – when we write, we separate our ideas from ourselves.

Writing is not simply a matter of putting down on paper ideas which we already have in our heads. Many ideas would not exist if they were not created on paper. Books never exist in an author's head (except as vague abstractions). It is true that authors shape books, but books shape authors, and ideas which never would have seen the light of day are born in this dynamic interaction called writing. We do not even know what we are *capable* of thinking unless we begin to manifest ideas in some observable way. When ideas are on paper we can do more than just contemplate them, we can work on them, mould and manipulate them, and build up a structure of new thought as complex and rich as a picture built up on canvas by an artist who started with little more than a generalized intention. Writing is truly creative – if we allow it to be.

There is nothing essentially different about writing; it is another way of discovering more about the world, about possible worlds, and about ourselves. Children should find nothing peculiar or exotic about writing; they should come to it as a natural means of expression and exploration like speech, music, play, and art. Children will strive to make sense of writing in the same way they strive to make sense of any activity – through the manner in which it satisfies purposes and achieves intentions.

As long as writing remains a natural and purposeful activity, made available without threat, then children will be willing to practise it and consequently will learn. Writing is then inevitably integrated in the learner's mind with every other productive aspect of language and every other worthwhile activity as well. It is only when writing is treated as a special and difficult kind of activity that it can remain separate from everything else, and therefore impossible to understand, in the learner's mind.

Conclusion

Our categories are arbitrary – reading, writing, speaking and understanding speech. They are useful perhaps in the way we want to organize our schools, but they are not a reflection of a categorization in the learner's mind. The question is not how the language arts should be brought together in the learner's mind, but why they should ever be separated. To a child, language and the world must be indivisible.

References

HALLIDAY, M. A. K. (1973) *Explorations in the Functions of Language* London: Edward Arnold

SMITH, F. (1975) *Comprehension and Learning* New York: Holt, Rinehart and Winston

SMITH, F. (1976) Learning to read by reading *Language Arts* 53, 297–9, 322

SMITH, F. (1979) The uses of language *Language Arts* 54, 638–44

YLISTO, I. P. (1977) Early reading responses of young Finnish children *The Reading Teacher* 31, 167–72

Acknowledgment

The publishers and UKRA would like to thank Frank Smith for his permission to include in this volume 'The language arts and the learner's mind' © F. Smith 1979, which first appeared in *Language Arts* 56, 2, February, 118–25.

Part 4

Research and
resources

Introduction

Research and resources, experimentation and application, have perhaps been unnecessarily regarded as separate in education. John Chapman, in the first paper in this section, examines various models of research and discusses their relevance for teachers. His emphasis is active classroom investigation but he argues that action researchers can usefully follow rigorous methods used in other types of research. To this end, the paper offers various suggestions, some based on discussions at the previous UKRA conference.

Gail Sharman and Angela Salfield are also concerned with classrooms, in particular with how to establish what are the formative influences on teachers' classroom behaviour. This area, which they consider unduly neglected, is the subject of a current research project and the paper, incidentally, gives a useful insight into problems encountered by researchers. Don Bouwhuis uses classical experimental methodology to examine the global versus analytic controversy about word recognition. Drawing on his own research, but also providing some historical and comparative context, he provides support for advocates of phonics (cf Part 2 of this volume), but he also points to the need for more detailed theories of reading.

Derrick Stock provides an account of one of the increasingly important influences on classroom practice, in-service courses on reading. Cecelia Obrist reports on Family Reading Groups, emphasizing the cooperation there between UKRA and other organizations, but paying particular attention to the UKRA research contribution.

Elizabeth King deals with the selection of books and provides a list of criteria for choosing books for children. John Rawnsley is concerned with the contribution which broadcasting has to make to reading development. He gives particular attention to the preparation and piloting of *A Good Read*, a television series for ten- to twelve-year-olds to extend their skill and interest in reading.

16 How research methods and findings can help the classroom teacher of reading

L. John Chapman

Introduction

It is appropriate at a conference that is entitled 'The Reading Connection' that problems surrounding the connection between the teacher of reading and reading research should be discussed. Indeed it is ironic that research, whose definitions so resemble teaching procedures, e.g. 'diligent and careful search and study' or 'a way of thinking' (Weintraub and Farr 1976) should in the first place be considered problematic; for if anything should be connected for the betterment of reading standards, it ought to be teaching and research. Yet for so long there has been either misunderstanding of the purposes of research, apathy on the part of some teachers or what almost amounts to disdain on the part of some research workers. Yet it is clear that a close working relationship is not being fully achieved however desirable it may be. The note on research in the Bullock Report (DES 1975, pp. 532–4) for instance, speaks of an 'uneasy relationship that exists between research and teaching' and the 'need for research and teaching to become more closely interrelated' or as it could be worded at this conference 'more connected'. The same report also calls for 'more action research in which teachers are widely involved'.

While most would agree that research and teaching should be closely connected, and there is more agreement today on this amongst most teachers than there has been for some time, the achievement of an interrelationship is not as straightforward as some might suppose and attitudes do not change overnight.

It is necessary before attempting to show how research can help the classroom teacher, to review the present situation and to put the problem of research and the practitioner into perspective. Incidentally, it is not only the teaching profession that has these problems but many other professions where research and practice meet. And, as will be shown later, the problems are much the same in some other countries as our European colleagues in the Council of Europe have shown.

An effort was made at the Fourteenth Annual UKRA Conference (Chapman 1977) to spell out some of the facets involved in the so-called 'uneasy relationship' and to show that when the problem is set in an historical context and the purposes of various research projects categorized, some of the difficulties are lessened and some of the fears (and some practitioners do find some elements of research disturbing) assuaged.

Types of research

At that Conference two years ago, four types of research were outlined:

R1   Research employing a classical experimental format.
R2   Survey and longitudinal research.
R3   Research for curriculum development.
R4   Action research or active classroom investigations.

This analysis took the discussion by Houghton (1966) extended and redeployed it.

These four types of research have evolved over the years and reflect, in the main, an increasing demand that research should be related to, or be connected with, practice. The research types R1–R4 differ because they are designed for different purposes and, because they have different purposes, they have different research methods and techniques. An understanding of those specific techniques is therefore required.

R1 type research

R1 type research uses the word research 'in its classical sense involving original thinking, the discovery of new data, the reinterpretation of existing theories or systems of thought, the critical analysis of existing assumptions' (Houghton 1966). This type of research is characterized by a model of research which comes from the 'pure' sciences, e.g. physical sciences, involving experiments and the stringent application of statistical methods. This type of research is performed mostly in universities and government establishments and is often very costly. In the main it has high prestige and has clearly demonstrated that it can 'deliver the goods' as any picture of an atomic explosion will testify. The experimental model of scientific research has influenced other branches of study and since education can never function in isolation the effect of this model of research is widespread.

R2 type research

Survey research (R2) investigates 'what actually happened at any point of time in any given field of education. This is in the nature of fact-finding inquiry which may, though not inevitably, point the way to deeper, more intensive consideration' (Houghton 1968). This type of research often involves sampling techniques which are claimed to be representative of large sections of the population. Surveys reveal, for instance, trends and attitudes and are often used by administrators in planning for educational developments. Research of a longitudinal nature is similar. This seeks, for example, to follow the development of children over a period of time. R2 research is different from R1 as to its purpose, and hence requires different methodologies which in turn require training in their techniques.

R3 type research
Research categorized as R3 involves curriculum development and often is an attempt by an outside agency to cause innovation to take place in schools. This type, of which the Nuffield Foundation's Mathematics project and the Schools Council's Humanities project are examples, is less common now than it was a few years ago. It has been the experience of some, that the innovations they propose do not take root and grow automatically in all school situations. And this is so, even when the proposals are developed as a result of teacher interaction during the project.

R4 type research
Research of the R4 type, action research or active classroom investigation, has evolved over the years and is the primary focus of this paper. It has importance for the following reasons:

1 It is probably true to say that research projects into areas of the curriculum that reflect practitioners' needs receive more attention now than they used to, or perhaps are needed more than formerly. As research methodology appears to evolve according to the purpose of the research, it is likely that action-type research, which is either a partnership of the practitioner and a full-time researcher, or the teacher assuming the role of both researcher and teacher, will become common in the eighties.

2 If teachers are to retain their present control of the curriculum there will be greater demands that they become more accountable to society and in more direct ways. If, for example, both parents and teachers have greater involvement on school governing or managing bodies (Taylor 1977) there will no doubt be calls for justification of the action of individual classroom teachers.

3 The increasing level of qualifications required for teaching will also enable many to take part in research, no matter what category.

4 It is noticeable that many innovations have been short-lived, but

because of the momentum that has been achieved in a variety of ways, many teachers have been swept along by the latest fashion in education. It is surprising how many of these innovations in teaching have not been researched, or even well argued, before they are launched upon the teaching force. To combat possible ill-effects of such proposals on the education of children requires an awareness of some elementary research techniques. From such a knowledge base, teachers can make critical appraisals and be able to stand firm when needs require it.

Comparisons in Europe
Before relating practical ways in which research methods and findings can assist the teacher of reading it is worth noting for comparison the research policies of some of our colleagues on the continent. Take, for example, the report on Educational Research Policy (Council of Europe 1978) prepared by the Netherlands in November 1978. Paragraph 1.3 is entitled: 'Researchers' collaboration at the local level with teacher, administrators and parents'. It reads, 'it is by no means common for researchers to cooperate with teachers, administrators and parents in the development of education at local level'. Two reasons are cited for this. Firstly the Dutch have organized their research as part of a national support-structure and 'within this structure', the report says, 'the research, development (curriculum development, test development), dissemination and consultancy sections are carefully separated at both policy-making and administrative levels'. Secondly, 'Action research is still a relatively small part of the total work'.

In the following paragraph, 1.4: 'Collaboration of research to reform in the classroom' which comes close to the kind of progress the Bullock Report had in mind, the authors report:

Many (research) contributions to reform in education, most of which are long-term occur as a result of diffusion rather than direct application. . . .The svo (the Dutch Educational Research Institute) is attempting to improve productivity by giving more emphasis to practical relevance in the assessment of research proposals by giving teachers and researchers the opportunity for discussion in drawing up research proposals (negotiated research) and by the organization of central scientific information services.

Paragraph 1.5: 'Main obstacles of greater impact of research in the classroom' makes interesting reading:

The main obstacles which prevent research from having a greater impact seem to vary considerably and include:
(a) the continuing relatively weak position of the social sciences;

(b) the paradox of the accent on practical research at the expense of so-called irrelevant theoretical research, which in fact endangers the formulation and testing of hypotheses and the ability of research to generalize in the long term and thereby also endangers the quality and significance of that same practical research;

(c) the jargon used by many social and behavioural scientists;

(d) the fact that research (notably evaluation research) is sometimes seen by policy-makers and teachers as a threat;

(e) the lack of coordination in programming research projects (see the English language version of the forthcoming svo memorandum Programming Educational Research);

(f) the credibility gap which has arisen as a result of expectations for the social sciences in the sixties following the post-Sputnik boom in the sciences; in the seventies, due to insufficient insight into long-term impacts, a certain degree of cultural pessimism (e.g. on the issue of equal opportunity) and the fact that the social sciences cannot really be compared with science and technology, have meant that these expectations are not being realized. Moreover, the departmentalization of the national educational support structure mentioned in 1.3 could also be an obstacle. International comparative evaluation research would probably shed more light on this aspect.

Teachers and research in Britain

In many ways the situation in the United Kingdom is similar to that in other European countries, with perhaps the Netherlands having the closest resemblance. (At the time of preparing this paper, however, the reports of Germany and France were not available.) Problems surrounding research and the classroom practitioner are not peculiar to the UK but reflect the experience of many of the advanced nations; for research, at one time very largely the province of universities or research bodies, has become practised by others outside those institutions.

Cortis (1977), for example, reviewing Cohen (1976) suggests that:

Historically, the development of the postwar educational-research tradition in England and Wales followed the usual 'closed' pattern obtaining in higher education at the time, namely that research was the prerogative of a cloistered élite, admittance to which could only be obtained after a novitiate of some severity in which, to quote a tract of the times, 'the appropriate choice of topic by the candidate forms an important element in his admission to a research degree'.

Candidates were often expected, certainly in terms of the dissertation mode alone and sometimes even where the dissertation came at the end of a taught course, to generate, describe and defend their topics without much, if any, guidance from their academic seniors. There were no such books as Cohen's to guide them. This produced, not surprisingly, a core of dedicated research workers, of varying degrees of originality, but essentially small in number, hard for aspirants to join and, like monastic communities, a minority group in the wider society. Such circumstances no longer exist. Now our concern in higher education generally, and in the study of educational research specifically, is with a broader band of ability and with a more open pattern of operation.

With the gradual increase in educational levels, the increase in establishments of higher education and the inclusion of research methodologies in the syllabuses of training institutions, many teachers have become researchers in their own right. In any case, as will be shown, research approaches to problems are useful procedures in general classroom practice.

Active classroom investigation
In what practical way then can research help the classroom teacher? To begin with, for the investigation of classroom problems the teacher can adopt the accepted methodology of sound research practice which has proved itself over time. This involves stating a problem in such a way that the teacher will know, after the investigation, that the problem has been solved. This clarification by explicit statement(s) helps in the first place to clear away misunderstandings that arise from the multifaceted nature of practical problems, and helps avoid woolly thinking. It is also most important to break the problem down into small manageable chunks. In the classroom there are always problems to be solved – some that are urgent and need immediate action and others that are medium and longer term. Many can, however, be resolved by careful analysis for these classroom problem statements are the equivalent of the statements of hypotheses of the (R1) laboratory experiments.

Let us take a problem of the classroom type as an example. At the Fifteenth UKRA Conference a problem was presented to a workshop group by a classroom teacher. She noticed, or thought she noticed, that some of her class and one boy in particular, read words from his reading book mechanically and monotonously and so she said 'without really understanding them'. In other words his mechanical word recognition was good but not his comprehension. She wondered how the position might be remedied. The workshop group who had met to discuss solving classroom problems were reminded that the task was to state her problem in such a way that the teacher would know, after carrying out certain procedures, that her problem had been solved. The group suggested that the problem was related to lack of motivation, that the lack of intonation, the monotonous reading, was only a symptom of an underlying reading problem. It might be due to uninteresting material or reading matter not related to purposes which the child could accept. After considerable discussion some of the group decided that the teacher would know that the problem had been solved when the child's oral reading showed more expression. Others in the group countered that this could still be so without the child really comprehending the passage.

A discussion of comprehension followed and ways of checking understanding were outlined. Most had heard of cloze procedure as a possible way of checking comprehension and it was decided that a cloze test could be arranged using the children's present reading material. Such a test would enable the teacher to have some idea whether the monotonous reading involving lack of comprehension was just lack of interest, or due to some other causes. The agreed statement was: 'That John could replace deletions in a cloze text constructed from his present reading materials at a level of 80 per cent correct'. The first action was to set a comprehension task using cloze procedure. This brought the group to a further step in standard research methodology. To find out how to do the job most efficiently, how to construct such a test, how many deletions, how long, required a search to be made in journals or books for information on cloze procedure. This is no more than an elementary literature search. Some will know that these can be extensive and costly if computers are involved, but it is possible to do a workmanlike job by looking at journals such as those of UKRA and IRA over the last few years for articles on cloze. These articles are bound to have lists of references and these will almost certainly indicate the main works on the topic.

The literature search is the nub of much of this classroom procedure, for in order for research findings to be of practical help to the teacher they must be closely related to actual classroom problems. In order to do this the investigator needs to state explicitly his or her needs first in a problem-solving format. It is important in the wider context for teachers to keep themselves informed by taking journals and reading articles regularly for in this way they will have a good idea where to find relevant materials when the need arises. And sometimes an article will alert you to the uncomfortable fact that you didn't know you had problems until you read more about the reading process and its teaching. Selectivity in reading is required, for some journals do not address themselves to teachers but to others involved only in research and not practice.

Next, the group proposed that as a result of this first procedure further statements would be needed before the teacher could be satisfied that her original problem was solved. It might be that John could perform adequately (i.e. 80 per cent correct) and still read in a monotonous fashion. The group then proposed further steps depending on the outcome of the first statement, such as: 'If John could replace deletions at an 80 per cent correct level, then would he be reading with comprehension; if he couldn't then he would not be reading with comprehension'. Action could now proceed from what, at this stage, is akin to a diagnostic process.

The group then saw the next stage as dependent on either (a) comprehension is satisfactory; or (b) comprehension is unsatisfactory. If (a) then a further problem-solving statement is required and it was proposed that 'the monotonous reading' might be: that the child has no idea how to read with expression; that the reading material is uninteresting to that child or that he has learned that school books in general are uninteresting.

If (b) then action designed to improve comprehension is called for, together with suitable methods. We are now well into action-research procedures where research methods and findings are involved in solving specific classroom procedures.

This is a report of discussions amongst teachers which must be left here; further steps require feedback from the real situation as the whole purpose is to encourage on-the-job investigation. However, further research elements now become desirable. Some kind of reporting is recommended so that both the teacher and other teachers can benefit. Again reports of research have a format that can be followed, and it is important that these reports are written in such a way that other teachers can read and understand them. This means that teachers reporting investigations they have carried out in their own classrooms should *not* try to use the type of technical language which, say, a psychologist or a sociologist who are addressing their own kind, might employ. The language should be as free as possible from technical terms and use made of only those expressions that a fellow teacher would use. If, on the other hand, teachers wish to have a report published in a journal intended for different professions, then to avoid misunderstanding and to have articles accepted the procedures of that particular journal must be followed.

Finally, and this became apparent during the early discussion on the results of the cloze test, more research or investigation becomes necessary. This is the nature of research and action research will not prove to be any different, so a final step needs to be suggested, namely, further research or continuation of the investigation, to accord with the ongoing nature of classroom teaching.

In this way, following an acceptable research format, teachers can be involved in action research in their own schools. But what of statistics? Some will have noticed that an elementary calculation was involved in the example given (the calculation of percentages), but statistical methods have not been introduced. When dealing with one child or a group of children in a classroom, there is not much need for statistical calculations. However, if general statements are required or one group is to be compared with other groups or one child with others, then some statistical operations will be needed to check whether the findings can be generalized or relied on. Teachers will also need to become acquainted with the methodology of one of the other types of research and the statistics that go with it. It may be that, in the decade that is about to begin, and with the microcomputer revolution, more specially-written statistical programmes can be made available in schools. This is another story, however, and would need another paper, but it is clearly an exciting possibility for schools, especially when connected with school-focused in-service education.

References

CHAPMAN, L. J. (1977) 'Classroom investigation: a reappraisal of research and the teacher' Paper presented to the Fourteenth Annual Conference of the United Kingdom Reading Association, Avery Hill College, London

COHEN, L. (1976) *Educational Research in Classrooms and Schools: A Manual of Materials and Methods* London, New York: Harper and Row

CORTIS, G. (1977) Book review *Educational Review 29*, 3, 221–3

COUNCIL OF EUROPE (1978) *Educational research policy in European Countries: 1978 Survey* Report submitted by the Ministry of Education Netherlands (DECS/Rech 82) Strasbourg: The Council of Europe

DES (1975) *A Language for Life* (The Bullock Report) London: HMSO

DES (1977) *A New Partnership for Our Schools* (The Taylor Report) London: HMSO

EVANS, K. M. (1978) *Planning Small-scale Research: A Practical Guide for Teachers and Students* Windsor: NFER

HOUGHTON, J. (1966) The role and function of educational research *Educational Research 9*, 1, 7–10

WEINTRAUB, S. and FARR, R. (1976) 'Introduction: What is research?' in R. Farr, S. Weintraub and B. Tone (eds) *Improving Reading Research* Newark, Delaware: International Reading Association

17 The formation of classroom reading practices

Angela Salfield and Gail Sharman

We think it would be fair to say that in *all* reading research there is one very simple underlying motive or aim and that is to help every person – child or adult – to read. How 'well', to what purpose etc can be and is argued about, but that reading is a positive goal to be achieved is, we would suggest, universally accepted.

The problem, then, is how to go about achieving this aim of universal literacy.

We can point to at least three dominant areas of research which attempt to do this for initial literacy.

The first centres around the debate on the best means of *instruction* – in terms of approach and/or materials – to use in the classroom. This debate is of course not new. A well-worn version of it – 'which is better, phonics or look-and-say?' – predominated for a long while, and Jeanne Chall's (1967) *Learning to Read: The Great Debate* is a comprehensive summary of this issue.

Although with the Bullock Report, the 'battle lines' were redrawn as the issues about reading were broadened, and with it an apparent acceptance that no one method, medium, or approach can hold the complete answer to success in reading, one can still note, in journals, new books, articles etc a steady stream of advice on what materials or approaches teachers should actually adopt in the classroom. We have called these 'prescriptions for *practice*' a term we return to.

(It's important to add here that there is a problem of definition with the term we've used – 'method', 'medium', 'approach', 'theory' – they tend to be used rather loosely and often interchangeably by teachers and researchers when discussing modes of instruction, and this may lead to confusion or misunderstanding.)

The point is that the notion of *practice* in most reading research of this type becomes or is reduced to an approach, method, particular use of a particular scheme or set of materials which teachers *use*.

The second way reading research attempts to reach its goal centres around the search for the *knowledge* thought to be essential for teachers and for the most part this knowledge is seen to be an understanding of what has been termed the *reading process*. This is usually defined as a cognitive, individual process, and underlying this is an assumption of a learning process universal to all individuals which will occur irrespective of context as they learn to read.

Frank Smith insisted in his earlier work on a split between these two areas we've outlined – knowledge of the reading process and instruction – stating that he felt that researchers' efforts should be less directed towards telling teachers what to *do*, i.e. what method to use, and more towards on what teachers should *know*. In his more recent work, however, he seems to be responding to the questions teachers and others have raised about the problems of this separation and to implications for classroom practice.

Both of these ways imply, it seems to us, that teachers have it within their power to create appropriate conditions in classrooms which will enable all children to read. Thus it has not been seen as important to investigate these classroom conditions in their own right.

The third area of research is different from the first two in that its findings place the school and indeed the teacher as being of secondary importance in determining a child's success or failure at reading. The research in this area points to external factors such as social class, home environment, etc as the strong determinants of a child's success or failure in reading; and in talking with teachers, these factors are regularly raised – either implicitly or explicitly – as being significant.

In this area we would place the recent work of the Bristol team (Wells, Raban *et al.*) which has indicated that preschool influences on children's reading attainment are in some cases significantly more important than school influences. There is also Jenny Hewison's work at the Thomas Coram Unit, Institute of Education, on the factors within the home environment which seem to bear on children's success or failure at reading. One finding is that success at reading relates to the child being read to at home.

It is necessary to mention here that there is a growing body of work from other areas of educational research – not looking at reading in particular, but more generally at children's success and failure in school – which argues against this position and asserts that it *is* what goes on in schools that influences their progress (e.g. *Fifteen Thousand Hours*, Rutter *et al.* 1979).

So, our problem when we came to plan our own research was an awareness of these different strands in the existing research, and the difficulties there were in trying to construct a framework which would enable us to intermesh them to provide what, for us, would be a more acceptable conceptualization of the relationship of the theories and practices of reading in schools.

The first two strands – the issue of instruction and what approach works best, and the issue of what knowledge teachers need of what has been defined as the reading process – both leave the issue of putting them into practice in the classroom assumed or unproblematic. This assumption is implicit in much of the research, but most teachers in classrooms every day are critically aware that the relationship between theory and practice is considerably more complicated.

The results of the third area of reading research indicate that what goes on in the classroom itself has less effect on children's reading attainment than outside influences. However, we felt that in all these approaches, the whole realm of practice had in effect been ignored in terms of any detailed investigations.

In the beginning we wanted to examine whether or how in fact different approaches or theories of reading produced different classroom practices. We attempted in our research to separate out broadly the main approaches to beginning reading. We felt that *theoretically* it could be argued that there were three main distinct theories of reading; phonics, psycholinguistics and *Breakthrough to Literacy*, each of which was either implicitly or explicitly based on a different theory of language and learning. Secondly, we argued that if a particular theory was adopted by a teacher it would result in a particular practice in the classroom. We therefore wanted to find classrooms using each approach and to examine in detail whether or not these arguments could be sustained.

We gave a questionnaire to in-service teachers, did a small pilot-study, had many discussions with teachers and advisory teachers, and in fact found that our initial formulation was not a workable one. There was no 'one-to-one' correspondence between what teachers describe as their own theory of reading, and either what they describe as their practice or what they actually *do*.

At the International Reading Association conference in Atlanta in April 1979 we found that this view is supported by some larger-scale research projects in progress there. So, we changed our formulation and began to concentrate on the *practice* side of the theory/practice relationship. Practice must be analysed in detail, in its own right and with its own set of determinants – theory being one, but only one of these determinants.

We hope that our research will: (1) produce an account of the practices of reading in infant classrooms; and (2) construct a framework to explain the formation of these practices in classrooms as a consequence of prevailing ideologies, policies, forms of organization and administration.

There are many ways of justifying our claim for the importance of analysing the practices of the school and classroom and we will discuss a few of the most important ones.

Political and policy issues

Both the publication of the Bullock Report *A Language for Life* (DES 1975) and subsequent debates have raised the question of standards and the accountability of schools for these standards. For infant schools these issues are focused on initial literacy and numeracy. The recent publication of *Fifteen Thousand Hours* by Rutter *et al.* (1979), which argues that different school processes produce different effects on the children, continues the debate about the role of the school and classroom in understanding educational outcomes.

Teacher education

Both the initial and in-service training of teachers raise questions of content in teacher-education curricula and the relationship between the curriculum and the everyday needs of classroom practice.

Ethnographic studies

Such work points to the importance of both investigating educational activities in the social context in which they occur and of doing this through methods which recognize their infinite variability and complexity. Keith Gardner (1976) has claimed that too much time and effort has been spent enquiring into methods and materials in reading and too little attention has been given to processes of learning to read. He argues that 'the real data for attaining educational certainties lie in an understanding of what children actually do in the classroom'.

Current research

Two recent studies are of particular interest to us.

THE SOCIAL ORGANIZATION OF READING ACTIVITIES
This research, directed by James Heap at the Ontario Institute for Studies in Education, is concerned to realign reading theory and practice and argues that for students and teachers what reading is in the classroom is 'what counts as reading'. 'What counts as reading' doesn't come just from theories of reading or programmes of reading instruction, but gets defined in the actual situation by the social organization of the conventions, assumptions and practices that are required or used in order to apply theories or to implement programmes.

TEACHER CONCEPTIONS OF READING AND THE IMPACT ON INSTRUCTIONAL BEHAVIOUR

This research at the Institute for Research on Teaching, Michigan State University, was set up to investigate whether teachers had identifiable conceptions of reading and if so whether and how these conceptions influence instruction in the classroom.

The initial assumption was that *if* there was a relationship between conception and instruction it would be a direct one. After the researchers had made their first venture into classrooms they had to change this view. They found that although teachers had identifiable conceptions and that these had some influence on instruction, the situation was considerably more complex than they had anticipated.

The researchers reformulated their project which finally consisted of a naturalistic field-study in 23 schools across three states in America, and their conclusion was that although teachers' conceptions of reading are *reflected* in instruction, they cannot be said to *govern* it, and that there are other influences which must be taken into account in understanding classroom instruction.

Conclusion

We have used the above arguments to back up our assertion that one important and largely neglected area of reading research is the investigation of how reading practices get formed in the way that they do in the classroom. Having said this, however, there is a very important methodological issue which we haven't addressed here concerning the difficulties raised by doing such classroom analyses.

References

CHALL, J. (1967) *Learning to Read: The Great Debate* New York: McGraw Hill

DES (1975) *A Language for Life* (The Bullock Report) London: HMSO

GARDNER, K. (1976) After Bullock – whither reading research? *Research Intelligence 2*, 1, 2–5

RUTTER, M. *et al.* (1979) *Fifteen Thousand Hours* London: Open Books

SHARMAN, G. and SALFIELD, A. (1979) Views on reading *ILEA Contact 8*, 7, 6–7

Note

For further information on the following research projects contact G. Sharman, Department of Teaching Studies, Polytechnic of North London, Prince of Wales Road, London NW5.

Reading Practices in Infant Classrooms (A. Salfield and G. Sharman)
Polytechnic of North London
The Social Organization of Reading Activities (J. Heap) Ontario Institute
for Studies in Education
Teacher Conceptions of Reading and the Impact on Instructional Behaviour
(G. Duffy) Institute for Research on Teaching, Michigan State
University

18   The global and analytic view of word recognition

Don G. Bouwhuis

It may be that the distinction implied in the title of this paper is already obsolete in present-day reading education. The analytic way of reading entails the process in which all letters of the word are functional in evoking the word and its meaning. In a global way of reading the whole word, rather than its letters, would function as the mediating unit: the letters would hardly play a role. Visual properties of letter combinations, which could be called transgraphemic features, might be operating in such a case. In 1908 Huey called it a time-honoured question whether we read by letters or by words, and he added that much more is involved in reading than the settlement of this query. As it is, any sort of reading education requires some idea as to how reading proceeds, a theory of reading in order to optimize the early phases of reading. Theories of reading have never been very detailed, nor comprehensive. Thus, it comes as no surprise that approaches in reading education at one time reflect the analytic theory and at another time the global theory. Chall (1967) recorded that these periods followed each other at intervals of between 20 and 30 years. At present there are more comprehensive methods of reading education encompassing both aspects, either simultaneously or sequentially. In the Netherlands the most widely-used method of reading education is known as the structure method, combining analytic with global aspects. Only very few schools, usually in small, relatively isolated communities, are still teaching in the global way only.

From the Greek and Roman times theories of reading were analytic in nature. Reading was usually considered to be the isomorphic counterpart of writing, in which one letter was written down after the other, each one representing a part of the sound of the word. There was also the subjective impression that the eye was moving smoothly over the lines of text during reading, taking out each letter sequentially in reconstructing the word and its sound. These notions are primitive in the light of what we know now about information-processing during reading, but insight into the perceptual processes going on during reading only proceeded very gradually.

History of reading research

In 1867 the Paris ophthalmologist Javal (1938) discovered that the eyes move in jumps over the lines to be read, rather than proceeding smoothly as had been thought previously. These jumps, *saccades* as Javal called them, are not limited to reading at all, but characterize all our looking behaviour.

In reading the average jump will take 25 milliseconds (ms) while the ensuing fixation pause averages 200 ms, but is quite variable. The size of the *saccade*, or the extent of the jump, is variable as well but the average is 8 letters of normal text at normal reading distance. Both early work (Huey 1908) as well as recent research (Lévy-Schoen and O'Regan 1979) on eye movements show that they are to a great extent autonomous and independent of the linguistic properties of the text. This appears from the observation that most words are not directly looked at and some words are not even fixated. In general the fixation spots are randomly distributed over the letters of the words and may even land on spaces between them.

It was soon established by the research workers that this strongly influenced the way in which words are seen during reading, owing to elementary properties of the human visual system.

Figure 1 Probability of perceiving each one of the three letters of the word 'day' when it is presented left of the fixation point (+) for a period corresponding to a single glance (100 ms)

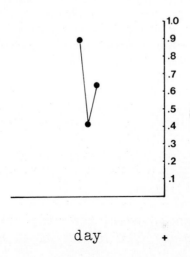

This is made clear in Figure 1, where the perceptibility of the letters of the word 'day' is indicated, presented at some distance from the fixation point. It is clear that the outward letters are best perceived, especially the one furthest from the fixation point. The letter closest to the fixation point is always perceived second best, while the middle letters can only be distinguished with much more difficulty. This difficulty will increase when the word is longer, or when it is further from the actual fixation point. This picture is reversed for a word presented right of the fixation point. The final letter would be most visible, the first slightly less, followed again by the middle letters. Words in the right visual-field are also somewhat better perceived than those in the left visual-field. Consequently, words look quite different, literally depending on the angle from which they are seen.

These observations present difficulties for a pure global view of word recognition because the same word has a different appearance in different locations of the visual field.

One of the first workers in the field of word recognition was Cattell. He went from the United States to Germany in 1883 to do experiments in Wundt's laboratory in Leipzig for three years. One of the first things he discovered was that a word was recognized as quickly as a single letter (Cattell 1886). Cattell concluded that a word is read as a whole. In fact this finding excluded the possibility that words are recognized by identifying or spelling the letters sequentially. Today we are tempted to say, in derived computer terminology, that letters may also be processed in parallel, or simultaneously. In that case we would also expect Cattell's finding to hold. Cattell further noted that subjects could usually report a maximum of five letters from a meaningless string of letters presented to them for a single fixation pause. But words of up to twelve letters could easily be reported in the same presentation time. He then argued that when you can see a word of, say, twelve letters in a single glance, you could not have seen all letters, but only five of them. This phenomenon would also point to the notion that words are read as a whole. Through the work of researchers such as Averbach and Sperling (1961) we now know that subjects can see many more than five letters in a single glance but are unable to report them all because of memory limitations. That is why present-day theorists assume that if the quickly-seen letters form a word, they are efficiently coded by that word, thus preventing the letters from being forgotten. This cannot be done when the letters form a meaningless arrangement.

A few years later another American, Raymond Dodge came to Germany and worked for two years at the University of Bonn in Erdmann's laboratory. That research showed strong evidence for whole-word perception in a range of well-designed experiments. However, in several of their experimental tasks the subjects knew the word responses beforehand, making recognition of the word, or in any case its letters, more or less superfluous. Close reading of the complete reports reveals that the subjects, who were the investigators themselves, knew many of the words to be recognized in the trials beforehand. If one knows which word will be presented it is not necessary to see all of its letters to recognize it; and such a phenomenon could aptly be called global perception. Nevertheless, they did not succeed in recognizing 26 very familiar short sentences presented under the same conditions as the words. So, while global reading of words might be possible given sufficient advance information, it did not work for well-known sentences. Meanwhile, other investigators found evidence for the important role of the constituent letters of words and they rejected the findings of Cattell, and of Erdmann and Dodge (1898), opting for whole-word perception. Wundt (1903) and Huey (1908) took more or less opposite views supported by accumulating experimental evidence. Yet the debate was unsettled at the time, since there was insufficient knowledge in general on human information-processing. Nor was the debate to be settled quickly. The study of perceptual processing during reading seemed almost to vanish from the experimental scene for several decades. Only in recent years has reading been attracting fresh interest from investigators in pattern recognition, psycholinguistics, memory and eye movements. At a time when memory factors especially are much better understood than before, it seems now that there is a strong case for analytic perception. Experimental evidence by Estes (1977), Massaro (1975), McClelland and Johnston (1977), and Bouwhuis (1979) points unequivocally to the prime importance of the constituent letters in word recognition.

Recent models of word recognition

An influential model of recognition put forward by Morton (1969) makes clear what kind of processes might operate in word recognition. Morton's so-called logogen model is actually meant to describe a broad range of recognition and listening tasks. The main point to be noted here is that in the model it is assumed that all information regarding the word combines independently and additively. A reader has word knowledge at his disposal and sees strings of letters when he is reading. As has been said before, both letter information and the knowledge that letters form words may be functional in recognizing the word in the sentence. If either of these were lacking we would not recognize the words.

This process is carried a step further in the letter-confusion model by Bouwhuis and Bouma (1979). They assume that when a word is presented to the subject (seen at some place in the visual field) a letter is seen in each of its letter positions. This assumption is reasonable in the case of three-letter words. Which letters will be seen then depends on how distinguishable they are (Figure 1) and their similarity to other letters. On each trial, one of a large number of different letter-strings may be seen, strings made up by the possibly perceived letters. Most of these strings are not real words, but some are. It is supposed that the subject responds with real words only, i.e. the reader employs his word knowledge to select the words from among the meaningless strings and responds with the most likely alternative. On the basis of a large amount of letter-recognition data the model can specify how letters in different positions in a word may be confused with each other. The model is also provided with a vocabulary, thought to be representative of the reader's lexicon, containing some 500 three-letter words. With these data the model can predict which responses may be given by subjects, and in addition how often they will be reported. Testing the model has shown that these predictions closely matched experimentally-obtained responses of subjects (Bouwhuis and Bouma 1979).

Though these results relate to three-letter words only, it has recently been shown that the same model reasonably predicts responses to five-letter words (Baggen 1979). The only alternative quantitative model, proposed by Rumelhart and Siple (1974) is mathematically quite similar to the letter-confusion model. Both models describe word recognition as an analytic process, where elementary visual information about all constituent letters teams up with word knowledge to enable us to recognize the word on the page.

Letters and word knowledge
When we are talking about constituent letters of words, it has to be realized that these have their proper position in the word. This position is of great importance. First (as one can see in Figure 1) from a sensory point of view, the initial and final letters of a word are almost all we can see of a word somewhat removed from the fixation point. But another important aspect can be demonstrated by the following example. In the sentence:

Cany our ead the sew ords

no letter is missing and all are in the right sequence. Typographically it is correct, the number of spaces is correct and even the way the segments are written does not violate English spelling rules. So, why is it so difficult? Apparently something is wrong – all the letters appear in improbable positions. In several experiments it has been shown that the frequency of a letter in a given position in a word to a large degree determines its familiarity. In English, for example, many more words begin with a *c*, *p* or *s* than with *x*, *y* or *z*. A vowel occurs in the middle position of 87.4 per cent of all Dutch three-letter words, but the first letter is a vowel in only 15.4 per cent of the cases. If letters were equiprobable in all positions, the vowels a, e, i, o and u would appear in $^{5}/_{26}$ (19.2 per cent) of the cases in both the first and the middle positions. The frequency of a letter in a position was shown to be connected with its subjective familiarity in an experiment by Bouwhuis (1979). The general finding can be illustrated as follows. Whenever a word contained a frequent letter in one of its positions, subjects recognized it faster and more accurately. Similar results were obtained in a number of letter-search tasks, devised by Mildred Mason (1975, 1978), also showing that poor readers were not very sensitive to letter-position frequency, but good readers were. From this it appears that it is not just letters which mediate word recognition but rather letters in their position. But the position of letters is a global word aspect, so whole-word properties assist in the recognition of the constituent letters.

Another implication of the importance of letter position is that spelling rules are probably less important for word perception than is sometimes thought (Massaro 1975). It is possible that the effect of spelling regularity is determined by the letter position rather than by abstract rules concerning letter sequences as they occur in the language.

Reading education

The preceding considerations do not give much hint as to how we should teach reading at school. It is clear that letters should be learned, as should where letters belong in a word. It is equally clear that whole words, with their meaning, should be learned to improve word knowledge, which would increase reading efficiency. These are neither new nor unexpected recommendations. It seems probable, however, that early reading of whole words – the pure global way – would generally favour only the prospective good readers, while being less suitable for poorer readers. When poor readers are being taught the whole pattern of a word rather than the detailed components, gross reading errors can result, examples of which are given by Henderson (1977). Of course reading errors typically occur in dyslexic children, who seem to read in a more or less global fashion, which is determined probably by their way of perceptual functioning. Somewhat paradoxically, spelling ability does not seem to typify good readers. Whereas Frith (1979) found that good readers, as well as poor readers, relied on the visual pattern of letters in their position for reading short sentences, some good readers could be very bad at spelling in writing. Frith (1979) concluded that writing words relies much more on the auditory representation than on the visual, or graphemic representation of words. Both phenomena, reading by graphemic form and writing by phonological form, suggest that phonics is probably not a very effective tool in reading or writing. This was actually the conclusion of the extensive study of Vera Southgate Booth and associates (this volume) on the writing ability of pupils in several age groups and proficiency levels.

Also, it may be desirable to employ somewhat more elaborate letter-shapes than are usually found in children's reading books. The letters printed are frequently large and clear, but lack serifs (the crossbars at the endings). For example, it was shown by Schiepers (1977) that omitting the upper serif of the letter k seriously degraded its recognizability in short presentations to adult readers. Simpler typefaces, like Helvetica or Univers, also contain symmetric pairs, e.g. b,d and q,p, which quite often tend to be reversed by young children. In general, serifed typefaces display much less symmetry, which could counter this tendency. It is generally agreed by typographers that serifed letters will continue to be used in books, newspapers and wherever large quantities of text have to be read. Therefore, it is not entirely clear why children should be confronted with the most simple and schematic letter shapes.

Yet firm recommendations on teaching to read cannot be expected from the present theories of reading, or word recognition. Much more detailed theories of reading are called for, as well as a good deal of supportive experimental evidence, before useful application of research findings can take place. Not only can experimental work be unknowingly repeated as Brooks (1979) has shown, it can often be interpreted in terms of contradictory theories. This can happen more easily when these theories are verbal rather than quantitative, or general rather than detailed. It is probably due more to the inexactitude of the theoretical stands than to their tenets that the global-analytic conflict could thrive for so long. Consequently, what should also be needed is research on the effectiveness of specific reading programmes under sufficiently controlled conditions. By 'sufficiently controlled' is meant that the research should involve larger numbers of students than has been the case, and also that different verbal abilities should be taken into account, as well as the usual safeguards which are employed in research on perception and memory. Follow-up research in the higher age-level brackets, particularly relevant for poor readers, seems now to be lacking completely. Such research could give valuable information on literacy in adults, as well as provide evidence on the long-term effects of a specific reading programme.

References

AVERBACH, E. and SPERLING, G. (1961) 'Short-term storage of information in vision' in C. Cherry (ed.) *Symposium on Information Theory* London: Butterworth

BAGGEN, C. P. M. (1979) The recognition of five-letter words *IPO Report no. 364* Eindhoven: Institute for Perception Research

BOUWHUIS, D. G. (1979) *Visual Recognition of Words* Doctoral thesis: University of Nijmegen

BOUWHUIS, D. G. and BOUMA, H. (1979) Visual recognition of three-letter words as derived from the recognition of the constituent letters *Perception and Psychophysics 25*, 12–21

BROOKS, G. (1979) *The Historical Reading Connection* Paper presented at the Sixteenth Annual UKRA Conference, Leeds. Revised version as The need for a historical dimension in research on reading *Journal of Research in Reading 3*, 1, 60–6, 1980

CATTELL, J. (1886) in R. S. Woodworth (1938) *Experimental Psychology* New York: Henry Holt

CHALL, J. (1967) *Learning to Read: The Great Debate* New York: McGraw-Hill

ERDMANN, B. and DODGE, R. (1898) *Psychologische Untersuchungen ueber das Lesen auf experimenteller Grundlage* Halle am Saale: Max Niemeyer

ESTES, W. K. (1977) 'On the interaction of perception and memory' in D. LaBerge and S. J. Samuels (eds) *Basic Processes in Reading* Hillsdale: Erlbaum

FRITH, U. (1979) 'Reading by eye and writing by ear' in P. A. Kolers, M. E. Wrolstad and H. Bouma (eds) *Processing of Visible Language I* New York: Plenum

HENDERSON, L. (1977) 'Word recognition' in N. S. Sutherland (ed.) *Tutorial Essays in Psychology I* Hillsdale: Erlbaum

HUEY, E. B. (1908, reprinted 1968) *The Psychology and Pedagogy of Reading* Cambridge, Mass.: MIT Press

JAVAL, E. (1938) in R. S. Woodworth *Experimental Psychology* New York: Henry Holt

LÉVY-SCHOEN, A. and O'REGAN, K. (1979) 'The control of eye movements in reading' in P. A. Kolers, M. Wrolstadt and H. Bouma (eds) *Processing of Visible Language I* New York: Plenum

MASSARO, D. W. (1975) 'Primary and secondary recognition in reading' in D. W. Massaro (ed.) *Understanding Language* New York: Academic Press

McCLELLAND, J. L. and JOHNSTON, J. C. (1977) The role of familiar units in perception of words and nonwords *Perception and Psychophysics 22*, 249–61

MORTON, J. (1969) Interaction of information in word recognition *Psychological Review 76*, 165–78

RUMELHART, D. E. and SIPLE, P. (1974) Process of recognizing tachistoscopically-presented words *Psychological Review 81*, 99–118

SCHIEPERS, C. W. J. (1977) *Global Attributes in Visual Word Recognition* Doctoral thesis: University of Nijmegen

WUNDT, W. (1903) *Grundzuege der Physiologischen Psychologie, Bd. 3* Leipzig: Wilhelm Engelman

19 In-service training: a course on aspects of the teaching of reading

Derrick Stock

This paper on in-service training will centre on an eighteen-hour course for teachers in ordinary schools who wish to bring themselves up-to-date on the teaching of reading.

This is the sixth occasion that the course has been run, and it is consistently oversubscribed.. Most of the applicants do not teach reading as a subject, but are aware of a situation developing in their schools in which children are failing to develop serious interest in the written word. As a result of this, certain skills, based on reading competence, are adversely affected. The course does not dwell on this, as the reasons may be deeply based in the structure of our present-day society, but rather concentrates on putting forward practical suggestions, based on sound theory, in order to increase teaching efficiency. This in turn would help children to increase their learning capacity and bring about the desired changes. Such an approach needs clear simple objectives, and the course is designed with the following three in mind:

1 It should concentrate on teaching technique. Much of today's knowledge so painstakingly developed in the universities seems to have little effect at classroom level. The best example is in reading itself. Here is a widely-researched subject, supported by plenty of written material, yet few would deny that there is little comparable improvement in reading standards.

2 The knowledge gained on the course should stimulate the course members to pursue their studies even when the course is finished. Course members must go away full of enthusiasm for their new skills and be anxious to apply them in the classroom situation. Without this the course is pointless. It is here that the book list plays an important part because a few selected examples can lead the reader on to more advanced concepts and thus extend the influence of the course still further.

3 The course members must be involved in their own course-programme planning. We present the basic content of the nine sessions to them at the beginning of the course and ask for

comments on its viability. If, in the subsequent discussion, specific suggestions are made which involve changes, then it is put to the vote. If it gets a majority we make the appropriate alteration. An important item here is that the course programme takes on a teacher-based format and as such is more likely to be effective when training colleagues.

We divide the course curriculum into nine subject elements, each of which is a full session. These subject elements are self-contained and are designed as an essential core of knowledge which can then be applied specifically to the teacher's own specialist area.

1 A general overview of teaching method
The first of the nine items relates to the general overview of teaching method. This is a brief survey and not intended to provide readymade solutions but to give course members essential background knowledge with which to start the programme. Most of them are not in a position to teach basic reading anyway, and to pursue this approach would be time wasting. Nevertheless, we mention the whole word, phonic, sentence, laboratory and language-experience methods, all with appropriate book references. We stress the importance of personal reading at this stage and recommend works that cover linguistics, psychology, and sociology.

2 Language skills
The second of the subject elements concerns language skills. We mention Chomsky and Halliday particularly because we find that both are helpful to the class teacher in the context of language usage and development. Language acquisition and subsequent development is studied and the associated problems of cultural disadvantage are investigated. From this come language enrichment schemes, and the need to increase children's lexical ability in every subject field.

3 Measurement
The third aspect is measurement. This is controversial at present and in our view justifiably so. We believe that the tendency to fix the child's reading level according to a statistical device locks him in a particular category and actuates a self-fulfilling prophecy effect which prevents further improvement. We prefer teachers to develop their own measuring techniques which can be used to diagnose individual reading problems and enable them to prescribe remedies which can be put into effect immediately. We use the readability index because we find that it

gives useful guidance to teachers on the difficulty level of the texts that they give children to read. Once teachers in specialist subjects realize how hard some of the textbooks are, they gain a better appreciation of the children's problems.

4 Cloze procedure
Cloze procedure has uses in several areas and can be applied by teachers across the whole curriculum. The technique involves taking a selected text and deleting one word in ten. This text is then presented to the children, who have to fill in the appropriate spaces with the correct words. They have to appreciate the context of the sentence in order to complete the missing word. This can be a very subtle exercise and if children can be trained to carry it out then they are helping themselves to read, with the ensuing advantage of independence.

5 The comprehension taxonomy
We have observed that many teachers do not realize the potential of a text and miss opportunities for helping the children understand it fully. To overcome this problem we have adapted the Barrett taxonomy, and cut it down to five basic categories: literal, reorganizational, evaluative, inferential, and appreciative. We encourage course members to try this with their classes and report back to the group on the results. The advantage of such an approach is that it explores the written language in three ways: first, in selecting specific items within the text; second, in the values it expresses; third, in the way the author uses words to illustrate scenes, characters and situations.

6 The study of children's literature
We believe this to be a rich, but increasingly neglected, source of knowledge which may be, apart from the sheer enjoyment of a good story, an important factor in the development of moral thinking, identification, and the development of higher thought-processes. We usually invite a teacher-librarian to talk in this session because it is essential to keep up with the very latest publications in order to appreciate the wealth of material that comes onto the market. One other point in this field is important, and that is the popularity of such comics as *Beano*, and authors whose work seems to have such little apparent literary merit. We believe that teachers should be conversant with these, and perhaps incorporate some of them into the early stages of reading development.

7 Psychology

The psychological aspect needs to be interpreted very diplomatically to teachers. The reason for this is that many teachers tend to scorn this discipline, possibly because it seems to have failed to deliver the answers to many of the problems we experience in school. Nevertheless, much of the work done by psychologists is very relevant to the field of education, and those of us involved in the teaching of reading need all the help we can get. The course programme stresses the stimulus-response approach to learning and the importance it gives to the careful preparation of tasks for children. Where children appear to have limited ability which prevents them from acquiring basic reading skills, it is essential that the tasks they are given are within their capabilities to ensure 100 per cent success. It surprises some teachers to learn that the correction of mistakes made by children is not as efficient a teaching device as had been thought. It may work well for the highly motivated, but it would seem to have only a discouraging effect on most others. We encourage the more precise preparation of tasks by reference to the readability index, cloze, comprehension taxonomies, and a careful personal analysis of the children's abilities.

8 Dyslexia

Dyslexia, the controversial aspect of reading difficulty, forms the basis of the eighth session. Many teachers do not agree that such a state exists, and attribute it to the desire of some parents to have a respectable title for their child's backwardness. We prefer to have an open mind on the subject. There is evidence to suggest that some children with a severe reading disability manage to cover it up by appearing to respond normally in other subject areas, whereas the normal expectation we have of a backward reader is that his deficit is reflected throughout the curriculum.

9 Reading schemes

The ninth and final part of the course is taken in the reading centre which is part of the John Taylor Teacher's Centre in Leeds. We examine a number of reading schemes which are readily available in order to assess their suitability for classroom use. We encourage criticism provided it is fair and accompanied by logical reasoning. Our reason for this is that we believe many of the schemes being marketed do not come up to the standards required for the purposes for which they were designed. Some are arid, others have parts that are easily lost, whilst a high proportion favour the middle-class social group. Perhaps the most inexcusable is the failure of most schemes to include an indication that our population contains any but white-skinned people. Even if we ignore the value of encouraging coloured children to identify with similar characters in the book as an aid to the learning process, why do we give white children the impression that their coloured friends do not exist in print? We put forward the view that all schemes should be revised to give recognition to the cultures and racial groups that in other ways are firmly recognized as members of our society.

These nine points represent our interpretation of the needs of local teachers who are keen to rekindle the enthusiasm of children for the printed word. There are, of course, many other solutions to the problem, and the variations on the theme of in-service training in the teaching of reading are endless. We have developed this particular format because it is practical, suited to the needs of this city, and supplies the teachers with the information they require.

20   The Family Reading Groups

Cecelia Obrist

The first Family Reading Groups evolved gradually and they are still developing and growing. The first meeting of parents and children to choose and read and discuss books together came about through the South Bedfordshire Children's Book Group, a member of the Federation of Children's Book Groups. The County Schools' Librarian, the late Christine Wright, suggested she might come to a meeting of the group in the local library to bring a selection of modern children's literature and talk about it to parents and children. This she did and allowed each family to take books home to read and discuss. Then after a few weeks everyone came back and gave an opinion on the book of their choice.

Shortly after, the United Kingdom Reading Association Research Committee decided to find out teachers' opinions on how children failed in learning to read and how teachers thought the teaching of reading might be improved.

A pilot study was carried out in North Bedfordshire, with 23 head-teachers taking part. From the answers it seemed the greatest concern was a lack of books in the home and lack of parental involvement with school. As the Family Reading Group already in existence involved parents and children going into the library together and reading books together, it was decided to try a similar venture in a school. It was discovered later that in the East Riding area there had been experiments with a similar project which had been instigated by the late Eva Astbury, County Schools' Librarian. Their experiment began with four families only, all reading the same book. But soon other groups were formed and the enthusiasm of Eva Astbury and her team inspired many people.

In Bedfordshire the first to form a group was a JMI school in a rural area, serving a cross-section of the community. It was thought that the rather widespread catchment area might militate against meetings after school but the response was excellent. The headmaster, Mr Price, devised review forms to be filled in by both parent and child. In this case they were very successful and nearly all families filled them in. It seems to give some children confidence to have a reminder of their thoughts on a book to start them off in giving their opinion.

All parents and children had been invited to take part and the age range covered five to eleven years. This wide age-range does not seem to give difficulties as long as the group is divided into subgroups, each with a leader, and the reviewing does not go on too long.

The Library Service, and the Bedford Council committee members of the United Kingdom Reading Association now encouraged other schools to participate, both urban and rural. At first these were not in areas where the need for reading books and parental involvement was greatest, and it was predicted that the meetings would not be as well attended in a more deprived area; however this turned out not to be the case, as in these areas there has perhaps been even greater enthusiasm. The first group in such an area was held in a middle school, where the headmaster thought no one would attend – but they did. A good link with the school book shop was established and children began to build up their own library. Parents from these areas said they enjoyed reading children's books much more than they expected, as they had not been able to do so when children themselves. They and the children spent a great deal of time in further discussion over tea and orangeade, when the more formal parts of discussion and choosing were over.

The organization of the groups is very fluid. Sometimes they are started by the headteacher in cooperation with the School Library Service or local library service. Sometimes a member of the teaching staff with responsibility for reading or English wishes to run a group. Many schools find it helpful to have parents involved in a committee to be responsible for the book collection and look after refreshments. Each school finds the way best suited to its circumstances and personnel.

Some teachers are disinclined to become involved with another pursuit which is as yet in its initial stages; some may feel that their lack of knowledge of modern children's books may be a handicap in participating. Those who do take part find they learn something about the books which librarians are choosing and recommending for children.

Librarians also learn a great deal about children's tastes in books. Some books which librarians consider proposing for an award would be read by only a few children. Indeed, from the written reviews it is plain that this happens. There are also certain books which children like very much, and which they constantly demand to have bought for them – such as those by Enid Blyton or H. E. Todd – which are excluded from libraries in some areas.

As a result of the group, families find that they talk to each other much more. Discussion takes place over the problems arising in books which may mirror the problems in the home or in life in general. For example, one child who was the middle child in a family, read a book in which a middle child was the main character. In the subsequent discussion with the parents the feelings of the child in such a situation were talked about and all parties understood each other much better.

In a sympathetic understanding group, with a skilled leader, subjects such as illness, cruelty and death can be examined at a safe distance. By the time children are in the middle school, their discussions go into greater depth on such subjects as loss of a parent, suffering of animals, deliberate human cruelty.

The folk stories handed down by storytellers to warn young children of possible dangers – stories like *Little Red Riding Hood* – have many modern counterparts. Glowing descriptions of a book can make other children want to read it. Indeed at 'choosing time' there can be several readers rushing for the same book!

There is much evidence from parents, particularly those of middle-school children, that there is an increased interest in books and eagerness to read selectively. Members of the family who had previously looked on reading as a 'chore' and on a book as a learning machine have come to look on reading in a new light, to see books as pleasure-giving and reading as an enjoyable pursuit.

Now there are two groups in upper schools. There had been doubts as to whether young people would wish to take part in activities with their parents. It seems that in favourable circumstances they do.

The Family Reading Groups are still finding their way but the more readers, librarians, parents, and teachers can come together the greater pleasure in reading, learning about life and communication there will be.

21   Book selection – how and why?

Elizabeth J. King

Unlike many other things, the price of a book in no way determines its worth. A bad book can cost as much as a good book, and in many cases may be more expensive. Books are the exception to the general rule that you get what you pay for! It is very easy to be taken in by an attractive cover, glossy illustrations or pictures of stage and television stars on the cover, but all these are just the packaging and in no way a guide to the real book inside the covers. Publishers are as well aware as supermarket managers of the value of eye-catching display and we must remember that children, parents and teachers are constantly subjected to a barrage of sophisticated advertising techniques, whether on television, as promotions in shops or in the outward appearance of the product to be sold.

It follows then, that for the person concerned with children and their reading, a conscious effort is needed to resist the blandishments of the marketing managers and look more closely at what is offered. This is in no way to suggest that books should not be attractive objects with eye-catching covers and good design, but only to reiterate that this aspect must not be the only judgment made on a book.

As the vast majority of children's books are bought by adults for children, it behoves us all to take this responsibility very seriously. If we believe that the enjoyment of reading, the fascination with books and the consequent enrichment of the child's future life is one of the most important gifts we as parents, teachers, or librarians can give to children, then the books that are put in front of children from a very early age will largely determine our success or failure.

This is not to suggest that we should exercise a repressive censorship over children's reading. We should always attempt to provide a wide variety of books, remembering as we do that children, as well as adults, are capable of reading on many different levels. This flexibility should always be encouraged and children should never be put into rigid reading categories and not allowed to explore the wonders that are available on the library shelves either above or below their strict reading age. Our prime responsibility is to try and ensure that all the children we provide for have a wealth of books available to them and that we encourage by all possible means their enjoyment in reading.

To this end, it is possible to draw up a list of basic criteria for book-selection. Though this is in no way a definitive list, the general criteria for book selection and for fiction in particular were taken as a theme for a meeting at the Conference. This concentrated on listing the most important areas of choice and in discussing these and their implications for library use. General guidelines felt to be important were:

1 Is the book so written that children will actively want to read it and find it both interesting and arresting?
2 Is the overall style appropriate for the book's purpose?
3 Does the sentence structure and paragraphing make the book easier or more difficult for the reader?
4 Are the chapters or subdivisions appropriate to the concentration span of the intended reader?
5 Is the vocabulary and language structure simple and direct, but also is it suitably demanding for its intended age group?
6 Is the total length of the book commensurate with the intended age range and purpose of the book? In general the younger the child, the shorter the book.
7 Is the typeface and physical layout suitable for your readers? Again the younger the reader, the more white space there should be.
8 Is the level of abstraction and conceptual difficulty suited to your readers?
9 If you practise the cloze procedure, how easy would it be for the children to fill in the gaps effectively, making use of any reading clues offered?
10 If illustrated, do the illustrations complement the text and help to carry it along?
11 Is the book physically attractive and pleasant to handle – this is essential these days with supermarket packaging and sophisticated colour-television.
12 Is the book physically robust enough to stand up to a number of children using it over a period of time?

The particular areas for choice in fiction were felt to be:

1 Does the book tell a good story – one that it is possible to believe in?
2 How well does the story feed the child's imagination, and is it possible for the child to enter a new world through the story?

3 Will children identify with the characters?
4 Do the characters develop and grow through the narrative?
5 How much enrichment will the children receive from the language and style of the book?
6 How far will the story extend a child's horizons and understanding of other people?
7 If the story takes the child into other worlds through fantasy, does it allow the child a secure point of return – this is especially important for young children.
8 Are the subject matter and background of the book ones which will interest the intended age group?
9 Does it enrich and extend the imagination of anyone, child or adult, who reads it?
10 If the book has a historical or particular geographical setting, how accurate is this?

It was felt that if libraries are going to fulfil the important aspect of introducing children to a wide range of literature, then they must exercise care and judgment in the books they offer.

22 Developing extension reading skills: a contribution via television

John Rawnsley

On the face of it neither television nor radio seem well-equipped to assist students to develop effective uses of reading. Television, that most ephemeral of media, whose images are imprisoned within the confines of the size of the television screen itself, would scarcely seem the most apt vehicle to carry reading text; and radio's distinctive strengths of sound effects, spoken language, music and dramatization, seem equally unpromising simply because radio scores best as a nonprint medium. Notwithstanding these apparent limitations, BBC Schools Television and Schools Radio have developed both television series and radio programmes in the area of extension reading skills.

In radio the BBC has for some years now produced *Listening and Reading 2*. This series, with ten specially-commissioned short stories each term, offers children help with extension reading skills. The stories are told simply on radio and pupils aural-scan the text as they listen. This has proved a highly successful use of radio and accompanying text to develop children's confidence in extension reading. In television there has been an even more recent innovation and this paper is concerned with the story of how this came about.

In spring 1979, BBC Schools Television produced *A Good Read*, whose aim was to help develop critical, efficient and habitual readers for whom reading is pleasurable both in and out of school. The series was designed for the ten- to twelve-year-old pupil who has learnt to read but who is failing to develop flexible reading strategies, particularly for textbooks and reference material, and who does not naturally turn to books for enjoyment: worthy aims well in line with the Bullock Report's (DES 1975) insistence on the need for developing later reading skills. But how could the objective be translated into television terms?

During the period of extensive consultation leading up to the production of the series three factors began to emerge clearly. Within the age range of the series teachers have a wide range of classroom situations to cope with and a wide variety of schemes of work. *A Good Read* would have to be planned possibly as a magazine programme containing several items with different emphasis as far as the potential for classroom follow-up was concerned. Teachers were interested in developing later reading skills and recognized the importance of reading to the development of learning of their pupils, but were themselves relatively unsure of how to go about it. Remember that the work of Lunzer and Gardner (1979) on *The Effective Use of Reading* was not then published. It was one thing for the BBC to extend its well-tried series *Look and Read* into reading for meaning for teachers confident in teaching code-cracking skills to failing readers aged about eight, and quite another to develop an entirely new series for competent readers aged ten to twelve in an area of little-understood and seldom-taught skills of extension reading. Thirdly, the adult literacy television programmes had clearly underscored the fact that television's strengths lay in motivating, arousing interest, modifying attitudes and triggering referrals, but not obviously in direct instructional aspects of reading.

A further hazard began to emerge: how to organize the reading elements within the programmes. For reference and information purposes teachers needed to be able to identify unequivocally whether an item was related to reading as a thinking skill, or dealt with the effective use of reading in study skills or in reference skills, or with reading as a source of pleasure. But conversely, the series had to communicate the heuristic and eclectic nature of the reading process. It needed to emphasize that the categorization of aspects of reading under separate headings did not indicate that the reading activities themselves were mutually exclusive. Many items would deliberately blur the compartmentalism of reading skills.

Pilot material for *A Good Read* was made and tried out extensively with teachers and teacher/librarians, and with groups of children in schools. The pilot tape did not represent a completed programme from the series but instead tested out five major items where any one programme would only contain three. It was a genuine attempt to indicate the style and intended approach of the series, however, and an attempt to present teachers with a real opportunity to influence the eventual programmes. Typical of these pilot segments was a 5 minute 10 second sequence on 'Looking for clues' in which one of the presenters read a short extract from the beginning of Chapter 2 of *Colour in the Creek* by Margaret Paise (published by Collins). The other two presenters were then invited to try and work out what the story might be about. Later in the pilot package in the 'study skills' element of the series, Gordon Astley worked on building a balsa-wood aeroplane from a construction kit and, failing to take enough account of the detailed instructions, he showed, in an amusing way, the need to adopt different reading strategies for various kinds of material. In the final pilot sequence Jan Mark filmed on location at RAF Coltishall talked about her approach to writing and how ideas come or fail to come. She discussed with children her book *Thunder and Lightnings* (published by Kestrel Books).

In the course of piloting, teachers and pupils commented on the overall plan for the series, noting how the pilot sections fitted into the proposed whole. The series plan was put before them with the items featured in the pilot cassette. You can see on p. 207 an example of how this was presented to the teachers who assisted in the piloting stage.

Teachers were invited to consider each section and to signal their response to specific questions. Did the teachers who were unfamiliar with prediction exercises feel that item 1 provided them with a reasonable starting point? Were the words readable on the screen? Where children aged ten to twelve were already familiar with library skills would these children still be entertained and helped further by the item? How many teachers were currently using sequencing to encourage close reading? etc. The piloting confirmed teachers' interest in the provision of such a series which they saw as timely, and the producer Geoff Wilson and his consultant Colin Harrison, lecturer in English in Education at the University of Nottingham School of Education and member of the Schools Council Effective Use of Reading project, were guided about what worked and what didn't. Only the successful sequences in the pilot programme survived, and even then many were considerably modified in the light of teachers' response. Overall it appeared that teachers welcomed a variety of items at different levels intended to stimulate different follow-up work. The piloting established that whilst the majority of teachers would use the series live, some would have access to videorecording, and teachers generally would wish to pick out and develop from the programme items which fitted into their own particular schemes of work.

Following the piloting, the pattern of the series and production strategies were fixed and it became clear that three proposed elements would occur in each programme in the same order each week. So each programme would attempt to provide material to stimulate work on:

1 *Reading as a thinking skill*

This element of the programmes would provide an introduction to a number of reading activities designed to encourage closer attention to text and therefore more responsive reading. Prediction activities, sequencing exercises and cloze procedure would be featured in a variety of ways.

Programme outlines for the first three programmes of *A Good Read*

1

How do you read?
A simple introduction to the thinking behind how the fluent reader does make sense of the written word.

What a lot of books!
An item filmed in the Bodleian Library, Oxford: to give viewers some idea of the vast numbers and range of printed books.

● The author at work
An interview with the author Jan Mark about how she writes, and an introduction to her first book *Thunder and Lightnings*.

● Items featured on the pilot cassette.

2

Chaos in the kitchen
One of the presenters makes a complete mess of making nutty chocolate cookies – the recipe has been written down in the wrong order: an introduction to the notion of sequencing as a classroom activity.

● How a library works
How to find your way to the right shelf of a library in search of books on a particular subject.

The book and the film
The book and the film of *James and the Giant Peach* by Roald Dahl are examined, to show how they must differ.

3

● Story time
A story is read in the wrong order and then reassembled by studying the text carefully. Another stimulus to sequencing activities, this time working from a narrative text.

Selecting and rejecting books
How to select, from a large number of books on the same basic subject, the ones most likely to be of use to the searcher.

Words into pictures
An interview with a well-known illustrator of children's books. How does she decide what to draw having read the words?

2 *Study skills*

The second main item in each programme would involve one of the presenters tackling a variety of activities designed to help children cope, as the Bullock Report states, with 'the reading required in each area of the curriculum'. This element would, to a certain extent, be cumulative. Thus it would begin with simple library skills and progress through such items as how to cope with indexes, an awareness of nonbook sources of information, coping with different kinds of reading strategies, guidance in reorganizing and summarizing material.

3 *Reading as a source of pleasure*

The third element of each programme would be an attempt to stimulate interest in books of all kinds by a variety of methods, all designed to encourage in children a questioning attitude to their reading. Thus, specific authors would be interviewed, the work of a children's book illustrator would be featured, a film made from a book examined and children themselves would be encouraged to talk about their reading preferences. A range of books and authors would be met within the series. These would include:

The author Jan Mark and her first published book *Thunder and Lightnings* (1976); *James and the Giant Peach* by Roald Dahl (1967); books illustrated by the artist Faith Jaques including *What the Neighbours Did and Other Stories* by Philippa Pearce (1972); the author Robert Leeson and *The Third Class Genie* (1975); the author Leon Garfield talking specifically about his latest book *The Confidence Man* (1978); and the poet Michael Rosen, author of *Mind Your Own Business* (1975) and *Wouldn't You Like to Know?* (1977).

In order to help teachers make more effective use of the programmes based on a selective approach to items which met the needs of a particular class, detailed teachers' notes were produced. These 24-page A4-size notes had a magazine format with illustrations and drawings. For ease of reference the notes of each programme were divided into three sections, under three separate titles, corresponding to the three basic programme elements.

Under each title, where appropriate, the programme item was outlined and the background thinking delineated. Suggestions for specific follow-up work were given in certain cases.

The centre four pages of the notes were designed to be pulled away. They did not refer to a specific programme but contained suggestions for classroom follow-up work related to the reading activities featured within the programmes.

The book list for each programme gave ten to twelve titles of children's books related in broad terms to those featured within the programme. The lists contained books likely to appeal to a wide range of reading interests and abilities; some almost certainly appeared on school reading lists, other did not. In any event, it was hoped that teachers would find it useful to have additional titles to hand in this way.

On the back page of these notes was a further reading list for teachers of books about reading and reading skills that they might find interesting as background material to the series.

On 15 January 1979 the first programme in this new series went on the air. 8,884 copies of the teachers' notes had been purchased by 5,695 schools and we awaited response from the classroom to what we saw as an innovatory series which itself was probing a relatively new area of the curriculum. The series has had one repeat showing in autumn term 1979 and attracted a similar-sized audience in another 5,398 schools.

Teachers have responded well to the transmissions of *A Good Read*, including the magazine format. The BBC have taken encouragement from this and are planning a further single-term series of ten programmes to be called *Read On* for 1980–1. It will be possible to incorporate feedback to *A Good Read* in the planning of this successor series. So, it is intended to retain the magazine style for *Read On* but to adopt a more flexible approach, allowing certain items to be developed in more detail and at greater length. The style of presentation, too, will be more direct in order to encourage greater use at a lower secondary level.

The series will include:

1 *Reading for meaning* Reading activities designed to encourage closer and more responsive involvement with text such as cloze procedure, prediction exercises, sequencing, etc.
2 *Reading textbooks and reading for reference* Greater emphasis in this series will be placed on library skills and the ability to locate and deal with material from a variety of sources. Help will be given not only in the area of understanding the layout and linguistic style of textbooks but also in assessing the information within them. There will also be items designed to encourage the skills of skimming and scanning, summarizing, note-taking and use of nonbook material.
3 *Reading for pleasure* A range of books and authors will be featured in the programmes and children themselves encouraged to talk about their reading preferences. Stress will be laid on the notion of rejecting as well as selecting books and on the acquisition of a questioning attitude to books in general.
4 *General interest* An element of the series will be devoted to material intended to create a general interest in the world of print, books and

reading, e.g. libraries of particular interest; the preparation and printing of books or newspapers.

References

DES (1975) *A Language for Life* (The Bullock Report) London: HMSO

GARFIELD, L. (1978) *The Confidence Man* Harmondsworth: Kestrel

LEESON, R. (1975) *The Third Class Genie* London: Collins

LUNZER, E. and GARDNER, K. (1979) *The Effective Use of Reading* London: Heinemann Educational for the Schools Council

MARK, J. (1976) *Thunder and Lightnings* Harmondsworth: Kestrel

PEARCE, P. (1972) *What the Neighbours Did and Other Stories* Harlow: Longman

ROSEN, M. (1975) *Mind Your Own Business* London: Collins

ROSEN, M. (1977) *Wouldn't You Like to Know?* London: Deutsch

Postscript: The reading connection

Gwen Bray

This Conference was concerned to highlight and encourage links of communication between all who are involved with the continuous development of literacy skills, from preschool to university level. To take the analogy of the railway connection, the teaching of reading and its related skills is given for the most part in a network of state-encouraged enterprises, in stations which vary in size and affluence. The travellers vary in age and stage of education and may travel without cost to themselves, and as far as they wish to go. Each traveller is an individual with special attitudes, aptitudes and abilities. The temperament, ability, and knowledge of the personnel responsible for the network varies considerably and may affect the journey of the inexperienced traveller for better or worse. The selection of trains and the planning of the journey require careful thought, and whilst some passengers arrive at Oxford or Cambridge, others may be attracted by the major cities. Others may be delayed for various reasons, and, regrettably, there are those who remain shunted onto sidings. The attitude of the general public becomes increasingly critical, and asks for accountability of a capital investment which, it is hoped, will yield immediate results.

That eminent station master, Sir Alan Bullock, has advised passengers that there is a lifetime of opportunity for those who wish to add to their skills by reading. In our increasingly automated and anonymous world, private reading in pursuit of one's own interests becomes more and more attractive, and there are those who follow the thinking of Robert Frost, on 'The road not taken';

> I shall be telling this with a sigh
> Somewhere ages and ages hence;
> Two roads diverged in a wood, and I –
> I took the one less travelled by,
> And that has made all the difference.

The International Year of the Child, 1979, has offered an opportunity for countries to review their provision for the all-round development of their children, especially the youngest ones. There are millions of children in the developing world who do not have the basic services that those in the industrialized countries enjoy, and their educational opportunities are negligible. The contribution made by certain members of the United Kingdom Reading Association in helping to develop literacy programmes for teachers and children requiring this help is considerable.

However, in connection with the International Year of the Child, one must ask whether there has been enough serious consideration as to whether our children are making the most of the opportunities that are available. Compulsory education begins at five years of age in this country, although it may be preceded by nursery education, and the minimum school-leaving age is sixteen. Whatever the differences in ability and aptitude between pupils, they must be able to read to some purpose if they are to derive benefit from at least eleven years in the educational system. The attitudes and expectations of parents, teachers, and the pupils themselves are vital in making the most of these years of opportunity. The enlargement of vocabulary and fluency of speech can only be achieved if there are sufficient interested and knowledgeable adults in a child's life, who are prepared to talk with and listen to him. Experiments with Family Reading Groups, in which teachers, parents, librarians and children cooperate, have been developed as action-research projects in several areas of the country, and a booklet prepared on behalf of the Research Committee of this Association, has been sent to every head librarian in the country. Adult literacy is an area in which many of our members have been involved. This work is important not only for the help it gives the adult students but for its effects on their homes and children.

The stress on parent involvement is less recent than we might think. In the first half of the century the Board of Education produced handbooks of *Suggestions, for Teachers concerned with Public Elementary Schools*. These were replaced by *Primary Education* in 1958; by *Children and Their Primary Schools* in 1967; and recently by *Primary Education in England*. The emphasis placed on home and school links, and the responsibility of the family in the 1905 publication has a familiar ring today: 'Each family has an inalienable duty in respect of its own members. . . . Education Authorities, working directly through official agencies or, it may be hoped, to an increasing extent with volunteer helpers, can promote the well-being of scholars, by reviving home interests and home influences'. In some schools, it was noted, 'the aid of parents has been successfully enlisted, and they have encouraged their children to read aloud for a few minutes each day'.

212

Links are not only within the UK of course, although here our Association, through its publications and activities, helps to keep attention on reading and publicize developments. I must also refer to the educational connection that the United Kingdom Reading Association has with countries represented at this conference: Australia, Canada, Denmark, France, Holland, and Italy. Earlier in 1979 we held a joint conference with representatives from Denmark, Finland and Sweden and the Faroes. With the International Reading Association, we are now extending our contacts with Europe, and the UKRA's *Journal of Research in Reading*, an international journal published in French and English, has been an important initiative in developing links between researchers in Europe.

These proceedings have shown many of the links which exist between those concerned with reading. They will also have suggested areas where the connection is not as strong as it might be and where new links need to be formed. Through its journals, its meetings and its individual contacts, the Association will continue to encourage the strengthening of the reading connection.

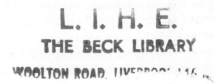

The contributors

Roger Beard
Nene College
Northampton

Don Bouwhuis
Institute for Perception Research
Eindhoven, Netherlands

Gwen Bray, President UKRA 1978–9
formerly General Adviser for Nursery and Primary Education
Leeds

Asher Cashdan
Head of Department of Communication Studies
City of Sheffield Polytechnic

L. John Chapman
Faculty of Educational Studies
The Open University

G. W. Elsmore
Staff Inspector
Department of Education and Science

Hans Grundin
Institute of Educational Technology
The Open University

Elizabeth Hunter-Grundin
Senior Lecturer in Reading Development
Avery Hill College, London

Jennie Ingham
Department of Research in Education
Bradford University

Sandra Johnson
Department of Education
University of Manchester

Elizabeth J. King
Tutor-Librarian
Leeds Education Service

Ethel M. King
Department of Curriculum and Instruction
University of Calgary, Canada

John Mann
Secretary
The Schools Council

Joyce M. Morris
Language Arts Consultant
London

Cecelia Obrist
Author and former headmistress

Eileen Pearsall
General Adviser for Primary Education
Leeds

A. K. Pugh
Faculty of Educational Studies
The Open University

John Rawnsley
Chief Education Officer
Schools Broadcasting Council

Angela Salfield
Department of Teaching Studies
Polytechnic of North London

Gail Sharman
Department of Teaching Studies
Polytechnic of North London

Frank Smith
Professor of Education
The Ontario Institute for Studies in Education
Canada

Vera Southgate Booth
Senior Lecturer in Curriculum Studies
Faculty of Education
University of Manchester

Derrick Stock
Director of Course on Education of Backward Children
Leeds Polytechnic

Derek Thackray
Honorary General Secretary UKRA

Christopher Tipple
Deputy Director of Education
Leeds

Marian J. Tonjes
Assistant Professor of Reading
Western Washington University
Bellingham, USA